Song of Exile

Song of Exile

The Enduring Mystery of Psalm 137

DAVID W. STOWE

OXFORD
UNIVERSITY PRESS

OXFORD
UNIVERSITY PRESS

Oxford University Press is a department of the University of Oxford. It furthers
the University's objective of excellence in research, scholarship, and education
by publishing worldwide. Oxford is a registered trade mark of Oxford University
Press in the UK and certain other countries.

Published in the United States of America by Oxford University Press
198 Madison Avenue, New York, NY 10016, United States of America.

Library of Congress Cataloging-in-Publication Data
Names: Stowe, David W. (David Ware) author.
Title: Song of exile : the enduring mystery of Psalm 137 / David W. Stowe.
Description: New York: Oxford University Press, 2016. |
Includes bibliographical references and index.
Identifiers: LCCN 2015044386| ISBN 978–0–19–046683–1 (cloth: alk. paper) |
ISBN 978–0–19–046685–5 (epub)
Subjects: LCSH: Bible. Psalms, CXXXVII—Criticism, interpretation, etc.
Classification: LCC BS1450 137th .S76 2016 | DDC 223/.206—dc23 LC record available
at http://lccn.loc.gov/2015044386

1 3 5 7 9 8 6 4 2
Printed in the United States of America on acid-free paper

Scripture quotations, unless otherwise noted, are from the New English Bible,
copyright 1961, 1970 by the Delegates of the Oxford University Press and the Syndics of the
Cambridge University Press. Used by permission.

For Clare

Contents

Preface

PSALM 137 BEGINS with one of the more lyrical lines in the Hebrew Bible: "By the rivers of Babylon, there we sat down, yea, we wept, when we remembered Zion." It ends eight lines later with one of the thorniest: "Happy shall he be, who taketh and dasheth thy little ones against the stones." Partly because it deals with music—another famous verse asks, "How shall we sing the LORD's song in a strange land?"—the psalm has been like poetic catnip, a siren song luring musicians and composers. But its cultural history is much richer than even those resonant lines would promise.

For over a decade I have inhabited Psalm 137. I don't remember exactly how I became aware of its remarkable musical legacy, although I found use for it in a history I wrote on music in the spiritual lives of Americans.[1] The psalm's full significance dawned on me only by degree; I would go so far as to say that it's grown on me. As a historian, I've been especially intrigued by one central question: Why, given the pervasive historical impact of the Bible on American culture, has the Babylonian Exile not registered a more significant presence in our culture?

Several books both popular and scholarly have documented the importance of Moses and the Israelite Exodus from Egypt. It has become a central thread in the national narrative, thought to epitomize a key element of the American experience: the escape from bondage. Psalm 137 has exercised a more subtle influence. No doubt, many Americans have identified with those lines. For Jews, Psalm 137 and the Exile remain central conceptions, marked especially during *Tisha B'av*, which commemorates the destruction of the second Jerusalem Temple and subsequent millennia of exile that continued into the twentieth century. But in the broader public culture of the United States, the Exile remains virtually unknown.

In a country populated by outsiders and migrants, why is the psalm—and the history it captures—not better known? What insights would we gain by placing the Exile alongside the Exodus as a foundational national narrative? Would U.S. history take on a different trajectory? Inscribed on the Statue of Liberty is a famous poem by Emma Lazarus, which dubbed the statue the "Mother of Exiles," linking it, and the national experience it symbolizes, to the events of Psalm 137.

Unique among the Hebrew Psalms, Psalm 137 transpires in a particular place and time. Like the Exodus, the Babylonian Exile to which the psalm refers dwells at the core of Judaism. The trauma served as a crucible, forcing the Israelites to rethink their relationship to Yahweh, revise their understanding of the Covenant, reassess their standing as a chosen people, rewrite their history. It inaugurated the Israelite sense of themselves as a nation of exile, a people who have somehow survived living in the diaspora for more than 2,500 years.

The psalm refers to a fifty-year period after Jerusalem was destroyed by Nebuchadnezzar's army and many of its leading Judeans were taken northeast into captivity. At first glance, the Hebrew Bible tells us little about the experiences of that period, either among the exiles in Babylon or the majority of the "people of the land" not considered important enough to relocate. But my research impressed on me how central the Exile is to several key texts: Isaiah, Jeremiah, Ezekiel, Daniel, Lamentations. For Jews and Christians of most persuasions, these are among the most important books of the Bible.

Psalm 137 has been highly adaptable for members of those religions, but for others as well. It has served as North America's longest-running protest song, lending rhetorical support to anticolonial movements from the American Revolution to Jamaican Rastafari. In the United States, its most distinctive use has come in antiracist movements from abolitionism to civil rights. Psalm 137 has also been used to articulate alienation and marginalization of a more private, existential variety. A pronounced undercurrent of nostalgia runs through its lines, reminding us of the word's Greek etymology: *nostos*, which means homecoming; and *algia*, meaning longing, and *algos*, pain or ache.

Though by training my research has focused primarily on North America, it was clear to me that pursuing these questions would require tracing threads from the Americas back to Europe and the Middle East. And the book itself would require a different kind of structure, not a straightforward historical narrative.

Eventually, with some inspiration from philosopher Paul Ricœur's final book, I fixed on a scheme of dividing the book into three parts, corresponding to the three sections of the psalm: *History, Memory, Forgetting.*[2] Historically, these three groups of verses have spoken to different situations and have been put to different social uses. My book draws together two distinct, interrelated narratives: the roughly fifty years of Exile following the destruction of Jerusalem in 586 B.C.E.; and the use of the psalm by Jews and Christians over the subsequent millennia. Each part works as a kind of extended essay, with its own loose narrative line linked by affinities of language, historical conjuncture, personal influence, and structure of feeling.

Part One, "History," examines the first four verses, rendered here in the ubiquitous language of the King James Bible:

> *By the rivers of Babylon, there we sat down, yea, we wept, when we remembered Zion.*
> *We hanged our harps upon the willows in the midst thereof.*
> *For there they that carried us away captive required of us a song; and they that wasted us required of us mirth, saying, Sing us one of the songs of Zion.*
> *How shall we sing the* LORD's *song in a strange land?*

These verses, in the first-person plural, evoke communal memories of better times remembered in moments of dislocation, ending with the question, "How shall we sing the Lord's song in a strange land?" They have generated by far the most musical settings, from classical—Bach, de Monte, Guerrero, Byrd, Dvořák, Verdi, Bloch, Alkan—to popular renditions sung by Don McLean and the cast of *Godspell.* But it was "Rivers of Babylon," an earlier, Rasta-tinged rendition by the Jamaican group the Melodians, that gave the psalm global exposure—and revived an established American tradition of antiracist and anticolonialist adaptations of the psalm that began during the American Revolution. The song has established a global presence through myriad cover versions and diegetic use in world cinema.

Part Two, "Memory," meditates on the middle verses of the psalm:

> *If I forget thee, O Jerusalem, let my right hand forget her cunning.*
> *If I do not remember thee, let my tongue cleave to the roof of my mouth;*
> *if I prefer not Jerusalem above my chief joy.*

These verses take the form of an inward-looking oath by the psalmist, calling for corporal punishment (paralysis of tongue and hand) if he forgets

Jerusalem; they have been of particular interest to political movements that invoke collective memory to mobilize social action. In North America, these verses were emphasized by composer William Billings and more famously by Frederick Douglass, who created the modern reading of the psalm as a broadside against slavery. His usage helped inspire sermons by prominent African American preachers such as C. L. Franklin, whose Detroit church we will visit, and Jeremiah Wright, who preached a sermon on the Babylonian Exile that echoed in the words of his most famous parishioner, Barack Obama. These verses prompt reflection on the different facets of memory: intentional and unbidden, individual and collective.

Part Three, "Forgetting," investigates the final lines of the psalm, least used in song or liturgy but most controversial:

> *Remember, O* LORD, *the children of Edom in the day of Jerusalem; who said, Rase it, rase it, even to the foundation thereof.*
>
> *O daughter of Babylon, who art to be destroyed; happy shall he be, that rewardeth thee as thou hast served us.*
>
> *Happy shall he be, that taketh and dasheth thy little ones against the stones.*

These final verses are addressed to Yahweh. With their call for vengeance against Edom and Babylon, climaxing with the infamous dashing of babies against the rocks, they have usually been excised (and forgotten) in liturgy. This despite the fact that vengeance has featured prominently in North American public life from the earliest conflicts with Native Americans through the triumphant takedown of Osama bin Laden. I trace the resonance of these lines, and the attempts to interpret them as commensurable with Christian doctrine, from Augustine through the convulsive violence of the Reformation to the present. Subtle gender overtones inflect the psalm's final verses—and the larger historical narrative in which it is embedded. In the original Hebrew, Jerusalem is depicted as a woman being sexually humiliated. We find echoes of these final verses invoked by modern episodes of genocide and ethnic cleansing, from the Holocaust to the Balkans.

These three sections of the psalm move through dramatic changes of tone, address, and emotional perspective. A reader might wonder what kind of through-line holds Psalm 137 together as a unified text. One possibility is that the psalm leads us through the stages of coming to grips with trauma or grief. First, the psalmist confronts his own disbelief, sadness, and uncertainty in the face of a cruel exile. Then comes an introspective turn, an adamant decision to remain faithful to one's calling and community in the face of adverse conditions. Last comes the expression of violent rage, a call to action, for God to blast the oppressor, a kind of psychic fuel for the challenge of maintaining one's identity in the face of oppression. These three stages are not necessarily sequential; they commingle and coexist, surfacing at different times in response to different internal and external circumstances. All are common human responses to the individual and collective suffering entailed by traumatic life changes like the Babylonian Exile. Taken together, they might be thought of as a natural process, culminating in the ability to take a stand, to declare a social identity worth defending.

Can a poem, even a Hebrew psalm, have a biography? Some would challenge the notion that a text can be a historical actor, exerting the sort of agency we chronicle in individuals and their biographies. It's people who make history, contriving and using texts. But if any text can be thought to have a life story amid myriad social contexts, acted upon by circumstances around it in diverse times and places even as it helped shape those circumstances, Psalm 137 would seem to fit. What follows will investigate some of the dramatic high-points of this narrative.

Readers interested in perusing the numerous musical examples and visual depictions of the psalm produced over the centuries are encouraged to visit the link for *Song of Exile* found at davidwstowe.com.

Song of Exile

PART ONE

History

*By the rivers of Babylon, there we sat down, yea, we wept,
when we remembered Zion.*

We hanged our harps upon the willows in the midst thereof.

*For there they that carried us away captive required of us a
song; and they that wasted us required of us mirth, saying,
Sing us one of the songs of Zion.*

How shall we sing the LORD*'s song in a strange land?*

(Psalm 137:1–4)

LIKE A FEW other psalms, Psalm 137 shows up in unexpected places. *Mad Men*, for instance.

Halfway through the first season, in an episode titled "Babylon," the Sterling Cooper advertising agency has just secured an account with the Israeli Tourism Bureau. Judging from the obtuse, mildly anti-Semitic office banter, it would appear that this is the first time anyone in the WASP-y agency has ever thought about Israel or the Jews. It's not clear they know the difference. But Leon Uris's *Exodus* is au courant, soon to be a major motion picture starring Paul Newman. We see the show's dashing protagonist Don Draper reading the book at bedtime to bone up for his new client.[1]

Draper has also been working closely with Rachel, a Jewish department store heiress. They meet for coffee, ostensibly to discuss the new account with Israel, although Draper clearly has amorous intentions. "I'm the only Jew you know in New York City?" she asks incredulously. Rachel explains that Jews have been living in exile for a very long time. "We've managed to make a go of it," she tells Draper. "It might have something to do with the fact that we thrive at doing business with people who hate us."

In the same episode, Draper is cautiously sampling the bohemian world of his girlfriend, Midge. They make their way to the Gaslight, a subterranean cabaret on Macdougal Street in Greenwich Village. After they endure a couple of cringe-inducing avant-garde poets, a folk trio comes onstage and plays a haunting round in a minor key. The banjo player wears a cap in the style made famous by the young Bob Dylan, who actually performed at the Gaslight. He sings:

> By the waters, the waters, of Babylon
> We sat down and wept, and wept, for thee Zion.
> We remember, we remember, we remember thee Zion.

Some viewers may have remembered this song from the iconic Don McLean album, *American Pie* (1971).[2] A few may have even sung it around campfires in youth groups. As the eerie music continues in the club, the camera cuts to vignettes suggesting Draper's stream of consciousness: scenes of Rachel, his wife and children, his boss leaving a tryst with a mistress.

These few lines of text provide an elegant lyrical thread connecting New York City at the dawn of the JFK era to the Middle East some 2500 years earlier. Unique among the Hebrew Psalms, Psalm 137 transpires in a specific geographic location at a particular time. The setting is Mesopotamia on the banks of the Euphrates River, or more likely one of the irrigation canals connected with the Euphrates. Verb endings tell us the time is the past: *We sat, we wept, we hanged; they carried us, required of us.* Very specifically, it's 586 B.C.E. The psalm is uncompromising in its historicity; unlike other laments, we don't have to guess which crisis of Israel is being invoked. Note the asymmetry: Judeans sat and remembered; their captors, as yet unnamed, carried out their actions on the Judeans—carried, wasted, required.

To the psalmist, is that past recent or distant? Like so much else about the psalm, it's debatable. Dominant Jewish and Christian traditions assume King David as the poet of this psalm (as for most others), implying that he had prophetic vision into the future. Other traditions attribute the psalm to the prophet Jeremiah, who lived through the destruction of the Jerusalem Temple and the Exile to Babylon. It could have been created by some other unknown contemporary of Jeremiah; or even someone living after the Exile had ended, as many of the exiled Judeans returned west of the Jordan River to Palestine.[3]

This is a psalm we can picture in our mind's eye. Bedraggled and forlorn human detritus, huddling on a riverbank. Whatever the circumstances that have led them there, these people—men, women, children?—have at least found a reasonably congenial site in which to mourn. As water flows by, the tears flow down. Their salinity mixes with flows—muddy, brackish, clear, boggy, rapid—we're not told. Later translators would embellish this image of tears flowing into the river. In some traditions, the Euphrates was held to be poisonous, fatal to the Judean captives clustered on its bank.[4] This is altogether a different ambiance from that other fabled biblical river, the Jordan—site of miraculous crossings by Joshua and the Israelites, Elijah, Elisha, and Jacob; and also the waterway in which Jesus was baptized by John the Baptist and by which he conducted much of his ministry.

And there is shade, provided by willows (the weeping tree) or, as sometimes translated, poplar trees. But these trees hold, as Billie Holiday sang in a different context, a strange fruit: stringed instruments, harps, lyres—again, the language varies among translations. Who are these people with stringed instruments in their possession, and why would they go to the trouble of festooning the trees with them? We imagine them being put away for safekeeping, perhaps, to keep them from getting stepped on or encrusted with gravel. The word for hang, *toleinu*, might suggest, for some listeners, gruesome forms of hanging, like crucifixion.[5]

"We" are not alone. There are others there, and "they" are clearly not on the side of "we." They carried us away captive; they laid us waste. Then they required of us mirth and commanded us to perform. To sing a song that we could not or should not sing—in that place, under those circumstances. The command is made more vivid by being rendered in direct speech, as if quoting: *Sing us one of the songs of Zion.*

Can we sing? Should we sing? *How* should we sing? How *can* we sing, with our instruments put aside? As readers, we are asked to identify with the "we." Thus we become fleetingly part of a community constituted by its difficult experiences in the present and its memories of a better time.

"We" and "they" must share something in common. Language, at least, since the captors request not just a song, a directive that could be pantomimed, but a particular type of song. These captors must know that their captives make music and that this music is symbolically charged and closely guarded. They would have to know of the existence of meaning-laden songs of Zion, the singing of which poses a difficult dilemma for their prisoners.

Amid this scene of civil disobedience, of the relinquishing of physical activity, the real activity is internal: the work of memory. The excavation of the experienced past. It may have become cliché to compare time to a river, but it does flow relentlessly regardless of our fervent desires. (And sometimes that relentless flow is merciful.) We remain stationary and observe one stretch, but that water is forever on its way somewhere else. The pre-Socratic Greek thinker Heraclitus famously observed: a person can't step twice into the same river.

Yet testimony can freeze a moment in time. These few lines, the opening verses of Psalm 137, are testimony, and they have frozen this scene now for some two-and-a-half millennia. Let us join these captives in their memories and see what happens when recording memory through testimony transforms it into the rough material of history.

After all, it is memory alone that allows us to place this psalm in time and space. Despite all the active verbs used to describe this scene—sitting down, weeping, hanging up, carrying away, laying waste, requiring a song—it is the inward activity of remembering that grounds this psalm most concretely in space-time: remembering Zion.

Zion is the name of a hill in Jerusalem, outside the walls of the Old City, but for these captives it is also a symbol of Jerusalem, their homeland, of Israel understood as a chosen people with a unique covenant with the one true God. These people are Israelites, more properly inhabitants of Judah, the part of Israel that had survived the conquest of Assyrian invaders from the northeast.

Mapping History

A map can make a great difference.

I had pictured the mise en scéne of this psalm for a long time before imagining the physical route trod by the exiles. According to *The Macmillan Bible Atlas*, they were marched north past the Sea of Galilee, following the coast of the Mediterranean for about 300 miles. Then, at the northeast corner of the Mediterranean, near Aleppo, where Syria meets Turkey, the route veered in a hard right to the southeast, meeting up with the Euphrates River and following it to the southeast for another 500 miles. We might imagine the rivers of Babylon anywhere along that stretch. Or near the settlement of Nippur, on the bank of another waterway, the Kebar, an outpost well known by the most famous Babylonian exile of all, Ezekiel (see Fig. 1).[6]

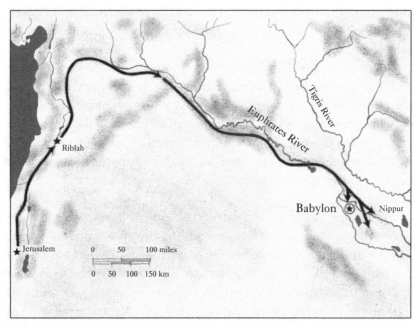

FIGURE I Route of the exiles from Judah to Babylonia. Courtesy of Nate Sensel.

How accurate could this map be? It bears the mark of reputable scholarship, but it doesn't include sources or any companion text explaining how cartographers arrived at it. I had always imagined the captives trudging directly east to Babylon. It would have saved almost 300 miles but also would have entailed crossing a brutal desert. The atlas map makes much more sense. But as soon as we open its pages and get drawn into its world, we are confronted by the specter of two histories: mythic history, or sacred history, as recorded in the Hebrew Bible; and historiography, which is conducted according to contemporary standards of scholarship.

By sacred history, I mean a version of the past that takes the Hebrew Bible as the sole and sufficient source of information about events that took place in Palestine and its environs (Egypt, Mesopotamia) between the creation of the world and the point when the narrative tapers off in the centuries before the Common Era. This is the history of the Holy Land that has shaped the perspective of the great majority of Jews and Christians over the past three millennia.

This sacred history differs from historiography because it doesn't depend on being corroborated by external sources. There may be extensive creativity applied to explaining apparent contradictions and inconsistencies, as in the Midrash and Talmud, but those scholars and exegetes don't typically look for supporting evidence elsewhere, let alone accept the possibility that the facts of scripture might be contradicted by the evidence.

From the perspective of sacred history, it matters little who left Judah and who stayed behind; how the captives got to Babylon; what they did when they got there; how many eventually returned home to Judah after Cyrus conquered Babylonia; how they reintegrated into their old homeland; or when they rebuilt the Jerusalem Temple. A few of these issues are touched on briefly in the Hebrew Bible, but for the most part the events of the Exile are an historical void, "the most profound caesura of all eras in Israel's history."[7]

For historiography, these questions matter a great deal. Apart from the basic curiosity of historians to uncover the texture of daily life, the roughly half-century that followed the first forced migrations of Judeans to Babylon is thought to be decisive in shaping the religion that has come to be called "Judaism." The experience of the Exile forced the Israelites to rethink their relationship to Yahweh, revise their understanding of the Covenant, reassess their standing as a chosen people, and rewrite their history. The Exile served as the crucible that transformed the followers of Yahweh from an innocent people who took their chosenness for granted to a nation aware that its continued existence was highly contingent.

More concretely, the Exile produced the Hebrew Bible. Some scholars believe that fully *one half* of that congeries of texts was composed, revised, and redacted during the Exile decades.[8] Exactly how and where this was occurring will probably always remain a mystery—it's not as if some attic will cough up a long-forgotten trunk of old letters that would add to what scholars already know. Still, knowing more about the historical circumstances of the Judeans both in their homeland and in Babylonia would help us better interpret books like Isaiah, Jeremiah, Ezekiel, Daniel, Ezra, and Nehemiah (see Fig. 2).

Thematically, the Exile is even more dominant. One scholar estimates that "about 70 percent of the Hebrew Bible tackles the questions of how the catastrophe of exile was possible and what Israel can learn from it. Without the impact of this catastrophe, the Hebrew Bible would have received a completely different shape."[9]

Working with what strike me, a historian of more recent times, as the most fragmentary shreds of evidence, biblical scholars in recent decades have achieved major feats in reconstructing the history and meaning of the Exile. The significance of their work can be roughly divided into two

Timeline of Israel and Judah

C. 2000 B.C.E	Abraham
c. 1280	Moses and the Exodus from Egypt
c. 1000	David unifies Israel and makes Jerusalem capital
722	Assyria conquers northern kingdom of Israel
597	First exile to Babylon
587–586	Babylon conquers northern kingdom, destroys Jerusalem temple
582	Third exile (to Egypt)
538	Persia conquers Babylon, many exiles return to Judah
198–167	Maccabean uprising against Hellenization
63	Beginning of Roman rule
70 C.E	Destruction of second Jerusalem temple by Rome

FIGURE 2 Timeline of Israel and Judah.

camps: one offers a better understanding of the experience of the exiles in Babylonia; and the other revises our understanding of those Judeans who stayed behind, "on the land." Both bodies of work are revisionist in that they challenge prevailing understandings of what was happening in both theaters. And both lines of work are predicated not on new discoveries of artifacts and documents but on applying new scholarly methods of analysis to familiar materials.

First, there's a major sea-change in our understanding of the Judeans who ended up in Babylon, often referred to in the literature as the *Golah* (Hebrew for "exile"). The experience of the Exile was undoubtedly a lot more punishing—involving a lot more suffering—than has been acknowledged. Earlier generations of scholars worked from the few terse accounts in the Hebrew Bible that suggested the conditions were actually quite benign. After the hardship of dislocation, the earlier account goes, the Golah community were treated humanely enough—allowed to assimilate into the host society and to enjoy a certain cosmopolitan identity.[10]

The Bible's historical books, Kings and Chronicles, which otherwise provide nearly all the material we have on the events of the Babylonian conquest and its aftermath, tell us very little about lives during the Golah. After recounting the dismal events of 586, both 2 Kings and Jeremiah end with a glimmer of rehabilitation at least for Judah's exiled king, Jehoiachin. Nebuchadnezzar's successor "brought him out of prison, treated him kindly and gave him a seat at table above the kings with him in Babylon.

So Jehoiachin discarded his prison clothes and lived as a pensioner of the king for the rest of his life. For his maintenance, a regular daily allowance was given him by the king as long as he lived" (2 Kings 25:28–29). Amazingly, this is the only part of the biblical account corroborated by nonbiblical evidence, in this case a Babylonian cuneiform administrative list naming Jehoiachin as a recipient of rations.[11]

The suggestion that Judah's monarch enjoyed special favor relative to other kings reminds us that Babylonia may have practiced a means of political control familiar from medieval Japan under the shogunate: keeping one's enemy close. Heads of state and their courts were held "in residence" in Babylon as a means of political control. Others seem to have been there for diplomacy and the opportunities provided by empire. Babylonia comes across as the great global city of its day.

"The court of Nebuchadnezzar was famous for its cosmopolitan society," writes an Assyriologist. "Phoenicians, Syrians, Elamites, and Egyptians rubbed shoulders with Ionians and Israelites, feasting together and conversing in Aramaic. Well-educated members of the nobility and well-travelled professional mercenaries shared experiences and ideas. Many Assyrians were drawn southwards, away from their damaged cities and abandoned courts, into the centre of world power in Babylon."[12]

This was the rich hub of knowledge and social capital in which appeared Daniel, certainly the most prominent individual in the Golah known to us from the Hebrew Bible. Daniel provides a stunning example of an improbable meritocratic rise: he develops a close relationship with King Nebuchadnezzar, becoming his close adviser, interpreter of dreams, and ultimately the figure who wins freedom of religious expression for his fellow Judeans.

The trouble is, a lack of detail about the Golah can't be taken as suggesting that living conditions were benign—or harsh, for that matter. A passing over in silence can just as easily reflect the effect of trauma. Certainly the Bible provides voices that resonate with pain caused by the experience of the Exile in Babylon. The Book of Ezekiel, another text well known because of its attractiveness to end-times-prophecy-believing Christians, is set by the Kebar, a tributary of the Euphrates River. The bizarre and disturbing visions that ensue from Ezekiel in its many chapters bear all the hallmarks of trauma.

Reading the biblical literature through the lens of trauma theory suggests an agonizing experience during the Golah. Recent work in trauma theory and post-traumatic stress disorder (PTSD) shows that symptoms formerly associated with psychosis and other mental illness are symptoms of the human psyche struggling against an overload of anguish. Distortions in verbal and written communication, even a failure to communicate at all—to become mute—reflect strategies of self-defense. Gaps in the historical record, the fact that the Babylonian period is virtually void, means not that nothing of consequence happened but that the psychic costs of recounting that history outweighed the benefits. Other empirically demonstrated responses include self-blame—we brought this on ourselves—and a heightened in-group identity with accompanying nationalist tendencies.[13]

Other scholarly methods produce different pictures of the Golah. The Bible itself gives little insight into what motivated Nebuchadnezzar to invade Judah. Nebuchadnezzar is simply a conqueror, it seems. His job is to subjugate Israel, because that's what foreign kings do: first Assyrians, then Babylonians. The Book of Chronicles provides a thin narrative of feeble resistance and costly miscalculations that provoke a full-scale invasion of Judah and destruction of the Temple, a cataclysm that may well have exceeded the Babylonians' original intentions.

So what did motivate them? Imperial expansion is one answer, although tautological; empires exist to expand. It's clear that Nebuchadnezzar wanted Judah partly to serve as a buffer zone between Babylon and that rival power to the south, Egypt. The more interesting question is, why carry the population away in captivity and relocate them several hundred miles to the northeast in Babylon? Here recent scholarship offers some intriguing hypotheses. Empires also exist to extract and consolidate wealth, of which labor is a major form. Babylon hoped to extract value from neighboring Judah by turning it into a vassal state. Their initial hope was to administer Judah as a colonial possession, leaving its political leadership intact, but when its kings showed a pesky independent streak Babylon had no choice but to destroy Judah's leadership and haul its leadership class away.

What to do with these captives? With a very arid ecosystem, Babylonia's agricultural production depended on irrigation, which required regular desalinization of its waterways. Hence, many in the Golah were pressed into service as corvée laborers—coerced unpaid workers, though technically not slaves—building and maintaining irrigation ditches and other public work projects, including the ambitious temples Nebuchadnezzar erected in Babylon and other cities, such as Etemenanki, the towering ziggurat dedicated to Marduk. Hence verse one of Psalm 137 is sometimes retranslated as "By the irrigation canals of Babylon," its prosaic literalness standing in ironic contrast to the usual poetic quality. "For the community in forced migration, beauty was lament," writes John J. Ahn; "the shade was the shadows in which they lived."[14]

How much more difficult was this plight than that of the Hebrews in Egypt, source of the other central narrative of the Yahweh religion? Again, the Bible itself is laconic. Because we learn so much about Moses' long attempts to win freedom from bondage for his compatriots, we assume that Egyptian slavery must have been harsher. But the actual textured history is elusive.

Comprehending Migration

To flesh out this monochromatic picture of the Golah experience, scholars have brought to bear analytic tools from the social sciences, in particular the recent field of migration studies. The premise is that using concepts and categories developed for the study of recent migrations will provide insights into the experiences of the forced migrants of Judah. An important contribution of the recent scholarship lies in drawing distinctions between different categories of people who formerly might have been simply labeled "exiles" or "refugees." These blanket terms obscure a host of subtle variations: between migrants, exiles, refugees, and members of a diaspora; between voluntary and involuntary migrations; between internal migration and migration that crosses political boundaries.[15]

For a nuanced understanding of an exile experience we would want to know about cultural practices in the homeland prior to departure, as well as the practices that developed in the host country through complex interactions with the native population. Easily overlooked is what Adelaida Schramm calls the "context of exit": the circumstances under which migrants leave their home country, which can vary widely among both voluntary and involuntary groups, that play a significant role in how individuals and communities locate themselves in their new environments.[16]

Undoubtedly there was hard, back-breaking labor—but who wasn't performing arduous labor in the sixth century B.C.E.? Life was unimaginably hard for everyone. Undoubtedly there were variations both within particular slices of time (synchronic) and over time (diachronic). From a twenty-first-century perspective, a fifty-year-long exile appears as a brief blip. But in the real time of lived experience, half a century is a lifetime—more accurately, given life expectancy of the time, multiple lifetimes. Then as now, people entered the Exile at different stages of life, from older people unable to survive the arduous trek to infants born to mothers carrying them while on their forced march to Babylon—assuming that the captive Judeans included women, a basic fact not specified in the Bible.

Close attention to how different generations experience migration offers another analytical lens that biblical scholars have deployed to flesh out the experiences of the Golah. We can assume that the initial group of exiles included both adults, who were fully formed by their upbringing in Judah, and children born in Judah but whose life experiences were formed by the ordeal of forced migration and growing up as a member of a minority group in Babylon. Ahn refers to these groups as the "first" and the "1.5" generations. The second generation would include those born in captivity, whom sociology teaches us are likely to assimilate to the host society and break radically with their homeland. Following that pattern, the third generation would have expressed an impulse to recover some of its lost cultural heritage, witnessed the later conquest of Babylon by the Persians from the East, and possibly have been part of the Golah that then voluntarily repatriated to Judah.[17]

Adopting an on-the-ground generational perspective on the Exile rather than a telescopic view, which is hard to avoid when glancing back so far in history, also heightens our awareness of how easy it is to collapse a series of discrete historical events into a catch-all category: *The Exile* (see Fig. 3). Even the broad-stroke narrative provided by the Hebrew Bible makes clear that there was no single Exile event but three discrete moments of forced migration.

The first occurred in 597 B.C.E., when Nebuchadnezzar invaded Judah but left its political structure intact, bringing an elite group to Babylon. The major conquest, 587–586, followed a foolhardy rebellion against Babylonian power led by Zedekiah. In crushing this rebellion, Nebuchadnezzar blinded the king (after executing his sons), razed the Jerusalem Temple, and transported a large contingent drawn from the Judean elite—priests, temple musicians, scribes, warriors, and artisans—to Babylonia. The third exile took place in 582, when a smaller group, including Jeremiah, who had made himself politically unpopular in Judah by urging acceptance of Babylonian sovereignty, fled to Egypt. (I'll continue to use the term "Exile" to refer to the cumulative experience of Judean subjugation, with an understanding that there were several deportations involved, that this period extended over sixty years, and that there was no unitary Exile experience.)

FIGURE 3 Gypsum wall panel relief from ca. 700 B.C.E. showing an Assyrian soldier and three captives, possibly Judeans, carrying harps in wooded terrain. © Trustees of the British Museum.

Combining this more nuanced view of different perspectives brought to the Exile by different generations with a more finely calibrated understanding of a historical process rather than a onetime cataclysm helps clear up some of the puzzles that surround biblical accounts of the period. For example, Jeremiah seems to hold sharply inconsistent views on the meaning of Babylon's conquest and the proper response of Israelites to this challenge. In a well-known passage from chapter 29, he advocated peaceful coexistence with the conquerors. But elsewhere he hurls the most violent vituperations against Babylon.

Accepting the likelihood that the Book of Jeremiah reflects a kind of composite voice only later compiled into a single book, the differences between chapters 29 and 50 likely reflect the varying perspectives of different generations. An adult who witnessed the destruction of the Temple and was forced into corvée labor would hold a different attitude toward

Babylonians than someone who grew up knowing nothing apart from the experience of the Exile and perhaps had benefited from it.

Paying attention to these variations in point of view and chronology can help suggest hypotheses about the most fundamental questions of Psalm 137: Who wrote it, and when? The specificity of the text's *Sitz im Leben*—setting in life—sharpens its quality of eyewitness testimony. We imagine it having been composed by someone who actually sat down by the rivers, wept, hung his harp—and later recorded the memory.

The question of the authorship of the psalms as a group has generated widely different answers, for reasons raised vividly by Psalm 137. The long-standing Jewish and Christian assumption was that all were composed by King David, known for his musical and poetic gifts. Given that he lived four centuries before the events of the Exile naturally casts that in doubt—unless the psalms were proleptic, a possibility not easily dismissed by the faithful. For more historically attuned readers, the leading candidate was Jeremiah, who certainly experienced the Babylonian catastrophe and whose writings echo the sentiments and tone of the psalm.[18]

The consensus of most recent scholars is that Psalm 137 was composed during or shortly after the Exile. This begs the question, which exile? The first verses make no reference to the destruction of the Temple and therefore reflect the sensibility of the first deportation of 597, while the final verses focus on that traumatic episode. Embedded within this one short poem, therefore, are multiple perspectives, and likely generational differences. There are even grounds for believing the psalm could have been written centuries later, in response to the Roman subjugation of Israel, but that will be taken up in part 3 of this book.

Another tantalizing question remains: If such a significant chunk of the Hebrew Bible was being inscribed and redacted during the sixth century, who was doing this work? Where and how? Unfortunately, the earliest original texts date from centuries later. William Schniedewind makes a plausible case that the Exile narrative found in 2 Kings and Jeremiah (and Psalm 137) was compiled in Babylon by the royal court of the exiled king, Jehoiachin, which had "not only the vested interest but also the means to write and preserve this literature."[19] But no smoking gun will surface to resolve this question conclusively.

Which is not to say that no new evidence on life during the Exile can emerge, even at this late date. In recent years scholars have begun publishing new findings on freshly analyzed cuneiform tablets from Babylonia. For the most part, this research supports the view that the Golah was a less

traumatic rupture than biblical accounts insist. Rather than being ghet-
toized, Judeans were surprisingly well integrated into the economic and
administrative systems of imperial Babylon. And there was a significant
presence of Judean tenant farmers in rural Babylonia, apart from the elites
like deposed king Jehoiachin located in the capital. These settlers appear
to have been part of a land-for-service system that provided them land in
exchange for taxes and corvée labor. Many of the tablets concern life in a
settlement called āl-Yāhūdu—"Judahtown"—likely located in the vicinity
of Nippur, a war-devastated rural region southeast of Babylon, near the
Kebar canal where Ezekiel issued his prophecies.[20]

"Far from portraying a deported, old but impoverished, Judean elite,
these documents provide glimpses into the lives of ordinary people in a
rural setting: they till the land and build houses, pay taxes, and render
services to the king," conclude two scholars who have worked most closely
with the cuneiform documents. "At the same time that this shows adaptation to local and changed circumstances, a strong sense of Judean identity and attachment to their cultural and religious heritage emerges from
the name-giving patterns preserved across as many as four generations of
exilic life."[21]

Babylonia

I rarely meet people who can immediately identify Psalm 137; unheard of
are those who would regard it as a life-changer. I was fortunate to meet one,
a theologian named Marie, almost by chance. Her singular interest began
when she was in the eighth grade, living in Norway, writing a term paper
for a history class. Marie's mother had emigrated from Baghdad, and her
grandfather had owned orchards in Palestine that were confiscated. Marie
decided to research the 1948 war that led to the creation of Israel.

"And I found on the bookshelf at home this book called *O Jerusalem!*
by Larry Collins and Dominique Lapierre," she remembers. "And they not
only tell this sort of very vivid and vibrant story about the Arab-Israeli war,
but they quote Psalm 137 there. And this line just stuck with me, right: 'If
I forget thee O Jerusalem, may my right hand forget its cunning, may my
tongue cleave to the roof of my mouth if I do not remember thee, if I prefer not Jerusalem above my chief joy.' "[22]

Marie recalls becoming captivated by these lines. "And I used to dream
about it in the way that one does imaginatively at the age of twelve or

thirteen, you know, about sitting by the rivers of Babylon in exile, and what that was like. And I correlated that both to my mother's experience when I was growing up in Norway—that she was always in exile. And she is permanently in exile, right, she will never go back to Iraq till the day she dies. I've tried everything I could think of to convince her that maybe we could go once it's safe and she's never going back.

"And then I understood myself as well as living in some ways in exile. This had to do with my family background—I was born in the US when my parents were students here but I grew up in Norway from very small childhood." Marie's mother left Iraq to attend a small Seventh-Day Adventist college just outside Beirut, Lebanon. There she met her Norwegian husband. Both of them enrolled in medical school in the United States, then returned to Norway when Marie's father accepted a call as a medical missionary.

"We were also part of this very odd religious community. That is, we were Seventh-Day Adventists, and very passionately such—very, very passionate. I used to grow up with my father doing all these evangelist events, and trying to get Norwegians to become Seventh-Day Adventists, which is weirdly not a very successful practice, bless his heart. But the point being there were just a lot of points of contact for me with that psalm, and that's where it started.

"It became a site of obsession to me in the way that things often do in your early teens when you're trying to figure out who you are in the world and what your place is going to be in the world, and there were three primary sort of sites or events where that happened for me. One was—this is not going to be super-shocking—reading *Lord of the Rings* for the first time and becoming *one of those people.* Another was reading the *Rise and Fall of the Third Reich.* And then the third book that I read that became this kind of obsession was this *O Jerusalem.*

"I ended up writing a project that was two, three times longer than I was instructed to, and just trying to cram as much of the excitement and interest that I was feeling from that book. I was also memorizing a lot of poetry at the time, and so memorizing the psalm, then again, became part of that. These lines just become kind of touchstones for something. Especially the incongruity between the sense of exile and the longing for revenge. That twist.

"And its inexplicability to me in terms of how I then thought about the Bible as well. I was very much raised as an inerrantist [someone who believes that every detail in the Bible is literally true], and was starting to very gently move away from that, but only very, very gently. So at the time it was more of a question, how do you go from here to there in terms of this imagery? And then it became so bound up with contemporary events. With thinking of Jerusalem as a site of longing. With thinking what it means to be Jewish and in exile versus what it means to be Arab and in exile. And the obvious structural similarities between those experiences, and at the same time the ongoing contestations that are inside that lack of relationship, in some ways."

Marie visited Jerusalem at age sixteen, and she drove her family crazy by reciting Psalm 137 constantly, "looking sad and longing at any number of important sites." The Israel Museum in Jerusalem made a particular impression. The ancient Torah scrolls and robes, which she remembers as being among the most spectacular objects in the museum, made her aware of how extremely old and sophisticated the Jewish community in Baghdad was. She learned from her mother, who grew up in the Jewish quarter of Baghdad, that two schoolmates had disappeared from the class-room in the mid-1950s, repatriated to Israel during a time of rising tension between Israel and the Arab countries.

Babylon came first. When Marie was three the family traveled to Iraq, of which she has her very first memories, including being terrified of fall-ing into a hole in which she was sure lions would be lurking.

"At age three you knew about Daniel and the lion's den?" I ask.

"I am a throwback in this regard," Marie explains. "I was raised with the Bible in a way that very few children are anymore. It was the first thing I ever read, that was read to me from my earliest days. I'd read the Bible myself cover to cover before turning nine years old. So yes, I did know about Daniel, very much so! Very, very much so. I even knew about Nebuchadnezzar."

For its part, the Hebrew Bible tells us next to nothing about the experi-ence of deportation to Babylon; about the living conditions faced by the migrants in their host country; or about whom was reworking the Bible and under what conditions. Or even what language they spoke, and how they communicated with their oppressors. These are all questions about which literary and social historians might sell their souls to know more.

Hebrew scripture does, however, contain a fair amount of detail on who was displaced. In 597, the first displacement, 2 Kings 24 reports that some 10,000 officers and soldiers were taken away, including Jehoiachin's mother "and his wives [there may have been a consider-able number], his eunuchs and the foremost men of the land." Also deported were "all men of substance, seven thousand in number, and a thousand craftsmen and smiths, all of them able-bodied men and skilled armourers."

Ten years later, when Jerusalem was besieged and its Temple razed, the exiled included all who were left in the city, those who had deserted to Nebuchadnezzar, and remaining artisans. (Jeremiah 52 gives us significantly lower totals for three distinct deportations: 3,023, 832, and 745, totaling 4,600.)

After which the Deuteronomic history is silent. Until thirty-seven years later, when, on assuming the throne, Nebuchadnezzar's successor Evil-Merodach released Jehoiachin from prison, gave him a seat of honor at the dining table, and provided a lifetime allowance.

While our focus has been on the human cost of the Exile, we should note that the Bible focuses significant attention on the treasures taken to Babylonia, in particular the precious objects of Temple worship. There is as much detailed attention to loss of bronze, silver, and gold as to the particulars of human displacement.

The Bible also contains two ostensibly eyewitness accounts of life in Babylon from the Judean perspective: the books of Daniel and Ezekiel. Interestingly, these are two of the best-known books among dispensationalist Christians, who read them carefully alongside the final book of the New Testament, Revelation, for their intricate trails of chronometric clues about the End Times: rapture, apocalypse, millennium, Second Coming.

In Nebuchadnezzar's Court

Daniel gets Bible readers close to the heart of Babylonian power. Like Jacob's son Joseph, another good-looking and resourceful Hebrew who ascended to the top of an empire (Pharaoh's Egypt), indirectly setting in motion the sacred history of Israel, Daniel made good working in the master's house. Both were self-made or, more accurately, Yahweh-made men. While Joseph gets in close with Pharaoh, Daniel makes himself invaluable to Nebuchadnezzar, mainly through the same uncanny ability to interpret dreams. Proximity to power does nothing to corrupt either man.

After conquering and deporting the Judeans, Nebuchadnezzar picks a handful of the best and brightest exiles of noble birth, intelligent and attractive, to join his court and be groomed in Chaldean language and art. Daniel is one of four who make the cut. All are given new Babylonian names: Daniel becomes Belteshazzar.

Daniel's first achievement, according to the biblical account, is to establish a healthy diet. Rather than risk eating pork, Daniel abstains from meat
and issues a challenge to the Babylonian court: compare the health of the
Judean vegetarians with the men assigned royal food. After ten days the
four Judeans looked healthier, and as a result wine and meat were elimi-
nated from the court; all were served vegetables (the reaction of the non-
Judeans to this new diet isn't recorded).

Later, afflicted by troubling dreams, the king asks his magicians and
astrologers to interpret them. They demur, enraging Nebuchadnezzar,
who then orders the execution of all the kingdom's wise men. Facing
execution himself, Daniel requests the chance to offer his own interpretation. After conferring with his Judean comrades, and taking care to credit
Yahweh, Daniel proceeds to recount in vivid detail the dazzling and fearful
imagery at the center of the king's dream. It turns out to be an allegory of
the rise and fall of four kingdoms, to be followed by a fifth that will bring
history to an end.

Nebuchadnezzar is suitably impressed, noting that Daniel's god is in
fact supreme. He promotes Daniel, making him regent over Babylonia and
chief prefect over all its wise men. Daniel intervenes to win promotions
for his Judean comrades. Certain Chaldeans, possibly disgruntled wise
men, orchestrate another showdown between the king and the exiles, this
time over a huge golden image, ninety feet tall, to which Nebuchadnezzar
has commanded all his subjects to prostrate themselves and worship. The
three Judeans refuse to obey and are cast into a blazing furnace so hot it
kills the executioners; the men survive. The king is even more intrigued,
issuing a decree that anyone who speaks blasphemy against this mysterious god will be "torn to pieces" (Daniel 3:29).

Having proved the supremacy of his god to Nebuchadnezzar (there
is yet a third dream-interpretation sequence), Daniel faces the same
challenge with the king's successors, Belshazzar and Darius. Identified
as Nebuchadnezzar's son, Belshazzar commits a new crime against
Yahweh: he throws a lavish banquet at which the assembled nobles drink
wine in vessels looted from the Jerusalem Temple. A mysterious hand
appears to write cryptic and ominous graffiti on the wall of the palace, leaving the king nonplussed. Daniel interprets the saying to mean the end of
Belshazzar, who promotes Daniel yet again—but ends up being slain that
night by the Persian conqueror, Darius.

As before, the chief ministers and satraps conspire against Daniel by
exposing the fact that he disobeys a royal edict by praying three times a day

to Yahweh. He is famously hurled into the lion's den but is protected by his god; his accusers, along with their wives and children, are then thrown in and instantly devoured.

The Book of Daniel continues through more dreams and visions experienced not by a foreign king but by Daniel himself. These later chapters interweave numerous military campaigns waged by Alexander the Great and his successors with prophecies of the Apocalypse and Rapture. In these chapters, Daniel is the one troubled and in need of soothsaying, which is provided by the angel Gabriel. Tellingly, these final revelations come to Daniel on the bank of a great river in Babylon—not a tributary of the Euphrates, where Psalm 137 is set, but the Tigris.

There are major problems with relying on Daniel as eyewitness to the Exile, the most important being that scholars believe most of the Book of Daniel was written four centuries later.[23] It is generally dated during the reign of Antiochus IV, a Greek Seleucid ruler, who responded to a rebellion/civil war in Judah by massacring and selling into slavery a large group of the population. Antiochus also desecrated the Temple (though it was not fully demolished for another 200 years, by the Romans), banned required rites and customs like circumcision and keeping the Sabbath, and required worship of Zeus.

There's no question that when compared with the available historiography, the Book of Daniel starts with fuzzy chronology and garbles basic facts about the succession of leaders from Nebuchadnezzar through Darius. Daniel is sacred history in its purest form, a book that can just as easily be taken as a reflection of the second century B.C.E. as the sixth. But for nearly all Jews and Christians, who until recently had no access to or particular interest in methods of historical criticism, there would have been no reason not to read Daniel as documenting the facts of Nebuchadnezzar's court. As Robert Allen Warrior observes about the Hebrew Bible, "People who read the narratives read them as they are, not as scholars and experts would *like* them to be read and interpreted. History is no longer with us. The narrative remains."[24]

What would such readers take away from the Book of Daniel about Babylon?

First, they would see that it was a cosmopolitan empire comprising all peoples, nations, and languages, and that it was possible for an exiled Judean to distinguish himself in this cosmopolitan foreign court without compromising his devotion to Yahweh. In fact, Daniel's success depended on faithful submission, acknowledging Yahweh as the source of all his gifts. Readers would notice that his hard-won position would be constantly challenged by Chaldean wise men—sorcerers, magicians, exorcists, diviners, and astrologers—setting up a showdown with life-or-death stakes. They would see that Daniel consistently prevailed, whether in the right to a healthy vegetable diet or to freely worship his god. Babylon's rulers, prone to caprice and towering rages, would repeatedly accept the supremacy of Daniel's god but would continue to resist Yahweh's power, seemingly despite themselves.

Prophecy turned out to be a useful way of speaking truth to power, the Book of Daniel suggests. The sort of prophecy given to Daniel could pay both short-term benefits (surviving court intrigue, understanding the violent confusion of current events in which Judeans found themselves passively caught up) and long-term benefits (seeing how history would unfold until the end of time).

These are, to be sure, twenty-first-century projections about what readers of earlier ages might have found noteworthy about Daniel. For the sake of this project, though, some reasonable speculation along these lines seems justified.

By the Kebar

If Daniel makes his way to the inner sanctum of power, Ezekiel provides the perspective of someone closer to Babylon's irrigation canals.

A temple priest before he became a prophet, by nearly any standard Ezekiel is outrageous, over-the-top. To call him the "wild man" of the Hebrew Bible would not be an exaggeration. Scholars have suggested that Ezekiel's bizarre behavior and hallucinatory prophecies are the mark of someone with the psychic scars of a trauma survivor or a post-traumatic stress disorder (PTSD) sufferer, possibly a person with epilepsy.[25] The Book of Ezekiel is highly unusual among ancient texts in narrating one of history's less prepossessing characters.

The book opens with the prophet beside the Kebar River, one of the irrigation canals near Nippur and slightly downriver from Babylon. Chapter three places Ezekiel in Tel-abib, one of the labor camps populated by the Judean exiles and located in present-day Syria. Ezekiel is a Zakhovite priest, part of the social elite taken in the initial displacement of 597, when he was twenty-five. Five years later he is commanded by Yahweh to begin his oracles to Judah.

Yahweh first appears to Ezekiel in one of the most extraordinary visions recorded in the Hebrew Bible, a visitation by a winged creature

with multiple visages—human, lion, ox, eagle—almost like a Cubist painting, surrounded by radiant fire and flashes of lightning. Alongside the
figure are sparkling wheels with eyes along their rims that spin and move
in synchrony (inspiring modern theories of flying saucers). A sound of
wings "like the noise of a great torrent or of a cloud-burst, like the noise
of a crowd or of an armed camp" (1:24). Above all, a glittering vault holds
a sapphire throne in which is seated a form in human likeness: Yahweh.
The image brings to mind a kind of enormous intergalactic battle chariot.

Ezekiel throws himself on his face but is commanded: "Man, he said,
stand up, and let me talk with you .... Man, I am sending you to the
Israelites, a nation of rebels who have rebelled against me. Past generations of them have been in revolt against me to this very day, and this
generation to which I am sending you is stubborn" (2:2–3). Yahweh orders
Ezekiel to open his mouth and eat a scroll "written all over on both sides
with dirges and laments and words of woe" (2:10).

Stubborn and rebellious these Israelites may be, like scorpions, but at
least they share a language. "You are sent not to people whose speech is
thick and difficult, but to Israelites .... The Israelites will refuse to listen
to you, for they refuse to listen to me, so brazen are they all and stubborn. But I will make you a match for them. I will make you as brazen as
they are and as stubborn as they are. I will make your brow like adamant,
harder than flint" (3:5–9). This turns out to be the case; Ezekiel becomes
an uncompromising oracle.

Then Ezekiel is carried off to share his revelations to his fellow exiles at
Tel-abib. For seven days he is dumbfounded, unable to speak. "Man, I have
made you a watchman for the Israelites," Yahweh finally instructs him;
"you will take messages from me and carry my warnings to them" (3:17).
He is commanded to be tied up with ropes in his house. "I will fasten your
tongue to the roof of your mouth and you will be unable to speak," advises
a spirit, echoing a trope from Psalm 137. "But when I have something to
say to you, I will give you back the power of speech" (3:26–27).

Ezekiel is commanded to eat bread baked in ovens fueled by human
dung (he convinces Yahweh to relent) and to shear his hair and beard with
a sharp sword. Then commences a series of revelations about the destruction of Jerusalem, brought on by its many "monstrous abominations," its
violation of God's laws and statutes, failure to honor the Sabbath, and,
most damning of all, its seduction by foreign gods and idols.

Jerusalem is infamously compared in some detail to a harlot. Even
worse than a prostitute—Jerusalem doesn't even take payment but bribes

her lovers to fornicate with her. In a later, nearly pornographic passage, Jerusalem is condemned as a nymphomaniac who lusts after foreign men, Chaldeans and Egyptians. "She was infatuated with their male prostitutes, whose members were like those of asses and whose seed came in floods like that of horses," Ezekiel is commanded to recount (23:20).

T. M. Lemos argues that in passages like this Ezekiel has internalized the masculine ideas of the Babylonian conquerors at the expense of Judean men, who become feminized and whorish. "Texts such as Ezekiel, written by a vanquished, debased man and for an audience of vanquished, debased people, are exceedingly rare in the ancient world," she writes. More typically, history records the boasts of conquering kings who take pride in torturing and mutilating their foes.[26] In later oracles relayed to Ezekiel, Yahweh turns his considerable wrath against Judah's neighbors: Ammon, Moab, Edom, Tyre, Sidon, Egypt.

In Ezekiel's ninth year of exile, and shortly before the conquest of Jerusalem and destruction of its Temple, Yahweh announces: "Man, I am taking from you at one blow the dearest thing you have, but you must not wail or weep or give way to tears. Keep in good heart; be quiet, and make no mourning for the dead; cover your head as usual and put sandals on your feet. You shall not cover your upper lip in mourning nor eat the bread of despair" (24:17).

That evening Ezekiel's wife dies; the following year Babylon invades Judah and destroys the Temple. Ezekiel's last prophecy occurred in 571, quite early in the Exile period. These oracles clearly had distinct audiences. The initial audience was composed of fellow exiles in Babylon, but the hard messages were directed at people remaining in Judah, particularly Jerusalem, which had not yet been destroyed.

What might we glean from Ezekiel about the Exile experience?

Very little, apart from confirming that Judeans were concentrated in settlements along still-existing waterways. We learn nothing of others in the community or of the labor they were doing. For Assyriologists, there is some evidence of the creative cultural intercourse we expect in global cities. "Once again we see a situation in which the exchange of information and close cultural contact could take place at the highest levels of society as a direct result of deportation," Stephanie Dalley writes. "Ezekiel's famous vision of the Chariot of God which he saw while he lived in Babylonia almost certainly uses imagery from the great temples and their rituals which he witnessed in exile. His tomb in lower Mesopotamia is still a place of pilgrimage for people of different faiths."[27]

Not in recent decades, though. In 2010, the *New York Times* reported efforts to reinvigorate this history of interreligious cooperation by restoring Ezekiel's tomb, now in the small town of Kifl, about twenty miles south of what was Babylon.

Dating from the fourteenth century, the tomb's interior features Hebrew carvings and old photographs of the Jews who once worshipped in the synagogue that surrounds it; atop the tomb rises a characteristically Islamic conical dome. A precariously leaning minaret stands nearby in the ancient city center, a latter-day Tower of Babel. "Muslims, too, revere the site as the tomb of Dhul Kifl, a prophet mentioned twice in the Koran who gave the town its name and who has long been assumed to be the same man as Ezekiel," explains Stephen Farrell of the *New York Times*. An upgraded Kifl could be a major tourist draw for millions of Shiite pilgrims who annually visit other holy sites of Islam.[28]

The last Jewish families left Kifl by 1951. "It was a very small place, and filled with date palms," recalls Zvi Yehuda, born there in 1936 and now research director at the Babylonian Jewry Heritage Center in Israel. "The Euphrates, the colors of the waters. As a child, near our house, we had a horse, and we had a cow and we had milk. We had everything." Iraqi officials hope to win World Heritage status from UNESCO and lure both Jewish and Christian tourists back. "We can prove to the world that this place is one of the cultural places that promote civilization and peaceful coexistence between peoples," the director of the State Board of Antiquities told the *Times*.[29] Not surprisingly, these efforts face daunting, and worsening, challenges on all sides.

People of the Land

Having sketched something of life in the Golah, what can we say about the homeland, Zion?

Judging from the Hebrew Bible, Judah was basically evacuated of anyone of significance. Following the 587 conquest, and the capture and blinding of Zedekiah, 2 Kings 25 reports, "the army of the Chaldeans who were with the captain of the guard carried into exile the rest of the people who were left in the city and the deserters who had defected to the king of Babylon—all the rest of the population. But the captain of the guard left some of the poorest people of the land to be vinedressers and toilers of the soil."

Challenging this "myth of the empty land" has been the other major focus of the past generation of scholars of the Exile. Just as studies of the Golah reflect the impact of new work on migration, refugees, and diaspora, scholarship on Judah during the Exile decades reflects the influence of fields like subaltern studies and history written from the bottom up. The challenge of recovering the history of people whose voices were lost to an already meager documentary record could hardly be greater than for Judeans left behind. By definition they were marginal, irrelevant to the narrative that took shape among the scribes and scholars who compiled scripture in exile. Their voices were silenced both because they weren't part of a formative experience and because they were regarded with suspicion by their compatriots who were carried away in captivity.[30]

In other words, theirs was an ideological erasure. There is an advantage to be gained by believing, perhaps ingenuously, and then creating a historical record that removes other people from the realm of historical actors.

This may have been the first instance of this empty-land myth in recorded history, but the claim has recurred frequently in recent colonial contexts. The belief that North America was essentially uninhabited, virgin land, and therefore free for colonial possession, undergirds a tenacious narrative of American history, developed most influentially by Frederick Jackson Turner in what came to be known as the "frontier thesis": that American democracy in all its exceptional glory emerged from the struggle to push the frontier west.

A myth of the empty land also buttresses the ideology that led to the colonization of South Africa by Boers and Brits. And the myth circled back to its origin point in Palestine, after World War II, where the establishment of Israel was premised on the notion that the region was being wasted, with a small population and less economic development. How ironic, then, that two-and-a-half millennia earlier the argument was advanced in the Bible, if obliquely, referring to fellow Judeans who stayed on the land.[31]

If the land wasn't empty, why did that myth get started? Who was there, what were they doing, and how do we know any of it? Estimates by historical demographers of total numbers displaced from Judah to Babylonia range from a high of 20,000 people, roughly one-quarter of the population, to only half that many. But losses from warfare and the inevitable sequellae, epidemics and famine, would have carried off larger numbers. Estimates of *total* loss of population, then, range from 60 percent to as high as 80 or 90 percent.[32]

As the Temple was destroyed in a blow against the sacred cynosure of Judean culture, the proportion of population shifted north to the Benjamin region centered on Mizrah. Nebuchadnezzar designed the new capital city of Judah after the destruction of Jerusalem. Without its temple and the knowledge workers and artisans who went along with it, Judah was a completely different place. Scholars have proposed a new appellation for the region: Templeless Judah. With the Jerusalem-based population deported to the northeast, the remaining population would have been those who lived off the land. The little we think we know about them comes through painstaking extrapolation from the scant existing records.

Jeremiah

What we know also comes from the biblical eyewitnesses. If the exiles included Daniel and Ezekiel as putative participants, Judah presents us with the testimony of Jeremiah and the Book of Lamentations.

Probably the best known of all Hebrew prophets, Jeremiah is slightly older than Ezekiel. Born to a priest in a village just north of Jerusalem, he is called to prophecy by Yahweh in 627, forty years before the conquest of Jerusalem, and continues his oracles a few years beyond 587. So Jeremiah prophesies under four Judean monarchs: Josiah, Jehoiakim, Zedekiah, and the exiled king Jehoiachin. He witnesses, harangues, and tries in vain to alter the historical events that lead to the massive displacement of Judeans and destruction of the Temple.

Jeremiah is a reluctant prophet who at times expressed self-pity for being continually thrust into harrowing, often life-threatening situations. He is also deprived of the ordinary comforts of a wife and children, practically condemned to a solitary life. He blasts his people for the same offenses— unfaithfulness to Yahweh, idolatry, breaking laws and statutes—and in much the same language as Ezekiel, though somewhat more subdued. Judah is described in Jeremiah as a harlot, for example, but also as a twice-divorced woman who attempts to return to her first husband.

Jeremiah takes Yahweh's message to the Temple itself. "You steal, you murder, you commit adultery and perjury, you burn sacrifices to Baal, you run after other gods whom you have not known," Jeremiah is commanded to say; "then you come and stand before me in this house, which bears my name, and say, 'We are safe;' safe, you think, to indulge in all these abominations" (7:9–10). A message of social justice sometimes seeps through, as Yahweh urges the assembled temple worshipers: "Mend your ways and doings, deal fairly with one another, do not oppress the alien, the orphan, and the widow, shed no innocent blood in this place" (7:5–6).

In a particularly dramatic performance, Jeremiah smashes an earthenware jar in front of an audience of Judean elders and priests, then returns to Jerusalem to issue a bloody oracle. This initiates a long showdown with the Jerusalem establishment during which Jeremiah is imprisoned; flogged; placed in stocks at the city gate; and almost condemned to death for sedition under two different kings, Jehoiakim and Zedekiah, the latter nearly allowing him to be killed by immersion in a murky cesspool.

He also contends with challenges from assorted rivals whose prophecies contradict his own. Most hurtful to his vocation as Yahweh's prophet is that Jeremiah is ignored—for thirty years, until Nebuchadnezzar invades in 597. The Babylonian ruler replaces Jehoiakim with Zedekiah, and takes the young king Jehoiachin to Babylon as a royal hostage along with the first contingent of the Judean elite.

Jeremiah's messages are received no more favorably by Zedekiah than they were by Jehoiakim, though. In addition to the message of Judah's corruption that he has been delivering for thirty years, Jeremiah is given the prophecy that the nation must submit to Babylon: "If any nation or kingdom will not serve Nebuchadnezzar king of Babylon or submit to his yoke, I will punish them with sword, famine, and pestilence, says the LORD, until I leave them entirely in his power" (27:8). Jeremiah underscores this divine message in a famous letter he sends via royal envoys to the exiles in Babylon:

> Build houses and live in them; plant gardens and eat their produce. Marry wives and beget sons and daughters; take wives for your sons and give your daughters to husbands, so that they may bear sons and daughters and you may increase there and not dwindle away. Seek the welfare of any city to which I have carried you off, and pray to the LORD for it; on its welfare your welfare will depend. (29:5–7)

It's difficult not to read this as advocating some degree of assimilation and acceptance of intermarriage.[33]

With this encouragement of the Judeans in Exile—Yahweh regards them as "good figs"—comes condemnation of those remaining in Judah: the "bad figs." "I will make them repugnant to all the kingdoms of the earth,"

Yahweh communicates through Jeremiah, "a reproach, a by-word, an object-lesson and a thing of ridicule wherever I drive them" (24:9).[34]

This prophecy does not go over well with official Jerusalem, which wants Jeremiah put to death for sedition. Zedekiah takes the prophet seriously enough to have a private conversation with him, asking his advice on how to respond to Babylon, but in the end rejects the divine message of submission.

The outcome for Jerusalem is, of course, cataclysm. When the city falls, Jeremiah is released from detention by Nebuchadnezzar's captain of the guard, who treats him notably well. As he is being marched north toward Babylon, he is unchained and given the choice of relocating to Babylon or settling anywhere he chooses in Judah. He ends up north of Jerusalem, in Mizpah, which would serve as the new capital of the war-devastated Judah. Here he is under the charge of Gedaliah, appointed by Nebuchadnezzar as a puppet governor. The already muddy ethical milieu that Jeremiah has been navigating becomes even more complex. Is Judah still a covenanted people or a corrupt abomination? Is Babylon an evil oppressor or Yahweh's vehicle for carrying out justice against his once-chosen people?

At which point a band of Judeans assassinates Gedaliah and is in turn massacred by fellow Judeans; there is more killing and political maneuvering. They then approach Jeremiah about whether to flee to Egypt to escape expected reprisals from Nebuchadnezzar. Jeremiah conveys Yahweh's answer: Stay in Judah. Once again, Jeremiah's oracle is rejected. By this point, confusingly, Jeremiah himself is reported to be in Egypt, where he issues a savage prophecy forecasting Nebuchadnezzar's invasion of, now, Egypt and destruction of its own temples.

Moreover, the wives of his fellow refugees have been worshipping a female deity: burning sacrifices, pouring drink-offerings, and baking crescent-cakes marked with her image. Jeremiah then makes his final prophecy: that like Zedekiah, Pharaoh will be deposed and the Judeans who fled to Egypt destroyed.

In light of Jeremiah's intimate personal involvement with the fall of Jerusalem, it's not surprising that Jewish rabbinic and prerabbinic commentators ascribed authorship of Psalm 137 to the prophet. In fact, the Book of Jeremiah contains a number of passages reminiscent of the psalm: foretelling destruction of the Edomites, "repaying" Babylon for her crimes, "dashing" various evildoers. An account by the first-century Jewish historian Josephus reports that the aforementioned Judean exiles who sought refuge in Egypt were themselves deported to Babylon after

Nebuchadnezzar's successful conquest of Egypt. Rabbinic exegetes specu-
lated that Jeremiah was among these exiles, thus making possible his presence by the proverbial Babylonian waters.[35]

"Surely Jeremiah, the author of Lamentations, was a fit candidate for
authorship of this brief lament as well," observes James Kugel, paraphrasing the Midrashic tradition, "all the more so because, as a prophet, he
had announced in his oracles the same vengeance on Babylon and Edom
that our psalm speaks of—and in strikingly similar language. And if we
locate the time of its composition toward the end of the exile, it will further accord with the curious mixture found in the psalm of retrospective
contemplation of suffering ('. . . we sat down and wept') with the prospective (because apparently still unfulfilled) contemplation of a return to
Jerusalem ('If I forget you, O Jerusalem . . .') and the vengeance still to be
wreaked on Israel's enemies."[36]

Lamentations

In many ways the most compelling account of the Exile, whether experienced in Babylon or Judah, is found in the book that directly follows
Jeremiah.

Some Midrashic traditions even attribute the poems in Lamentations
to Jeremiah, based on affinities of style and outlook. While the Book of
Jeremiah includes prose sections alternating with poetry, Lamentations is
pure poetry. Still, it is a complex fugue of voices: a narrator who describes
the devastation of Jerusalem; a man of affliction who retains a glimmer
of hope despite being crushed by the conditions of war-torn Judah; a collective first-person narrative reminiscent of the captives who mourn in
Psalm 137; and most memorably, Lady Jerusalem, widowed and childless,
narrating her own harrowing plight in a voice numb with grief.

Unlike the other texts we've considered, which feature prophets passing on edicts from Yahweh and then narrating the usually unsatisfactory
results, Lamentations provides neither a divine voice nor the focused point-
of-view of a strong personality. It offers instead a polyphony of voices. As
poetry, it was easier to transmit and preserve orally, and has lent itself to
liturgical uses as an expression of mourning.

Stark details emerge from the war-torn landscape. "Her priests groan
and sigh, her virgins are cruelly treated" (1:4). Gentiles are seen entering
the sanctuary, violating Jerusalem's sacred space (also an allusion to sexual
violation). The built city has been ruined: "Her gates are sunk into the

earth, he has shattered and broken their bars." This wrecked landscape reveals immense human suffering, most sharply exposed in the plight of children. "The sucking infant's / tongue cleaves to its palate from thirst," echoing verse six of Psalm 137; "young children beg for bread / but not one offers them a crumb" (4:4).

The narrator observes as "children and infants faint / in the streets of the town / and cry to their mothers, / 'Where can we get corn and wine?'— when they faint like wounded things / in the streets of the city, / gasping out their lives / in their mothers' bosom" (2:11–12).

More horrifying, "Tender-hearted women with their own hands / boiled their own children; their children became their food / in the day of my people's wounding" (4:10). In addition to these post-Holocaust images are passages in the first person, reporting a more subjective experience of suffering.

Daughter Jerusalem, the personification of the city, reports of illness sent by Yahweh: "He sent down fire from heaven, it ran through my bones; he spread out a net to catch my feet, / it turned me back; / he made me an example of desolation, / racked with sickness all day long" (1:13). "My bowels writhe in anguish and my stomach turns within me" (1:20); this trope of gastrointestinal anguish, either from hunger or disease, is repeated in other testimony (2:11). "He has wasted away my flesh and my skin / and broken all my bones," laments the man of affliction. "He has broken my teeth on gravel; fed on ashes, I am racked with pain" (3:4, 16).

A passage from the final communal lament captures well the damage inflicted on different sectors of the population:

> Slaves have become our rulers,
> And there is no one to rescue us from them.
> We must bring in our food from the wilderness,
> Risking our lives in the scorching heat.
> Our skins are blackened as in a furnace
> By the ravages of starvation.
> Women were raped in Zion,
> Virgins raped in the cities of Judah.
> Princes were hung up by their hands,
> And elders received no honour.
> Young men toil to grind corn,
> And boys stumble under loads of wood.
> Elders have left off their session in the gate,
> And young men no longer pluck the strings. (5:8–14)

As before, music serves as an index of suffering and defeat. Whether hung up or not, harps have been given up. Instead, the victors' music becomes a weapon. "I have become a laughing-stock to all nations / the target of their mocking songs all day" (3:14).

Again, through the logic of metonymy, the Hebrew Bible directs us to read the experience of the inhabitants of Jerusalem as that of Judeans, the people of Yahweh. We find this pattern throughout the Bible: Lady Jerusalem (or Zion) symbolizes Israel, which in turn stands for an ethnic community defined by its covenant with Yahweh. Texts composed and reworked under conditions of exile rivet the attention of readers on those Judeans whose experience most clearly reflects the political theology through which the exiles made sense of their tumultuous history.

My point is not to dismiss the perspective of the Golah as ideological illusion, but to reiterate that the requirements of historiography are different from those of sacred history.

A careful reading of both biblical and extrabiblical evidence suggests that the exiled Judean royal family in Babylon—King Jehoiachin and his entourage—decisively influenced the texts that narrate the Exile: 2 Kings, Isaiah, Jeremiah, Ezekiel, Ezra. These books tend to give a favorable account of Jehoiachin, who lived a privileged life in Babylon, in comparison to two other potential Judean kings: Jehoiachin's grandfather Jehoahaz, exiled in Egypt, and Jehoiachin's uncle Zedekiah, who rebelled against Nebuchadnezzar and paid dearly for it with his life (and his sons') and destruction of the Jerusalem Temple.

"Why is the fate of King Jehoiachin, a prisoner in Babylon for some thirty-seven years before his release in 550 B.C.E., so important to this narrative of the exile?" asks William Schniedewind. "The obvious answer is that this same Jehoiachin was behind the writing of the Bible during the exile."[37]

In effect, the exiled king was a collaborator with the power that had conquered his people and destroyed the temple. "Jehoiachin probably also served as a counselor to King Nebuchadnezzar," according to Schniedewind, "giving information as required about this remote region of the Babylonian Empire. It is out of this royal family, and the support afforded them in the Babylonian court, that the preservation and writing of biblical literature continued, though on a limited basis, in the exilic period."[38]

In fact, Babylon was the only place that could have supported any kind of sustained Judean literary activity; after the conquest, even if Judah was not literally an "empty land," living conditions were too challenging to support literacy and textuality. Ironically, then, it was fortunate for the development of the Hebrew Bible that it enjoyed the patronage of its Babylonian nemesis.

Let me emphasize again that this discussion of Daniel, Ezekiel, Jeremiah, and Lamentations is not an effort to reconstruct "what really happened" in Palestine and Mesopotamia in the early decades of the sixth century B.C.E. While these texts may in some cases reference actual events, the lengthy process of redaction renders dubious their value as historical sources. But these accounts clearly have shaped the sacred history of the Exile—the grainy details that have colored Jewish and Christian understandings for nearly two millennia. Detail matters as much, if not more so, in fictional narratives as in historical ones.

Strange Lands

The salient questions raised by the psalm's opening lines are not, from the view of the psalmist, What have we done wrong? Why are we here, and Why is God punishing us? The questions are rather: Given the situation in which we find ourselves, this disturbing time and place, how are we expected to act? Given our obligations to Yahweh, how should we respond to our captors? Is there any place for sacred song in this setting, for this audience of people who manifestly do not wish us well? Note the emphasis on first-person plural; this is a collective challenge through and through.

The dilemma comes to a head in verse four: How shall we sing the Lord's song in a strange land?

Surely this is one of the best-known questions posed by the Hebrew Bible. And it is also one of the most universal: several books have been published with that very title. *How shall we sing the Lord's song in a strange land?* practically begs for a colon followed by a subtitle. If we count variations, the number of titles multiplies: *Singing the Lord's Song ... or, In a Strange Land.* The number of books, dissertations, and song titles shoots up into the dozens if expanded to include variations of the first verse: *By the Rivers of Babylon; By the Waters of Babylon; Rivers of Babylon; Waters of Babylon.*

Psalm 137's language has found its way into titles of literature as well. Elizabeth Smart titled her path-breaking, searing prose poem about frustrated love and unwedded motherhood *By Grand Central Station I Sat Down and Wept* (1945). William Faulkner wanted to title his 1939 novel *If I Forget Thee, Jerusalem*; he was talked out of it by his editors for fear anti-Semitism might hurt book sales. It was released instead as *The Wild Palms* (and also deals with forbidden love, pregnancy, and childbirth). Stephen Vincent Benét titled one of his short stories "By the Waters of Babylon" (1925); Arthur Clarke published a short sketch, "'If I Forget Thee, Oh Earth . . .'" (1951), about interplanetary exile after nuclear Armageddon.[39]

There are many poems as well, in English alone. Emma Lazarus's last poem published in her lifetime was "By the Waters of Babylon," a prose poem in seven parts. Part 1, "The Exodus (August 3, 1492)," narrates the expulsion of Jews from Spain. Part 5 is titled "Currents":

1. Vast oceanic movements, the flux and reflux of immeasurable tides oversweep our continent.
2. From the far Caucasian steppes, from the squalid Ghettos of Europe,
3. From Odessa and Bucharest, from Kief and Ekaterinoslav,
4. Hark to the cry of the exiles of Babylon, the voice of Rachel mourning for her children, of Israel lamenting for Zion.
5. And lo, like a turbid stream, the long-pent flood bursts the dykes of oppression and rushes hitherward.
6. Unto her ample breast, the generous mother of nations welcomes them.
7. The herdsman of Canaan and the seed of Jerusalem's royal shepherd renew their youth amid the pastoral plains of Texas and the golden valleys of the Sierras.[40]

The experience of being exiled or displaced of course has been widely felt across civilizations, societies, and history, especially when the category is broadened to include migrants and refugees. Among the communities who have been compared to the Judeans in Babylon are Tibetan refugees; Maori prophets; Germans after World War II; black South Africans under apartheid; survivors of genocide in Auschwitz and Rwanda; people displaced by World Bank–sponsored hydroelectric dam projects; immigrants from Ireland, Scotland, Finland, Italy, and Mexico; modern-day emigrants to Australia, France, Germany, Norway, and the Netherlands.

Even narrowing the scope to migration to or within North America produces a remarkable range of examples, including Native American survivors of the Trail of Tears, Irish immigrants after the potato famine, Japanese Americans interned during World War II, Vietnamese refugees after 1975, and residents of New Orleans in the aftermath of Hurricane Katrina.

A sense of exile, it seems, has been a defining experience of a large proportion of Americans. It's no accident that Lazarus's most famous poem, "The New Colossus," inscribed on the base of the Statue of Liberty, refers to it as the *Mother of Exiles*:

> Here at our sea-washed, sunset gates shall stand
> A mighty woman with a torch, whose flame
> Is the imprisoned lightning, and her name
> Mother of Exiles. From her beacon-hand
> Glows world-wide welcome; her mild eyes command
> The air-bridged harbor that twin cities frame.[41]

What ethnic group in the United States has not occasionally felt itself unmoored in a strange or foreign land? We'll consider briefly three very different nationalities for whom Psalm 137 has been a touchstone.

First, the Irish.

"We hung our harps on the willows, and mourn ever the departed glories of our native land," wrote one Irish immigrant in an article in the *New York Freeman's Journal* in 1844. The theme of exile figured often in the Irish American songs published during the nineteenth century. Perhaps the most explicit occurs in a hymn written by Charles Constantine Pise, a well-known priest who, among other distinctions, was the first Catholic invited by the U.S. Senate to serve as its chaplain.

> Like the children of Sion on Babylon's shore,
> When Jerus'lem their country smiled round them no more;
> Their harps were all lonely and wet with their tears,
> And their bosoms were harrow'd with sorrow and fears.
>
> . . .
>
> O! when from the storms of this world shall I flee,
> And who would restore me Jerus'lem to thee. [42]

Set to music by Benjamin Cross of Philadelphia, the hymn was first published in 1826, just as Irish immigration was accelerating.

The Irish faced the classical dilemma of diaspora. They "are desir-
ous of becoming Americans and yet remaining Irish; and this serving of
two masters will not do," wrote a European visitor to the United States in
1835. They "clan more together" in large cities than other ethnic groups.
Moreover, he observed, "the Irish feel that they have been wronged in
their country; they have, in a degree, been driven from it, the feelings with
which they look back to it are, therefore, of a more intense character than
they would otherwise be; or, if this be not the case, they feel among themselves the strong tie of bearing one common wrong."[43]

In his irreverent *Why Catholics Can't Sing*, Thomas Day explains how
Americans of Irish descent have exerted a decisive influence on the
style of Catholic worship in the United States. Irish Catholics have had
a strikingly ambivalent attitude toward the value of music in the Mass.
He traces this tendency back through centuries of English oppression of
the Irish, during which time Roman Catholicism was essentially driven
underground.

"Throughout the worst years of English oppression," Day writes, "the
one institution which preserved a separate Irish identity was the outlawed
Roman Catholic church. During that period, a priest, someone who had
the same status as a criminal, would go down to the hedge in the fields or
perhaps set up a makeshift altar in a barn and celebrate an illegal Mass.
The faithful would come from miles around to attend."[44] Since religious
expression was blended with political defiance, "singing was risky."
Church bells, organs, and hearty congregational hymns became sonic
signifiers of political and religious oppression by English Protestants.
This sounds remarkably like the covert "hush harbors" in which enslaved
African Americans worshipped.

Irish immigrants of the nineteenth century brought these attitudes
toward music with them to America, according to Day. Cut off from cultural and musical developments in other Catholic countries, especially
Germany, Spain, and Italy, Irish Americans associated more sophisticated
church music with English Protestants. Given their historical longevity
and sheer numbers relative to other Catholic immigrants, an Irish liturgical style became the status quo in Catholic worship. "The Latin language
seemed to put everyone on an equal footing and ethnic parishes allowed
congregations to indulge in their old-world customs," according to Day,
thus avoiding "large-scale defections of the non-Irish."[45] Significant

regional differences also existed, with German Catholic musical influence much stronger in the Midwest than on the East Coast.

Day brings the acerbic perspective of a church organist and music director. Writing as a scholar, Robert Grimes finds a more cosmopolitan musical sensibility at work among Irish American Catholics during the decades before the Civil War. As he concludes a book titled *How Shall We Sing in a Foreign Land?*: "The harps may have been hung on the willows, but only to allow free hands to play the piano and organ, the guitar and horn .... The immigrant retained some traditions, adapted others, and accepted entirely new ideas. The Irish in America would have a profound effect on the development of popular music in America, as performers and consumers of American culture. And the musical traditions that developed made the immigrants feel less and less that they were singing in a foreign land."[46]

Like the Irish, Koreans have survived in the orbit of a powerful island hegemony, Japan, that since the nineteenth century has exerted a strong will to dominate.

In popular stereotype, Koreans, like the Irish, love to sing, dance, drink, and fight—all carnivalesque activities indulged in with trepidation by their more buttoned-up island neighbors, England and Japan. Even today, singing is often central in gatherings of Koreans and first-generation Korean Americans, with attendees expected to belt out at least one song regardless of his or her singing ability or willingness. This is equally true in religious settings. For Christians, who represent a sizable minority of South Koreans and nearly three of four Korean Americans, Western hymns and gospel songs serve as the core repertoire of communal singing whether in worship or not.

Koreans endured several forms of exile and displacement over the course of the twentieth century, with music serving as a survival strategy. Beginning in 1903 Koreans began migrating to the United States, most serving as laborers on sugar plantations in Hawaii before moving on to the mainland or, in many cases, returning to Korea. Roughly half of these first immigrants were already Christians, having been converted by American Protestant missionaries active in Korea since the late nineteenth century. Most came from the same port cities in Korea and had been members of the same Christian churches. Immigration was halted by U.S. law between 1924 and 1950.[47]

Meanwhile, beginning in 1910, Koreans confronted colonial occupation by Japan. As Imperial Japan gathered force, the Korean language was suppressed and people were forced to take Japanese names. Millions of Koreans were involuntarily deported to Japan as conscript labor; tens of thousands of men were forced to serve in the armed forces while at least 100,000 Koreans were forced to serve as "comfort women" for the Japanese military.[48] Korean Christians were often leaders of resistance to Japanese occupation, looking to the Exodus story for inspiration.

After 1950, immigration to the United States resumed, initially comprising war orphans, Korean wives of U.S. military personnel, and students. "At the time of the political and economic upheaval in the divided Korea, many (male) Koreans made decisions to put their souls in the hands of U.S. missionaries as an exchange for a ticket to the land 'flowing with milk and honey,'" according to a study of Korean American religion titled (aptly) *Singing the Lord's Song in a New Land*.[49]

Most had already adopted Western hymns at their churches in Korea. "In this sense, Korean immigrants were already made strangers to their tradition in their own land even before they left Korea."[50] Traditional Korean melodies, musical modes, and instruments were rejected because of their associations with Korean shamanism, which Christians were encouraged to forcefully break. The bilingual hymnal published in 1984 and used by most congregations in Korea and the United States includes very few non-Western hymns.

The South Korean campaign to recover or reinvent traditional culture in past decades has inspired attempts to include more indigenous musical elements and instruments, including a composer who wrote a new Korean-inflected melody for every hymn contained in the standard hymnal. These efforts have generated some pushback from Christians who consider traditional Korean music not sacred enough, not Christian enough, or simply inferior.

Not uncommonly, where migrating people encounter world religions with a missionary impulse, the coordinates of "home" and "foreign" get remapped; for many Korean Christians, regardless of where they happen to be living, Western hymns have become the "songs of Zion," while traditional Korean music and instruments signify the "strange land" that has been forsaken in favor of the new spiritual identity.

Latin America offers a third analogy to the Judean Golah.

Cuban Americans in particular have recognized the narrative outlines of Psalm 137 in their experience. Feminist theologian Ada Maria Isasi-Díaz recalls first reading Psalm 137 as a young woman in 1961, shortly after leaving Cuba. The Cuban missile crisis of 1962, and the change in status of her tourist visa, brought home the fact that she was now a refugee, unlikely to return. (She did return to Cuba for two weeks in 1987.)

"I recall vividly the day I dared to mention to a friend how much I identified with Psalm 137," she writes. "Jokingly she answered me, 'Are you going to hang your guitar from some palm tree?' I knew that though she and many others around me intended no harm, in reality they were incapable of understanding the sorrow of being away from *la tierra que me vió nacer* (the land that witnessed my birth)." They couldn't understand why Isasi-Díaz wouldn't sing "Guantanamera," based on a poem by the great Cuban patriot José Martí, the equivalent for her of "Yahweh's song in a foreign land."[51]

Isasi-Díaz's reading of the psalm was shaped by her experiences living in a convent, working for three years with the very poor in Lima; by divinity studies that opened her eyes to sexism and pushed her toward liberation and womanist theology (she called it *Mujerista* theology); and by finding her identity as a Hispanic woman in the United States. She writes:

> As the years have gone by, it has become harder and harder to make others understand that though I am a USA citizen and have lived here longer than the eighteen years I lived in Cuba, I continue to live in *el exilio*. It is today more difficult than ever to convince my friends that if I could I would move to Cuba immediately. It is much more challenging now than it was in 1960 to explain to those who love me that I would go back because I want to, and that of wanting to has to do with remaining faithful to who I am. And I often continue to turn to Psalm 137, not to try to understand what exile meant for the Israelites and to learn from them, but to find someone who understands me![52]

Another Cuban-born theologian, Miguel A. De La Torre, extends this analogy with an ingenious reading of Cuban-American relations since the Batista regime fell on New Year's Eve in 1959. "Those who were able to leave arrived in this country [the United States] still in their tuxedos and dress uniforms, their wives in formal gowns and high heels," he writes. "Unlike other contemporary examples of refugees, both the Babylonian-bound Jews and the U.S.-bound Cubans belonged to the privileged upper class."[53]

The parallels continue. Like the Judean exiles, Cuban refugees arrived in three waves: 1959–1962, 1962–1973, and the Mariel boat lift of 1980. "In both cases, the hegemonic northern power was responsible for the circumstances that led to refugee status . . . . As vassals, both Cuba and Judea were desirable prizes: Judah as a buffer zone between the powers of the north and south, and Cuba as a key to the entire hemisphere."[54]

The Caribbean exile produced many of the same effects as the biblical one. "Judaism was constructed in Babylon through the pain of questioning the sovereignty of a God who would tear God's people from their homes and plant them in a foreign land," De La Torre writes. "Likewise, we exilic Cubans subconsciously reconstructed ourselves in Lacan's mirror . . . . Cuba became more than just the old country; it was the mythological world of our origins. Cuba is an ethereal place where every conceivable item es mejor (is better), from the food to the skies to pests. Everything aquí (here) when contrasted with allá (there) is found lacking."[55]

Jeremiah urged his exiled compatriots to build houses and settle down, just as exilic Cubans have built Little Havana and a shrine in Miami for their patron saint. The Hebrew psalmist yearns for violent revenge; Cubans on both sides threaten retribution against each other. "Each Cuba sees itself in the mirror as the true remnant. Resident Cubans see themselves as the true Cubans just as King Zedekiah's nobles who remained in Judah saw themselves as true Jews (Ez. 11:14, 33:24)." Exilic Cubans regard themselves as the "good basket of figs" in contrast to the "bad figs" who remained under Castro and need remedial work in capitalism and democracy.[56]

Just as Judah's suffering was caused by their own corruption, according to Jeremiah, Cuba brought about its plight largely through its own corruption. Havana allowed itself to become a kind of fantasy playground "where the repressed libidinous appetites of the Anglos could be fulfilled . . . . La Habana of 1958 was a United States brothel with Mafia-controlled casinos, holding the infamous distinction of being the sex-and-abortion capital of the Western Hemisphere."[57]

And in the same way Persia manipulated Judean politics in order to advance its national interests, so the United States is positioning itself to exploit the market potential of postcommunist Cuba. "The biblical paradigm of domination will repeat itself," De La Torre insists. "The planned post-Castro community will lead to the subjugation of resident Cubans by exilic Cubans, who in turn will be subjugated to U.S. hegemony."[58]

Exilic Cubans have a choice, the same choice faced by the Golah exiles before their return to Judah: whether to exploit their advantage in power and wealth or to follow the egalitarian vision of Isaiah. Like Isasi-Díaz, De La Torre finds Psalm 137 deeply stirring.

> We fully comprehend the tragic pain of sitting by the rivers of an alien land unable to sing to a God the Psalter secretly holds responsible. The hope of returning to our land becomes a foundational building block for the construction of our exilic Cuban ethnicity; yet with the passing of each year, the cemeteries of Miami increase with headstones engraved with Cuban surnames. Rather than proclaiming "next year in Jerusalem," we tell each other, "this year Castro will fall," as though this one person is the only thing that prevents us from "going home." In reality, the hope of returning home has been replaced with a private desire to adapt and capitalize on our presence in this country.[59]

Irish, Korean, Cuban: this comparative work demonstrates that modern exilic communities have understood their experiences through categories recognizable from the Babylonian exile. But there is also the hope that the abundant information we have about the forced migrations of recent times can shed some light on the Babylonian exile, about which our sources are so meager. The exile experience can be generalized even further. Even people and communities who appear settled in geographical space can feel alienated or estranged.

Existential Exile

Redolent of the pleasures of power and vice, Babylon is an evocative marker of social space. Close proximity can be titillating. Everything else being equal, habitations near waterways tend to offer more opportunities for worldly pleasure. That perilous conjunction of temptation and the holy is especially ripe for religious groups that emphasize personal piety.

Christians in particular have made extensive use of the Exile as an analogy for living in troubled times, and Babylon as a symbol of oppressive power. African American Pentecostals, for example, may feel like exiles in a strange land. Cheryl Sanders offers her own interpretation of how African American sanctified church members would answer the question of singing the Lord's song in a strange land. "The saints in exile are religious communities of African Americans upon whom the

North American Babylon has imposed alien status on account of their race, culture, class, and, in some cases, their sex," Sanders writes in *Saints in Exile*. "Moreover, they have further exiled themselves in significant ways by virtue of their codes of morality and their peculiar liturgies of song, speech, and dance."[60]

Deprived of "a prideful place of origin and a firm sense of belonging," Sanders observes, "African Americans have been forced to live lives as perennial outsiders, finding a home only in a dynamic language and mobile music, as Cornel West has lamented, and never in a secure land, safe territory, or welcome nation. In this perspective, migration and emigration eclipse integration and separation as the fundamental themes of African American life."[61]

Sanders spent years as a participant-observer at her own church, a Church of God congregation in northwest Washington, D.C. She explains the particular practices through which this Holiness church provides its members a place of refuge and homecoming amid the alienation many of them experience as working-class African Americans in the United States. All members, whether homeless or relatively well off, are expected to repent and be transformed. "Perhaps the best hope the Sanctified church tradition has to offer to the world," Sanders writes, "is the preservation of a divinely anointed and authorized space in this North American Babylon and beyond, where the privileged can deal with their resentments and the dispossessed can dispel their doubts and where both can learn to celebrate homecoming with compassion and conviction."[62]

Black preaching has often explicitly identified the "strange land" of Babylon with the familiar alienation of urban existence. "In most of our metropolitan cities we are captives in a strange land of eccentric, erratic, odd, psychotic, unfamiliar people," preached Sandy F. Ray, minister of the Cornerstone Baptist Church in Brooklyn, probably in the 1960s. Or in families bereft of love and communication, or even in the church itself, often roiled at the local level by factions and cliques, "troubled by the 'confusion of tongues,' theological controversies, divisions by race, class, cults, and splits within denominations."[63]

The most formidable Babylon, however, is the American nation, with its myriad forms of injustice and inequality.

Joseph E. Lowery, a Methodist minister, colleague of Martin Luther King Jr. and a founder of the Southern Christian Leadership Conference: "Any society blessed with resources a-plenty and yet endures hunger, homelessness, and encyclical poverty in the midst of abundance *is a strange land*,"

Lowery preached. "Any culture that claims to love the Creator while devastating his creation is a confused culture and subsequently *a strange land*. Any civilization that chooses violence over nonviolence, war above peace, military rather than diplomatic solutions, is a mad, *strange land*. A social order wherein we have deserted the good spouse of spirituality and carry on an affair with the prostitute of materialism and greed, an incestuous affair producing offspring with congenital defects—racism, sexism, economic exploitation, drug addiction, gun addiction—*is a strange land*."[64]

American exceptionalism cuts both ways. Usually it suggests that the United States is uniquely virtuous or blessed, but it can also be taken to mean that the nation is exceptionally flawed: America as Babylon. We can find traces of this exilic sensibility in the early Christian church. The Book of Revelation, which concludes the New Testament, was written by a man named John living in exile on the Aegean island of Patmos toward the end of the first century C.E., about the time the Romans destroyed the Second Temple in Jerusalem and were persecuting Christians in Rome. John of Patmos experienced urgently the early church besieged by Roman persecution as well as pressure to conform to the surrounding Greco-Roman pagan culture.

Modeling itself on the prophetic style of Ezekiel and Jeremiah, Revelation refers repeatedly to Babylon as a personification of evil, either the whore of Babylon—"In her hand she held a gold cup, full of obscenities and the foulness of her fornication; and written on her forehead was a name with a secret meaning: 'Babylon the great, the mother of whores and of every obscenity on earth'"—or the city itself, standing for Rome, which will be spectacularly destroyed in the end times (17:4–5; 18). This destruction was actually witnessed by the great theologian Augustine, who developed a very different, influential interpretation of Psalm 137.

At the end of the Middle Ages, the language and sense of the psalm could still be adapted by individuals attempting to balance the competing loyalties of state, church, and individual conscience. Fourteenth-century humanist Francesco Petrarch, considered the "father of the Renaissance," also navigated perilous tension between Rome and its challengers, in his case the French monarchy. A native of Florence who fled political conflict in the city, Petrarch identified with the exiled Judeans. He was an unwilling resident of Avignon, where the French King Philip "the Fair" had succeeded in relocating the papacy—exiled from Rome, in effect. In a letter published after his death, Petrarch concludes, "I, an angry exile from

Jerusalem, living by the rivers of Babylon, have written these things to you in great haste."[65]

Petrarch himself was a strong champion of Rome, however; it was Avignon that he regarded with distaste. In his view, the papacy was effectively in exile from its proper home. He links Avignon and its pope to Nimrod, the king who erected the Tower of Babel described in Genesis; to the Assyrian queen Semiramis, alleged to have built the hanging gardens of Babylon; and to the mad Babylonian king Cambyses. Petrarch also invokes Augustine's sermon on Psalm 137, and a comment made by Ambrose regarding the emperors Gratian and Valentinian: "How are the mighty fallen? How are both fallen by those rivers of Babylon? How much swifter for both men has been their course of life than the waters of the Rhone itself?" Exile is in this sense doubled for Petrarch: himself an exile as he observes the church in exile from its rightful locale.[66]

At the tail end of the Renaissance, another Italian artist, Salomone Rossi, drew on Psalm 137. In his case, the link was even more poignant; Rossi was Jewish. A supremely gifted violinist and composer, Rossi came to the attention of the powerful Gonzaga family that had ruled Mantua for centuries; he was hired as a court musician and composer by Duke Vicenzo I. Working directly alongside Monteverdi and others, Rossi composed music for wedding feasts, banquets, chapel services, and other court functions. He was so highly regarded that he was allowed to travel freely in and out of Mantua's Jewish ghetto (which was located nearby, behind the ducal palace), a rare privilege. Moreover, he was excused from wearing the required yellow badge of Jews even in that relatively tolerant city. Though he composed madrigals, galliards, canzonettes, and instrumental sonatas, Rossi is best remembered for his pioneering work, *Hashirim ásher lish'lomo* ("The Songs of Solomon").[67]

A pun on his first name, since the piece doesn't include texts from that particular book, *Hashirim* sets Hebrew psalms, hymns, and other sacred texts to contemporary music, including popular tunes from the Jewish ghetto. It was written in Hebrew, for use in synagogue liturgy, but the melodies were Rossi's rather than derived from traditional Jewish cantorial songs. Susan Gillingham suggests that some of the melodies came from popular tunes of the Jewish ghetto. "In Psalm 137 the chorus is unaccompanied," she writes. "Rossi still adhered to the ban on music in synagogue liturgy to observe the destruction of the second Temple: metaphorically speaking, the harps were still hung on the trees."[68] His setting is one of the most beautiful of all settings of the psalm, and also one of the few to include the harsh final verses.

In 1630, Mantua was invaded by German mercenaries. The Jewish ghetto was sacked, its inhabitants driven out. Rossi is thought to have died in the invasion or from the plague that followed, along with his sister, the opera singer Madama Europa, also a court musician for the Gonzagas.

By this time, the Protestant Reformation was well underway across the Continent. Because of the real possibility that a person of some station might actually be exiled at some point, the Reformation was a milieu in which Psalm 137 carried a particular charge. For Europe as a whole, the wars of religion that began in the sixteenth century created enormous dislocation and suffering, ranking among the most bloody conflicts in history. Feeling themselves enmeshed in a righteous crusade against the entrenched power of the Roman Catholic Church, Protestants readily drew an analogy between their own plight and the plight of Judeans in the face of Babylonian power.

The primary architect of the Reformation, Martin Luther, titled one of his sharpest polemics *De captivitate Babylonica ecclesiae praeludium* (The Babylonian Captivity of the Church) in 1520, months before he was excommunicated—spiritually exiled—by the Pope. Luther's target was the Roman Catholic system of seven sacraments; he argues that there are properly only two, baptism and the Eucharist, and is most exercised by the Church's doctrine of transubstantiation, the literal transformation of the bread and wine into the body and blood of Christ. These rigidly enforced restrictions are the spiritual equivalent of spiritual captivity for right-minded Christians. Though at one point, like Petrarch, Luther compares the pope to ancient Babel's Nimrod, he more often draws an analogy to the Babylon of Nebuchadnezzar, paraphrasing Psalm 137: "Truly, 'by the waters of Babylon we sit down and weep, when we remember thee, O Zion. On the willows there we hang up our lyres.' May the Lord curse the barren willows of those streams! Amen!"[69] As with so many biblical exegetes, Jewish and Christian, there is for Luther easy slippage between Babylon and Rome—and between the Rome of Caesar and the Rome of the Vatican.

Within a decade England saw the stirrings of its own Reformation, a conflict that would convulse the British Isles (and the Continent) for more than a century. England witnessed its share of conflict as the fortunes of Catholics and Protestants rose or fell from Henry VIII to the restoration of

King James. As always, the majority of suffering was borne by common-
ers, but elites faced the threat of exile or escape when political fortunes
in London changed. And this was an educated elite with the expertise in
language necessary to produce psalm translations.

English poets made various attempts to capture the evocative language of Psalm 137. Miles Coverdale's language was most influential, as it
became canonized in the *Book of Common Prayer*. Beyond translation, an
additional step was necessary to transform psalms into texts suitable for
congregational singing. The poetic lines needed to be rendered into rhym-
ing meters that matched the cadences of hymn tunes.

Among English Protestants who moved in and out of exile on the
Continent, the Puritans offer the most dramatic example of migration. The
first version of Psalm 137 sung in North America was carried by the Pilgrims
to Plymouth aboard the *Mayflower*. English Protestants had first encountered psalm singing in Switzerland, where they fled after the middle of
the sixteenth century to avoid persecution under the Catholic Queen Mary.
For these dissenting Protestants, congregational psalm singing became
the sole legitimate form of church music. The millennium-long tradition
of Roman Catholic hymn-singing was abruptly abandoned. With the emigration of English Puritans to North America in the seventeenth century,
metrical psalm singing became the foundation of American sacred song.

Because it laid out the standard and metrical versions of the psalms
side-by-side in parallel columns, Henry Ainsworth's 1612 psalter provides
a good introduction to the technique of metrical psalms. On the left column appear the first three verses of Ainsworth's translation of the Hebrew
psalm into English prose; on the right the rhymed, metrical version created for congregational singing:

1. By the rivers of Babel, there we sate, yea we wept: when remembred, Sion.	By Babels rivers, there sate wee, yea wept: when wee did mind, Sion.
2. Upon the willowes in the mids thereof: we hanged, our harps.	The willowes that amidds it *bee*: our harps, we hanged, *them* upon.
3. For there, they that led us captive asked of us, the words of a song: and they that threw us on heaps, mirth: sing unto us, of the song of Sion.	For songs of us, there ask did they that had us captive led-along, and mirth, they that us heaps did lay Sing unto us some Sions song.[70]

The musical setting Ainsworth provides is known as long meter double; the tune is divided into three eight-line stanzas, each line having eight syllables. The tune recommended by Ainsworth is a stately triple meter in D minor.[71]

Because Ainsworth was willing to subject the poetic flow of his translation to "strain now and then" rather than to violate the meaning of his original text, the phrasing is ungainly. The Puritans of Massachusetts Bay who arrived in Boston in 1630 took an even stricter line toward adapting psalms for worship. Their psalm collection, known as the *Bay Psalm Book* (1640), contains a thirteen-page preface laying out an elaborate rationale and criteria for creating metrical psalms.

Comparing the opening stanzas of the 1640 version with an earlier version shows the awkward phrasing accepted by Puritans at the cost of their adherence to a literal translation of the Hebrew Bible:

Sternhold and Hopkins (1562)	*Bay Psalm Book* (1640)
When we did sit in Babylon	The rivers on of Babilon
the rivers round about,	there when wee did sit downe:
There in remembrance of Sion	Yea even then wee mourned, when
the tears for grief burst out.	we remembered Sion.
We hanged our harps and instruments	Our Harps wee did hang it amid,
the willow trees upon,	upon the willow tree.
For in that place men for their use	Because there they that us away
had planted many one.	led in captivitee,
Then they to whom we pris'ners were	Requir'd of us a song, & thus
said to us tauntingly,	askt mirth: us waste who laid,
Now let us hear your Hebrew songs	sing us among a Sions song,
and pleasant melody.[72]	unto us then they said.[73]

New England's homegrown psalmists were content to twist syntax and let verses flow across stanzas. Despite this, the 1640 version dominated Sunday worship in the New England colonies for generations.

Given the psalters in use—Genevan, Sternhold and Hopkins, the *Bay Psalm Book*—how often was Psalm 137 actually sung in worship? Unfortunately, evidence on this point is nonexistent. It doesn't appear that the psalm was the subject of many sermons, either; neither Cotton Mather nor Jonathan Edwards had sermons on the topic.[74]

Literary scholar Sacvan Bercovitch has famously emphasized Puritan readings of Jeremiah as a distinctive ritual of judgment and repentance delivered by ministers against their congregations in New England.[75] Important as Jeremiah's prophecies may have been in shaping a distinctive American ritual of judgment and repentance, it was not the theme of Psalm 137—exile, memory, vengeance—that struck preachers as the most helpful for their congregations.

So why wouldn't ministers and other people of cultural influence have made more use of such a psalm?

One answer is that while the New England settlers may have experienced a sense of exile, their response was not to cling to memory. They were voluntary migrants and had no investment in a physical return to the homeland. The linkage of temple, promised land, and chosen people did not exist as it did for the subjects of Psalm 137. Like Moses and the Israelites, they had found their promised land—founded their New Jerusalem—in America. There was no longing, backward glance toward England—at least not for those preaching the sermons and publishing new psalm books.

Rivers of Watertown

With this perplexing heritage in mind—a people that loved psalms, experienced jarring dislocation, and by all rights should have been drawn to Psalm 137 but were not—I paid a visit to the Congregational Library on Beacon Street in Boston.

The library sits on the second floor of an elegant building within a stone's throw of the Boston Common. The windows of the reading room, with its high ceilings, burnished desks, and portraits and busts of Puritan divines, look down on the Granary Burial Ground, established in 1660, the third oldest burying ground in Boston. It's the final resting place of such luminaries as Paul Revere, Samuel Adams, John Hancock, and two notable African Americans: poet Phillis Wheatley (her grave is unmarked) and Crispus Attucks, killed in the Boston Massacre.

The library is the repository for some of the oldest documents of North America, the earliest papers of the Puritans who founded the Massachusetts Bay. The executive librarian, Margaret Bendroth, has written several books on American religious history and also directs the Congregational Historical Society. I'm half-hoping—but not really expecting—she might have uncovered some previously unknown (to me) sermon on Psalm 137—or, better yet, produce an according file of documents specifically devoted to the psalm in colonial times. As we talk in her office, though, she describes a much more personal encounter with the psalm.

As an undergraduate at Cornell in the 1970s, she sang a folksy version of Psalm 137 frequently as a round with Christian student groups. "Everybody knew this song," she told me. "It was like you would go to an Intervarsity or, you know, evangelical youth group, and people would just—it was one of those songs that people would just start singing. And it was beautiful. But I remember thinking, So, what am I supposed to feel? You know, when you sing those songs you are supposed to feel something. It's not any particular evangelical message, it was just beautiful music and beautiful words, but I always thought it was kind of odd."[76]

"So people were mostly attracted to the poetic line about the waters of Babylon—and the haunting tune?"

"Yeah, and singing in a round, and you can just do it over and over and over. And you feel like you're kind of together while you are doing it. But I remember thinking at the time, 'Why are we singing this?'"

"Why did you feel it was an odd choice?" I ask.

"I think—and this is true with a lot of the Bible—am I just kind of *feeling* what Jews felt when they were in exile? Or is Zion the United States— or Babylon? It's kind of—where am I standing when I'm singing this? So when we sang the round, it was this whole mournful thing and didn't really have any message at all, to anybody. While all the other things we sang were heavy on message, thin on melody."

"So you weren't necessarily identifying with the experience of the Judeans in exile or thinking, what is Babylon, really, in the 1970s? Is it the United States?"

"Yeah," she answers, "and of course these are evangelicals singing that, so a lot of people probably knew what Babylon was. I mean, more than I did."

"The real historical Babylon, you mean?"

"No, secular culture. Secular culture."

I finally get it. "Oh, so *that's* Babylon."

"We're exiled and we're born," she adds. "I mean, that's one of their metaphors."

I ask Bendroth if she had any idea where the tune came from.

"During that time there were so many of what we now call 'praise songs' that just kind of bubbled up. Sometimes it would be the group that you happened to be a part of. Somebody wrote this, and you didn't know that it was kind of local, until you realized no one else knew it. Or you were singing it and thinking it was local and then you realized everybody knows it. So there was a kind of musical vocabulary that people had back then, where one of the things about being evangelical, you had to know a certain repertoire of praise songs. And that was always there."

I know which version she's talking about from her college years: the one Don McLean sings on *American Pie*, the song performed in the folk club scene in *Mad Men*.

For such a simple round, the song has frequently been misattributed. Some hymnals identify it as a "traditional Jewish melody," even an "Israeli melody." *American Pie*'s liner notes mistakenly attribute the tune to William Billings, perhaps because it somewhat resembles "When Jesus Wept," a still-performed round set by Billings to a somber tune: *When Jesus wept, the falling tear / in mercy flowed beyond all bound ;/ when Jesus groaned, a trembling fear / seized all the guilty world around.*

The actual source of the version popularized by McLean is quite surprising: a piece titled "The Muses Delight: Catches, Glees, Canzonets and Canons," written in the late eighteenth century by an English composer and Oxford professor of music named Dr. Philip Hayes. Nothing the least bit ethnic, or American, about that pedigree.[77]

I ask Bendroth if she ever remembered singing it in church, as a hymn, before those college youth groups.

"Well, I grew up Christian Reformed, and so we had a psalter hymnal. The first part of the hymnal was every psalm set to music. So I must have sung it many times, and I'm trying to remember what the tune of it was. We had other stuff in the back, gospel hymns and stuff. But the front wasn't just metrical, it wasn't just Genevan Psalter kind of stuff, it was all kinds of tunes. I think if I walked out of here I would probably remember the tune to 137."

"Was your church one that especially identified with this psalm, its emphasis on exile?"

"I think Christian Reformed would be a good example, because they did have the psalter, and so they were committed to singing all of the psalms. And they had set them all to music and they were part of their repertoire, so they couldn't avoid certain things. And one of the reasons why the whole evangelical Moody Bible Institute gospel hymnody appealed to them in the late nineteenth century is because it had—George Marsden has written about this—the themes of alienation and loneliness. So that, and maybe even on a conscious level, *This world is not my home*. They could say: Well, yeah. My parents were second-generation, but that sense of, *We're not like those people.* They still talk like that."

Rivers of Reggae

The folk song popularized on *American Pie* was not the only version of Psalm 137 flowing through popular music in the seventies. The text found its way into one of the signature examples of the Jesus Movement, *Godspell.* A very young Stephen Schwartz wrote the piece "On the Willows" at the request of *Godspell*'s creator, John-Michael Tebelak. The two had met as students at Carnegie Mellon, in Pittsburgh, though their collaboration on the musical happened later, when both lived in New York City.

Tebelak had requested that the setting of Psalm 137 have an "oceanic quality," Schwartz recalls, "which I took to mean sort of waves cascading, and so that was what I tried to capture in the music I wrote for it." The words are to be sung by the band, providing an effect of "movie-like scoring" at a pivotal scene near the end of the show. "The other thing that may be of some interest is that in the original show, we changed one word. We changed the word 'lyres' to 'lives'—l-i-v-e-s—but now in most of the revivals they changed it back. In the most recent Broadway revival, for instance, they changed it back to 'lyres.'" The relevant line of the show goes thus: "On the willows there / We hung up our lives."[78]

Why the change? Again, Tebelak's idea. "I'm not sure I would make the same change today," Schwartz said, "but the reasoning behind it was that we wanted to be clear it was their entire life that had changed for each of the disciples. And we weren't sure the metaphor of the *lyres* would be clear enough, particularly since we don't get to the explanatory line about singing the Lord's song in a foreign land until much later in the song."[79]

I asked Schwartz why, when nearly all of the libretto comes from the Gospel of Matthew and the Book of Common Prayer, Tebelak wanted Psalm 137.

"Well, I think he chose that particular psalm because it speaks of loss and estrangement and feeling displaced. And he felt that, emotionally, that was appropriate for the moment when, as I said, Jesus is bidding goodbye to his disciples. And he has said to them, right before these lyrics commence, 'And I will never again drink of the fruit of the vine until I drink it with you in the kingdom of my Father.' So clearly he knows that it is in fact

the Last Supper." Which is actually a Passover Seder, the traditional blessing of the matzo and the wine, delivered in Hebrew by Jesus.

Through *Godspell*, Schwartz's "On the Willows" certainly has reached
a wide baby boomer audience. But the most influential of all popular versions came from Jamaica, an island nation that, like the United States,
began as a British colony. The vehicle was the 1973 film *The Harder They
Come*, which quickly became a campus cult classic, bringing its intoxi-
cating mix of reggae music, ganja, and gunslinging urban rudeboy style
to enthusiastic American and European youth. The soundtrack, featuring

FIGURE 4 The Melodians, "Rivers of Babylon," featured in *The Harder They Come*.
Author's collection.

songs by Jimmy Cliff and Toots and the Maytals, became a phenomenon in its own right and helped pave the way for the global success of Bob Marley (see Fig. 4).

For many outside Jamaica, this was an enticing introduction to reggae culture. It launched the international career of the film's star, Jimmy Cliff, as well as a Jamaican group called the Melodians. Based on the opening verses of Psalm 137, the song "Rivers of Babylon" is heard twice in the film. It offers a subtle commentary on an important conflict in the film, between Ivan, a young man recently arrived in Kingston from the countryside, and the autocratic Christian preacher he challenges.[80]

Diverse musical sources fed the musical mix that came to be called reggae. Its rhythmic underpinnings were laid by Burru and Kumina drumming, an African-derived form based on cross-rhythms created by a regular beat and a higher-pitched "repeater drum." Reggae also drew on successive traditions of Jamaican popular music: the mento of the thirties and forties, which was influenced by American big-band jazz; ska of the fifties and early sixties, with its echoes of American R & B; and blue beat and rocksteady of the late sixties. North American gospel hymns supplied many of the lyrics and tunes.[81]

But beginning around 1962, with a revival of homegrown culture led by the record producer and eventual prime minister Edward Seaga, Jamaican musicians began to turn away from North American influences to create a more intentionally nationalist sound. By the early seventies, Bob Marley's music and the soundtrack of *The Harder They Come* was putting into global circulation both Rastafarian religious ideas and Jamaican music.

Like Psalm 137 in the Hebrew Bible, "Rivers of Babylon" is divided into three sections, the divisions signaled as much by the music as by the lyrics. Propelled by a seven-note G major bass line, the song's hook features two identical rising phrases followed by two parallel falling ones. Its first two stanzas condense a modified version of the first four verses of Psalm 137, from "By the rivers of Babylon" through "How shall we sing the Lord's song in a strange land?" The image of harps hung from willows is dropped. A more pointed term, "the wicked," replaces the pronoun "they" found in the psalm.

More important, the Rastafarian version replaces "The Lord's song" with "King Alpha's song," a reference to Ras Tafari, Haile Selasie I, who was crowned emperor of Ethiopia in 1930 and is considered by Rastafarians to be the Messiah and resurrected Jesus Christ. "By the rivers of Babylon / Where we sat down / And there we wept / When we remembered Zion /

Cause the wicked carried us away in captivity / Required from us a song /
How can we sing King Alpha's song / In a strange land?"

With that final question, the Melodians' version diverges from the Bible
altogether. Instead of invoking memory ("If I forget thee, O Jerusalem . . . .
If I do not remember thee"), which characterizes the middle verses of the
psalm, "Rivers of Babylon" offers an exhortation to struggle and protest.
Again, lines are repeated for emphasis. The Rasta version replaces the
spirit of resignation and self-pity of the Babylonian exiles with militant
defiance expressed through shouts and songs. In the phrase, "Chanting
down Babylon," *Babylon* signifies oppressive power, whether referring to
colonial domination, racial subjugation, or economic exploitation—and
often all three.[82] Musically, the lyrics are shouted in exhortatory fashion
above the familiar bass line that sounds at the song's beginning:

> Sing it out loud
> Sing a song of freedom, sister
> Sing a song of freedom, brother
> We gotta sing and shout it
> We gotta talk and shout it
> Shout the song of freedom now.

The song's final stanza, repeated once, invokes the historic connection between Rastafari and Christianity. The former developed in a colonial society shaped by beliefs and practices of British Christianity, both
Anglican and Baptist, and by such indigenous African Jamaican forms
as Revival. Beginning without a distinctive sound of its own, the early
practitioners of Rastafari borrowed Baptist hymns as well as gospel songs
known as "Sankeys," in reference to Ira Sankey (1840–1908), musical side-
kick of Chicago-based evangelist Dwight Moody and prolific composer of
white gospel songs in the late nineteenth century.[83]

The expression "Let the words of our mouth / And the meditations
of our heart / Be acceptable in Thy sight" is taken from the end of Psalm
19 and is a familiar benediction among Protestant Christians; "Rivers of
Babylon" adds just the Rastafarian salutation "O FarI" to the traditional
formula.

On a bright Sunday afternoon in May I met Tony Brevett, one of the
founding Melodians, at his home in Queens. We talked in his kitchen
as he methodically cooked Jamaican chicken and rice, taking frequent
breaks to sweep the floor, sponge off dishes he had used, and load the

dishwasher. No longer sporting dreadlocks, his shaved head gave him the look of a puckish Michael Jordan. I asked him about the origin of the Melodians' most famous song. He reminisced about growing up Catholic in Kingston, being an altar boy and a choir boy, but identifying with the older Rastas who congregated in his neighborhood, known as the Dungle. He grew up near a site he called the Temple, a meeting place for artists, singers, musicians, and writers, especially during Ethiopian Christmas, when Rastafarians congregated from all over Jamaica.

"You see, at these functions, I love my guitar. I learned to play guitar when I was about thirteen. Sometimes the Rastafarians that would come with drums, playing and singing songs, you know, they sing songs like Bob Dylan . . . you know, because of British rule. So we call the cops "Bob Dylan," because they are working for Bob Dylan, and they don't like that.[84]

"So eventually, this song comes up to me. From all the songs that the Rastafarians are singing. And I said, a lot of Jamaican artists have been singing these songs. Bob Marley, Ethiopians, you know, and a lot of other groups, they sing those songs, because they are the same group of people. The same gathering, where all of us come together and praise Rastafari, His Imperial Majesty.

"When they were playing, my uncle also, who is Matt Brevett, you know, he formed a group called the Sons of Negroes—that was the original Sons of Negroes—and they sing songs like, 'In the Jungle, the Lion sleeps tonight.' You understand? And we sing,

> *By the Rivers of Babylon, there we sat down and there we wept,*
> *when we remembered Zion.*
> *Captive, required from us a song.*
> *How can we sing this song in a strange land?*

"It was when we were sitting down and we were smoking the chalice, smoking the peace pipe, as we call it. And after the songs, somebody said a psalm: 'May the words of my mouth and the meditations of my heart be acceptable in thy sight, oh most high, Rastafari.'" Playing around in this way, the group decided, "This is going to be our next verse of the song."

The Melodians were working with the legendary reggae producer, Leslie Kong, who produced Jimmy Cliff, Derrick Morgan, Desmond Dekker, and Bob Marley's first recordings. Kong offered Brevett and his two bandmates, Brent Dowe and Trevor McNaughton, twenty pounds a week each if they could generate songs. Brevett recalls that the band that recorded "Rivers of Babylon" included Jackie Jackson on bass, Malcolm Graham on drums, Langston Anderson on piano, and Ronnie Bock and Ox Brown on guitars.

The musical style was called rocksteady—"much slower than the ska," according to Brevett. "We used to listen to a lot of foreign artists. Sam Cooke is one of my favorites. The Temptations, we used to listen to them. The Beatles most of all. We said we wanted to create songs just like those guys. And with the slower rhythms of rocksteady, we could sing much more harmony, like country-and-western style harmony."[85]

"I started to play the song, 'Rivers of Babylon,'" Brevett told me, "and I gave Ox Brown the lead, and when it started, I took my guitar and started to play [sings the melody] and I said, 'That's it.' And he was trying to find it, for about fifteen, twenty minutes, he could not play it. So I said, 'Ox, look at my fingers' [sings the melody again], I had to call the notes to him, and he eventually got it, yeah? And now he got it. I said, 'All right, just sing slowly, sing softly, you know?' And he said, 'All right.' At Dynamic Studio."

Brevett recorded the lead vocal, but was dissatisfied with the song's arrangement. "I said, I think Brent Dowe should lead that song. You know, because he's got a higher-pitched voice than me, he sings tenor in the group. God bless his soul. He died. You know, Trevor the bass and I some-times sing falsetto. I sing alto, too, as a lead. So Brent Dowe took it up and did a good job of it.

"And then it came out. Mr. Kong loved it. He loved that song right away, you know? Because, you see, that's when they got 'Poor Me Israelites.' You know? And that was when ['Rivers of Babylon'] could follow up to a song like that, because that's a million seller, big selling song, 'Poor Me Israelites.' You know something, okay, I love this song. And he put it out right away. And it was going, going, going, going—it doesn't stop going. Everywhere I go, people just love the song, you know? All over the world. Even in Japan, all those places, you hear them singing it."

I ask Brevett about a story I'd heard, that the song had been banned in Jamaica. Shortly before his death in 2006, Brent Dowe said that he set the psalm to reggae to raise public awareness of Rastafari, with its calls for justice and liberation. When "Rivers" first hit the airwaves, according to Dowe, the government banned it, regarding its overt Rastafarian refer-ences as subversive and inflammatory. Leslie Kong then publicly criticized the government, pointing out that the song came straight from the Bible, and the ban was lifted; within three weeks it hit number-one on the local charts.[86]

"Never," said Brevett, without hesitation. "Because you see, what happened was Beverly Kong [meaning Leslie Kong; Beverly was the name of Kong's record label], he got his money. He's one of the rich guys. So he can pay us sixty pounds. And then Ken [Boothe] would come and get his twenty pounds, the Gaylads come and they would get they twenty pounds, and the other groups, everybody getting twenty pounds a week. We don't have to sing. We just be on the contract. That's Beverly Kong, he's one of the best. But it was never banned. No ban, because it was going so good. It was going so very good, on the label .... But you see, once it was from Beverly Kong, they would not ban it, because he's got the money to spend. It was on the radio for seven weeks number one. You know, so they did not ban it."

Did he think "Rivers of Babylon" was the group's best song?

"Well, I think it's the most recognizable song. Because it relates to different religions, different people. You know, it relates to the Israelites and the time when they are coming out of Egypt and all of that. And on the song they sing, Rivers of Babylon, that river, you know? I'm going to the Promised Land. And so it was, you know, it come from many ideas. And me as a man who goes to church; every Sunday, I had to go to church." Which he didn't like as a boy, he told me, because it began at 7 a.m. so he didn't have time to eat breakfast beforehand.

Brevett told me he was working on a sort of sequel to the song, to be titled "Still in Babylon." He sang me a few lines:

> We are still in Babylon
> Why must we be?
> We have sold our instruments
> And bought machines.

He explains, "We have forgotten how to be. We have forgotten the songs, in Babylon. You understand? But I'm still thinking. Yeah. I'm trying to put them together musically. The same formation. I'm going to take it slow. Or I'm going to take it faster. Whatever. But it's coming to me. On the next album. Or maybe it might be a song by itself that I put out. But it's working on. It's working on."

Chicken stewing away, we took a break from the kitchen. Tony played me songs from *Lyrics to Riddim*, the Melodians' soon-to-be-released album timed for the fiftieth anniversary of the group, which came together in

1963, when Tony was all of fourteen. Six tracks include vocals by Dowe, recorded before his sudden death in 2006. "We don't want to lose the roots of the reggae music like some guys who are taking it to the hip-hop rhythms," Brevett has said. "That's why we have the original musicians playing for us on this album. Bring back the grass roots. No computer."[87]

After Dowe's death, Brevett continued to perform live with Trevor McNaughton. As luck would have, on the night of our interview he was singing a solo show in Brooklyn, at the Pendergat Club. Accompanied by his gracious wife Cindy, Brevett looked bespoke in a white suit and hat. He sang for about half an hour, right on the pool deck, as a deejay played songs behind him. They urged me to stay the night with them, to stay with them any time I was in the area, but I had to get home.

Had he ever played "Rivers of Babylon" in the Holy Land?

"That's a nice place to be. Someone told me Jimmy Cliff did it down there, you understand? So, I get there. I'm just trying to keep alive. Keep strong. Take my vitamins. Do my exercises and all that. And I'll be there when the time comes. Yeah. Maybe next year. Hopefully."

About six months later, Tony Brevett died in Miami, of cancer. It came on suddenly; he probably had no inkling of it during our conversation in New York.

Popular as the Melodians' song was in Jamaica, "Rivers of Babylon" has reached its largest audience through the dozens of covers over the past forty years, ranging from Linda Ronstadt and the Neville Brothers to Culture Vulture and Sublime. Sweet Honey in the Rock links most directly to the song's political lineage. Taking its name from Psalm 82 ("with honey out of the rock should I have satisfied thee"), the group was founded in 1973. Its founder was Bernice Johnson Reagon, who first became nationally known through the Albany Freedom Singers, which helped recruit volunteers and raise funds for the famous Freedom Summer voter-registration drive of 1964.

Steve Earle's version, recorded in 1995 for *Train a Comin'*, offers a different crossing of genres. Great-grandson of a Methodist preacher who built a church in Texas that still stands but is himself a hard-living Texan with outspoken left politics, Earle is best known for the controversy over his song "John Walker's Blues" (2002), which offered a sympathetic account of the young American caught with the Taliban in Afghanistan after 9/11.

By far the bestselling version of "Rivers of Babylon" was recorded by the band Boney M. The group comprised four West Indians, three of them women and two from Jamaica, assembled by a German record producer in the seventies. Their 1978 cover version, with voices soaring over an infectious disco backbeat, did extremely well in Europe, becoming the second-biggest-selling single in U.K. chart history, and was the group's only song to reach the Top 40 in the United States. Boney M's version made two notable changes in the Melodians' text. First, it reverted to King James language, replacing "How can we sing King Alpha's song in a strange land?" with "How shall we sing the Lord's song in a strange land?" Second, it dropped the second section of the song—the part most clearly marked by a Rasta political sensibility, the exhortation to "Sing a song of freedom" and collectively shout down Babylon.

Like the Melodians' original "Rivers," heard in key scenes in *The Harder They Come*, Boney M's cover turns up in international films. In the somber Chinese film *Shanghai Dreams* (2005), a nineteen-year-old schoolgirl growing up in rural Guiyang during the early 1980s struggles against her father's restrictions. The family is in exile from Shanghai; the parents were persuaded to leave as part of China's Cold War "Third Front" policy to maintain an industrial base in the countryside in case of invasion. The father wants desperately to return to the city. They are internally displaced workers, in the language of social science.[88]

One evening the daughter sneaks out to a surreptitious dance party in a local factory. Boney M's cover of "Rivers" echoes through the industrial space, where boys dance in couples in the center while girls and less confident guys stand around the walls, smoking cigarettes and watching. Eventually, an obviously cool young man in designer shades and plaid bell-bottoms makes a dramatic entrance and takes a long look at the women. Soon he is the focus of attention, striking a Travolta-like stance in the center of the ring. The music shifts to another Boney M song, "Gotta Go Home," and the dance descends into chaos when a gang of locals cuts the power and breaks windows. In the film, clear status barriers divide the displaced urbanites who dream of returning to cities like Shanghai—like Judeans yearning for Jerusalem—from the locals.

Shanghai Dreams is driven by the pain of exile. The father in the film is obsessed with yearning to return to the city that represents home and opportunity. In the Khazak film *Tulpan* (2008), home is the steppes of Central Asia. The youthful protagonist, Asa, recently released from the navy, hopes to marry a local girl named Tulpan, live in a yurt, and establish himself as a sheep-herder. In a euphoric moment after the two families meet, and Asa and his friend see a glorious future on the steppes opening up, Boney M's "Rivers" booms through the dilapidated jeep. But suddenly the music cuts out and the mood is broken. Asa's uncle informs him that Tulpan has rejected him; his ears are too big.[89]

After struggling fruitlessly to change Tulpan's mind and to win some respect from his uncle, Asa finally concedes defeat and agrees to leave the steppes with his friend. Again "Rivers" blasts through the battered vehicle, festooned with photos of naked women his friend has cut out of magazines, as they leave his family behind. But something calls Asa back. He gets out of the jeep to rejoin his sister's family, in transit themselves, moving their yurt to a new site to avoid a mysterious illness that is killing the newborn sheep.

All three films, then, play off the theme of not-quite-voluntary migration. Of exile. In *The Harder They Come*, after Ivan's family property in the country is sold off, what follows is exile to Kingston. Drawn into the ganja trade, Ivan is killed trying to escape to Cuba from the urban Babylon. In *Shanghai Dreams*, the direction is reversed; the father nurses a bitter yearning to return to the city that represents home and opportunity. In *Tulpan*, the city is never actually seen; it exists as a kind of fantasy against which Asa struggles, wanting to establish himself in the traditional way, living in a yurt and raising sheep. In each case, a 1978 disco song based on a Hebrew psalm sounds through the film, not just background but diegetic music, woven into the plot.

Why would an ancient text like Psalm 137 have struck filmmakers as right for these films, set in widely varying national contexts? Reflecting on the modern persistence of nostalgia, Svetlana Boym notes that "progress didn't cure nostalgia but exacerbated it," and globalization, rather than dissolving local attachments, encouraged them. "In counterpoint to our fascination with cyberspace and the virtual global village," she writes, "there is a no less global epidemic of nostalgia, an affective yearning for a community with a collective memory, a longing for continuity in a fragmented world. Nostalgia inevitably reappears as a defense mechanism in a time of accelerated rhythms of life and historical upheavals."[90]

These films, and the characters they feature, fit Boym's category of "off-modernism," which challenges "both the modern fascination with newness and no less modern reinvention of tradition. In the off-modern tradition," she explains, "reflection and longing, estrangement and affection go together. Moreover, for some twentieth-century off-modernists who came from eccentric traditions . . . as well as for many displaced people from all over the world, creative rethinking of nostalgia was not merely an artistic device but a strategy of survival, a way of making sense of the impossibility of homecoming."[91]

The Melodians and Boney M have lost most of their band members over the decades since "Rivers of Babylon." With Brevett's passing, the Melodians are down to one original member, same as Boney M.

Maizie Williams still puts on a rousing show. In 2010 she played a concert in the West Bank city of Ramallah. Located about 10 kilometers north of Jerusalem, the city is the de facto center of the Palestinian National Authority. It is off-limits to Israelis, who are not checked on the way in but face interrogation, arrest, fines, even imprisonment if caught crossing back into Israel. "If there's anywhere that scares Israelis, it's Ramallah," wrote Yuval Ben-Ami, a journalist who braved the border crossing in order to see the last remaining member of Boney M.[92]

The concert took place at an open-air theater next to the Ramallah Cultural Palace. "There were less hijabs to be seen here than on the streets, both because there's something deeply un-Islamic about lines such as 'Rasputin, Rasputin, Russia's greatest love machine' and because at least 30 percent of those present were internationals." Fronted by Williams—"unbelievably energetic and lovely"—the band soared through a succession of thirty-year-old hits: "Daddy Cool," "Sunny," "Belfast." The power died for a few minutes during a rendition of Bob Marley's "No Woman, No Cry," though the audience kept singing until the lights and amps were restored.

"We had only one major disappointment," Ben-Ami reported. "'Babylon' was not sung. I can only assume that the festival organizers banned it for fear that the word 'Zion' (as in 'Zionism') would offend the audience. Sometimes deeper meanings are lost on people. The crowd chanted 'Babylon' harder than it chanted 'everything's gonna be alright' but to no avail."[93]

After the show Ben-Ami joined a house party with Palestinian friends, noting "the extraordinary hospitality of our neighbors, easing the shift between the glittery clothes we saw on stage and the uniforms we would meet at the checkpoint later."

With this performance on the outskirts of Jerusalem we circle back to Psalm 137's geographic origin. Before concluding Part 1, we can move even closer, with one more sounding of Boney M's cover version—a particularly shocking one.

In 2007, an Iraqi named Ali Shalal Qaissi testified under oath that he had been arrested by American troops in October 2003 and transferred to Abu Ghraib, where he was brutally tortured for weeks. One day his interrogators (he identified them as American and Israeli) jabbed a jagged wooden stick into his rectum, then the barrel of a rifle:

> The next morning, the Israeli interrogator came to my cell and tied me to the grill of the cell and he then played the pop song, "By the Rivers of Babylon" by Pop Group Boney M, continuously until the next morning. The effect on me was that I lost my hearing, and I lost my mind. It was very painful and I lost consciousness. When I regain (*sic*) consciousness, he started beating me again and demanded that I tell him of the names of resistance fighters and what activities that I did against the American soldiers. When I told him that I did not know any resistance fighters, he kicked me many times.[94]

Qaissi was mistakenly identified for a time as the "man behind the hood" in the famous photo of the torture victim standing on the box, with electrical wires springing out, at Abu Ghraib. He eventually acknowledged that he was not the prisoner in the famous photo, although he was reportedly subjected to the very same treatment. No one has questioned the rest of his testimony.[95]

For U.S. military personnel and their allies to play Boney M's "Rivers of Babylon" for this purpose, in the city that was once Babylon, raises disturbing questions. How did the various parties to the atrocities at Abu Ghraib identify with the song? Where, or what, is Babylon? Who is the oppressor and who is oppressed, the empire and the subjugated state?[96] And how do we ever begin to sort out the truth, evaluate the testimony? All questions to be taken up in Part 2.

PART TWO

Memory

*If I forget thee, O Jerusalem, let my right hand
forget her cunning.*

*If I do not remember thee, let my tongue cleave
to the roof of my mouth;*

if I prefer not Jerusalem above my chief joy.

(Psalm 137:5–6)

TOAD'S PLACE IN New Haven, Connecticut. Sunday night, two days before the Obama-Romney presidential election. Matisyahu, who made a name for himself as the first Hasidic rapper, has come to play a show. I go stag and get there much too early, so I'm forced to kill time with a couple of beers as the warmup band finishes and the headliner gets ready to take the stage. A vivacious young woman thinks I look lonely; she takes pity on me and draws me into conversation with her and a law-student boyfriend. Later I watch her bouncing around the club, talking and dancing with lots of guys. She's one of the most gregarious people I've ever met.

A respectable crowd begins to congregate on the floor. Some are wearing yarmulkes, but for the most part the crowd looks pretty generic—although pop fans look younger to me every year. There are several hundred fans of all ages. Matisyahu comes out wearing a baggy Jamaican-style cap, an overcoat, shades. As he warms up he strips off the shades and layers of clothing, and within a few songs is down to a plaid flannel shirt. Clean-cut, pleasant features, rather mainstream, very unlike the Hasidic look he rode to fame a few years ago (Figure 5).

Matisyahu breaks from a song, addressing the crowd directly for the first time: "It's good to be back in New Haven ... Toad's Place!" Then he launches into perhaps his best-known song, "Jerusalem." It's a defiant Zionist statement, laying out the plight of a diasporic people, "3,000 years with no place to be." The lyrics reference "milk and honey," ovens and gas, rebuilding the Temple, "Babylon burning in the place." "Don't you see,

FIGURE 5 Matisyahu performing live at Glavclub in Moscow, December 2014. © hurricanehank (Shutterstock).

it's not about the land or the sea / Not the country but the dwelling of his majesty." Then the chorus—a clear paraphrase of Psalm 137:

> Jerusalem, if I forget you
> Fire not gonna come from my tongue.
> Jerusalem, if I forget you
> Let my right hand forget what it's supposed to do.[1]

Many in the crowd seem to know and be energized by this song. The set wears on. Matisyahu does a careful stage dive into the crowd. At the end he invites the audience up on stage, and it quickly fills with audience members singing along; it's hard to find Matisyahu himself, lost in the crowd.

Afterward I join a line of fans who have paid extra for passes to meet Matisyahu in his dressing room. A somewhat intoxicated couple next to me carry on a bit about her having run the Hartford Marathon a few weeks earlier. Matisyahu receives his fans stoically, allowing them to take photos and generally gush over him. He seems to be expecting me and gestures that I sit down next to him. We talk for a few minutes as people mill around the dressing room. Maybe he's tired from the show, but there's not a trace of bling or attitude about him. He gives off the slightly remote, muffled quality of Robert Pattison, star of *Twilight* (whom he slightly resembles).

How did you develop an interest in Psalm 137? I ask. "I learned about it through the Hebrew," Matisyahu answers. "The first time I heard it was in Hebrew." Later he explains: "The experience of exile is something I really relate to; I have always related to that personally."[2]

I ask him how important the Babylonian exile was to his understanding of Judaism. "Very important," he said, "because we are a people of exile. The Dalai Lama, you know, he invited in a group of Jewish rabbis so that they could tell him about what it's like to be in exile."

Does he think it's a good or bad thing that Judaism has been so shaped by the experience of exile? "I don't think of it as a good thing or a bad thing; it just is. We are a people who have been in exile for our entire existence: Adam and Eve, Abraham and Sarah, Jacob and his sons, Joseph, Moses, the Sephardim and Ashkenazim .... I was playing at a music festival and a reggae musician there asked me where Zion was. The Rastafarians, you know, they think Zion is Ethiopia. And I said, no, it's here"—pointing to his chest—"it's in here, a point in the heart."

"Do you know where the word Jerusalem comes from?" Matisyahu asks me. "It's a composite of two words, *yireh* and *shalom*. *Yireh* means full of awe. *Shalom* is peace. So Jerusalem means awe-some peace ... the most awesome peace there is."

I thank Matisyahu for his time and head off into the night, leaving him with his remaining backstage well-wishers.

Commanding Memory

The two verses that form the chorus of Matisyahu's song fall at the very center of Psalm 137. As David Freedman demonstrates in elaborate detail, the psalm is constructed like an envelope, with outer verses folding around inner ones. Verses 5 and 6 are like a nucleus at the very heart of the psalm. "This nucleus," he writes, "is an *artfully designed chiastic couplet* which is at once the dramatic high point or apex of the poem and the axis linking the parts and exhibiting the essential structure of the whole." He renders the heart of the psalm this way:

> If I forget thee, Jerusalem,
>   May my right arm wither
>   May my tongue stick
> To my palate, if I remember thee not!

The symmetry is remarkable: "remember thee not" balances "forget thee"; the oaths back up the psalmist's promise of fidelity to Israel with bodily collateral, one offering the arm, the other the tongue. Even the Hebrew syllable counts balance out: 9, 5, 5, 9.[3]

A distinct change of tone marks this middle section of the psalm. Sketching out a scene of mourning and humiliation beside a waterway, the first four verses are retrospective; all the verbs are past tense. And they are first-person plural: we sat down, we wept, we remembered, we hanged; how shall we? In the two middle verses that follow, the verbs are future-conditional and singular. The sense of a communal plight shifts to one of individual resolve and self-admonition.

And both oaths are addressed to Jerusalem, a synechdoche that stands for a sacred place, a chosen people, and their god. The sense of a collective bond with one's fellow exiles shifts to a notion of responsibility to the city that's been destroyed, symbolizing the covenant between the Judeans, as traumatically disrupted as their lives might be, and Yahweh, who still requires obedience and honor. We can imagine the loyalty oaths being made in the plural: If *we* forget thee, O Jerusalem. But they are not. There is a sense of the covenant being internalized.

The consequences of failure are starkly individualized. Rather than sanctions against the group, like forced displacement, what's threatened here is the loss of two abilities that define what it is to be a human being: manual dexterity and speech. (A colleague pointed out to me that both of these penalties are common sequellae of strokes.)[4] It's not Yahweh threatening these penalties; the psalmist is calling them down. It is the only instance in the Bible where punishment invoked by the speaker against himself for disloyalty to God is made explicit.[5]

We are left with the sense that in the psalmist's circumstances, it might be very easy to forget Jerusalem. We get a sense of the internal war that often ties religious folk into knots. The roots of so much popular music come out of that tantalizing dialectic between piety and temptation.

Johnny Cash's "I Walk the Line" comes to mind: "I keep a close watch on this heart of mine / I keep my eyes wide open all the time," sings Cash. And, "As sure as night is dark and day is light / I keep you on my mind both day and night." He's got a woman in mind, clearly, but could easily be singing to Jerusalem.

For musicians, either penalty could be incapacitating; neither singing nor playing an instrument would be possible, leading commentators to suggest that the psalmist could be a musician, possibly a Levite, a musician of the Jerusalem Temple. ("There were no left-handed Temple musicians," another colleague joked.) This conjecture has the advantage of creating a subtle linkage to the psalm's first section, where harps are put away as useless ("hanged . . . upon the willows") and singing becomes difficult or impossible: How shall we sing? Should we—can we—even sing at all? As we will see, American composer William Billings found these lines especially congenial in his own paraphrase of the psalm: "If I forget thee, yea if I do not remember thee / Then let my numbers cease to flow . . . / Then let my Tongue forget to move and ever be confin'd."

The way the Jewish Midrash elaborates on this possibility is interesting. As James Kugel shows, rabbinical exegeses included extensive commentary on what exactly the harps were, and what it meant to hang them up. One tradition held that the exiles foreclosed the possibility of playing for their captors by actually mutilating their thumbs in their teeth—actually gnawing their own flesh to make it impossible to play any instrument. In a way, then, these musicians of the Midrash carry out on their own digits the oath given in verse five—for the right hand to lose its cunning if Jerusalem is forgotten.

When Nebuchadnezzar orders the lamenting captives to provide background music for a banquet, the Judeans "looked at one another and said, 'is it not enough that we have destroyed His sanctuary by the multitude of our sins, but now must we go and play our harps before this dwarf?' Whereupon they all conferred and hung up their harps on the willows that were there and mastered themselves and put their thumbs in their mouths and crushed them and mutilated them." When the royal request for entertainment comes, the Levites can truthfully answer, "We shall not sing, we shall say nothing but 'How can we sing?'—and they showed them their fingers."[6]

While considering this extreme literalistic enactment of the musicians' oath, it's worth considering briefly the different perspective expressed by Christian theologians like Augustine, who interprets the harps allegorically. "The citizens of Jerusalem have their harps— God's scriptures, God's commandments, God's promises, the habit of pondering on the world to come—but when they live in the middle of Babylon they hang up their harps on Babylon's willows," Augustine explains. Willow trees bear no fruit and are effectively worthless, like the Babylonians: "The people who live there are greedy, miserly, and barren with respect to good works, and so they are like the trees of their region, for the citizens of Babylon feed on the pleasures derived from transient things, like trees irrigated by Babylon's rivers." Christians would be wasting their time to offer their scriptures to such people; a more opportune time will come.[7]

In short, we can read verses five and six as continuing the perspective of those Temple musicians who hung up their harps in verse two and hesitated to sing in verse four. But what if those middle verses are actually an answer to the question, "How should we sing the Lord's song in a foreign land?" Some interpreters offer an ingenious theory: that the songlike structure of verses five and six indicates it is the captives' reply to the just-posed question. "The 'captors' have asked for a song, and they get it—in a language they don't understand," suggests Christopher Hays. "The Jews 'show their defiance to their captor not by refusing to sing, but by what they sing,' they 'fill a recognizable form with an unexpected content.' They wanted to lay aside their harps; but now they are compelled to sing, so they take comfort in this song of national pride. In the temple, the Lord's song comes out as praise; but in exile, everything is inverted, and it comes out as anger." Hays observes that the Babylonians appear "blissfully unaware that they are being cursed," and relates a comment made by an acquaintance: "I might have had that experience, listening to a Korean choir. We had no idea what they were singing."[8]

Be that as it may (and some question whether the captives' language would be unintelligible to captors), the psalm's middle verses introduce a subtle shift in the meaning of memory from the way it is used in the opening section.

In his final book, *Memory, History, Forgetting*, Paul Ricœur draws out the difference between memory as image—something we recall in our mind's eye—and memory as a faculty that we can cultivate and command. In the first four verses, the psalmist freely evokes a scene, sketching an entire historical scenario in just a few lines. The "we" of the psalm is remembering Zion and weeping; psalmist is remembering what it felt like to be in that place at the time, the disorientation compounded by mockery. But in verses five and six we are reminded that memory is not arbitrary but intentional. It is a faculty that can be commanded and practiced.

As Yosef Yerushalmi has written, "The Hebrew Bible seems to have no hesitations in commanding memory. Its injunctions to remember are unconditional, and even when not commanded, remembrance is always pivotal. Altogether the verb *zakhar* appears in its various declensions in the Bible no less than one hundred and sixty-nine times, usually with either Israel or God as the subject, for memory is incumbent upon both. The verb is complemented by its obverse—forgetting. As Israel is enjoined to remember, so is it adjured not to forget. Both imperatives have resounded with enduring effect among the Jews since biblical times."[9]

The *Midrash Tehillim*, a collection of Jewish psalm commentaries compiled during the early Middle Ages, includes this prescription for observant Jews:

> If a man covers his house with plaster, he must leave uncovered a small space as a mourning reminder of Jerusalem. If a man prepares all that goes with a feast, he must leave out some small thing as a reminder of Jerusalem. If a woman is adorning herself, she must leave off some small thing as a reminder of Jerusalem, for it is said *If I forget thee, O Jerusalem, let my right hand forget her cunning.*[10]

These verses also figure in Jewish ritual life: invoked at weddings, where verse six is recited by the bridegroom, "who, with symbolic ashes on his head to represent the devastated Jerusalem, remembers 'Jerusalem, my *highest* joy,' as he awaits another joy—his bride." Or as a grace after meals, reminding the observant diner that the satisfaction of a meal must not distract from mourning the destruction of the Jerusalem Temple.[11]

This dynamic interplay between memory as image and memory as faculty will be explored at greater length below. These two verses, which enjoin the Judeans both to remember and not to forget, have held particular appeal for leaders of movements and those committed to causes. They are the verses Matisyahu chose for the chorus of "Jerusalem," with its Zionist yearning for milk and honey, its call for rebuilding the Temple.

"Fire not gonna come from my tongue . . . . Let my right hand forget what it's supposed to do."

They are the particular lines that captured the imagination of the thirteen-year-old Marie. "I found on the bookshelf at home this book called *O Jerusalem!* by Larry Collins and Dominique Lapierre," she told me. "And they not only tell this sort of very vivid and vibrant story about the Arab-Israeli war, but they quote Psalm 137 there. And this line just stuck with me, right: 'If I forget thee O Jerusalem, may my right hand forget its cunning, may my tongue cleave to the roof of my mouth if I do not remember thee, if I prefer not Jerusalem above my chief joy.'

"I was obsessed with this. So I not only became very interested in the conflict, but specifically the actual lines of the psalm became part of the poetry I was memorizing."

New World Babylon

It would be hard to identify a more dramatic musical adaptation of Psalm 137 than the one created by American composer William Billings. One of the truly fascinating characters of the Revolutionary era, Billings considered himself both a musical visionary and a political leader: someone laboring heroically to create a vernacular American music virtually from scratch as well as a diehard patriot during the Revolutionary War. He ended his anthem "Lamentation over Boston" (1778) with these bracing lines:

> If I forget thee, yea if I do not remember thee
> Then let my numbers cease to flow
> Then be my Muse unkind.
> Then let my Tongue forget to move & ever be confin'd.
> Let horrid Jargon split the Air & rive my nerves asunder.
> Let hateful discord greet my ear as terrible as Thunder.
> Let harmony be banish'd hence and Consonance depart.
> Let dissonance erect her throne and reign within my Heart.[12]

What is Billings driving at here? As with the Hebrew psalmist, we are aware that these self-imprecations are especially punishing for a composer and musician, for whom an unkind muse and paralyzed tongue could prove debilitating. In addition to his day job as a tanner, Billings was also an active teacher in singing schools; a paralyzed tongue would clearly disqualify him from that line of work. Whether composing or teaching others to sing, "horrid Jargon" and "hateful discord," the banishing of harmony and the ascendance of dissonance, all seem a musician's worst nightmare.

"Blind with one eye, one leg shorter than the other," Billings emerges as the quaintly uncouth hero of Nathaniel D. Gould's *Church Music in America* (1853), where he is described as grabbing snuff from his coat pocket and snorting it by the fistful. "We might infer, from this circumstance, that his voice could not have been very pleasant and delicate," Gould observes. But "stentorian" it was, according to a friend of Billings, who when singing next to the irrepressible composer, "could not hear his own voice."[13]

Billings was unfortunately not well appreciated by many of his contemporaries. The single most flattering review he ever received came from an unnamed Philadelphia critic in 1788. The critic comments in passing that Billings's "style, upon the whole bears a strong resemblance to that of Handel, and nature seems to have made him just such a musician, as she made Shakespeare a poet."[14] There is in fact an uncanny echo of Shakespeare's psalm language in "Lamentation over Boston." In *Richard II*, Thomas Mowbray, the Duke of Norfolk, has just been banished for life by the king:

> The language I have learnt these forty years,
> My native English, now I must forgo,
> And now my tongue's use is to me no more
> Than an unstringed viol or a harp,
> Or like a cunning instrument cas'd up—
> Or being open, put into his hands
> That knows no touch to tune the harmony.
> Within my mouth you have enjail'd my tongue,
> Doubly portcullis'd with my teeth and lips,
> And dull unfeeling barren ignorance
> Is made my jailer to attend on me.

This trope recurs in Act 2, when one character comments on someone recently deceased: "His tongue is now a stringless instrument." And in the play's final act:

> For ever may my knees grow to the earth,
> My tongue cleave to my roof within my mouth,
> Unless a pardon ere I rise or speak.

"The England of *Richard II*," writes Hannibal Hamlin, "like the biblical Jerusalem, is in ruins because of the sins of her people and, especially, her king."[15]

The analogy certainly fit the Boston of Billings, whose residents also suffered a kind of exile and bondage imposed by George III. "Lamentation over Boston" makes sense only when placed in the context of Revolutionary Boston. Billings was deeply rooted in the resistance to the Stamp Act (1765), Townshend Acts (1767), Boston Massacre (1770), Boston Tea Party (1773), Intolerable Acts (1774), and siege of Boston (1775–1776). A personal friend of both Paul Revere, who engraved the frontispiece to Billings's first publication, and Samuel Adams, next to whom he reportedly sang in church, it's no challenge to gauge Billings's politics, especially in view of patriotic tunes like "Chester": "Let tyrants shake their iron rod /And slav'ry Clank her galling Chains / We fear them not we trust in God / New Englands God for ever reigns."[16]

The Provincial Congress of Massachusetts was actually "exiled" and met in Watertown beginning in 1775, during the siege of Boston. Musically, Billings may have been influenced by Caleb Ashworth, a Baptist minister and headmaster from Daventry, England, whose anthem, "By the Rivers of Babylon," was published in no fewer than five North American songbooks beginning in 1766.[17]

But unlike Ashworth, who follows the biblical text in his anthem, Billings offers perhaps the most topical treatment of Psalm 137 it ever received. "By the Rivers of Watertown we sat down & wept," the anthem begins, "when we remember'd thee O Boston." Rather than merely requiring a song of humiliation, the unnamed Babylonian oppressor—Britain—forces Bostonians to take up arms against one another.

> As for our Friends Lord God of Heaven
>   preserve them, defend them,
>   deliver and restore them unto us again;
>   For they that held them in Bondage
>   Requir'd of them to take up Arms against their Brethren.[18]

Pushing his paraphrase well beyond the vitriol of the Hebrew psalmist, Billings introduces graphic imagery of Babylon thirsting for both milk and blood: "Forbid it Lord God that those who have sucked Bostonian Breasts should thirst for American Blood." Here Billings intersperses a trope from Jeremiah: "A voice was heard in Roxbury which echo'd thro' the Continent / weeping for Boston because of their Danger." The passage from Jeremiah 31—"A voice was heard in Ramah, lamentation, and bitter weeping; Rachel weeping for her children refused to be comforted for her children, because they were not"—is itself echoed in Matthew 2:18. There it stands as a fulfillment of prophecy, referring to the appalling incident known as the Massacre of the Innocents, in which Herod the Great, fearing the existence of Jesus, ordered the death of all boys age two and under.

The anthem then takes up the theme of memory: "Is Boston my dear Town? is it my Native Place? for since their Calamity I do earnestly remember it still." Again Billings is paraphrasing Jeremiah: "Is Ephraim my dear son? Is he a pleasant child? For since I spake against him, I do earnestly remember him still" (31:20). These lines lead into the dramatic finale, with the composer's oath and self-imprecations to guarantee his memory of Boston: the threat of unkind muse and frozen tongue, horrid jargon and hateful discord.

Musically, Billings's anthem is somewhat stolid and ponderous. It runs 133 measures in length, with the final section repeated, and takes about five minutes to perform. Following the text, the anthem divides into seven sections, each of which resolves to the tonic, A minor. This is no fuging tune, with the exuberant contrapuntal lines of which Billings was so fond; the anthem is mainly homophonic, with all four voice parts mainly singing the same phrases at the same time (though on different notes). The exception comes about midway through, where the word "weeping" is sung in a descending pattern by treble and bass, then echoed by the other voices, which gradually assemble into the phrase, "weeping for Boston because of their Danger."[19]

How often was "Lamentation over Boston" sung, and where? Nobody knows; there are no traces of it in the archives. Not included in *The Sacred Harp* or any of the tunebooks commonly used by contemporary shape-note singers, the anthem is rarely performed today.[20]

Musicians like Billings were not the only New England patriots to take up Psalm 137. For ministers, it was part of the scriptural rhetoric for the cause of independence. Ministers preached on the text; published sermons and tracts drew an analogy between the plight of Boston and that of the Judean exiles. In a sermon preached in December 1774 on a congressionally prescribed day of thanksgiving, Reverend Samuel Williams of Bradford, Massachusetts, began his sermon with a reminder of what happened to Judah.

As the just punishment of their sin and folly, God gave them up
to the power of their enemies. Nebuchadnezzar king of Babylon
prevailed over them in battle. Being brought under his power, they
soon found what the insolence of victory, and what the fate of a
conquered people generally is. From liberty, peace, and plenty, in
their own land, they were carried away to endure all the miseries of
subjection and slavery, in a kingdom where no other law or liberty
was known to them, but the arbitrary will of a proud, cruel, despotic
monarch.

Williams recounts the image of the captives mourning beside the rivers.

The idea of their former happy days, was constantly returning to
their minds. But amidst all their gloomy prospects, the interest and
welfare of their country lay nearest to their hearts. With a beauty,
force, and energy, that nothing but this noble patriotic passion
could inspire, the author of the psalm, in the language of his own
feelings thus expresseth the love, regard, and attachment, they all
bore to her.[21]

After quoting verses five and six verbatim, Williams offers his own
gloss: "Wheresoever I am carried, or whatever I endure, I shall never forget my native country. The right hand might as well forget her motion; the
tongue might as well lie dumb, as that I should cease to remember and
love her. For in her welfare and prosperity, my chief joy and pleasure lies."[22]

The following year appeared in Connecticut a pamphlet known to be
the work of Moses Mather, minister and inveterate patriot, of the famous
family of New England divines. Mather rehearses a scorching indictment
of British policy toward the colonies before turning, very much in the
spirit of Billings's anthem, to Psalm 137:

In a word, are not all our rights and liberties, natural, religious and
civil, made a mark for their arrows, and threatened to be laid in the
dust? And to compleat our ruin, are not our harbours blocked up?
our coasts lined with fleets? our country filled with armed troops? our
towns sacked? inhabitants plundered? friends slaughtered? our
pleasant places desolated with fire and sword? all announced
rebels? our estates declared forfeit, and our blood eagerly panted

for? When I think of Boston, that unhappy capital; what she once was, and the miserable captive state, to which she is now reduced, I am almost ready to adopt the plaintive strains of captive Israel concerning her.[23]

Mather then quotes verbatim the first seven verses of Psalm 137. (Interestingly, even in this heated rhetoric, Mather holds back from citing the two vengeful final verses of the psalm.)

In addition to ministers, hymn-writers made topical mention of Psalm 137. Noting that Isaac Watts had excised the text from his influential 1719 collection, *The Songs of David Imitated in the Language of the New Testament*, Joel Barlow included it in his 1785 publication, *Psalms Carefully Suited to the Christian Worship in the United States of America, Being Dr. Watts' Imitation of the Psalms of David, as Improved by Mr. Barlow*. He begins, "Along the banks where Babel's current flows / Our captive bands in deep despondence strayed / While Zion's all in sad remembrance rose, Her friends, her children, mingled with the dead." This is how Barlow paraphrases the middle verses:

> If e'er my memory lose thy lovely name,
> If my cold heart neglect my kindred race,
> Let dire destruction seize this guilty frame;
> My hand shall perish and my voice shall cease.[24]

Barlow found his own work "improved" fifteen years later by Timothy Dwight, the formidable minister, poet, and educator. Both Barlow and Dwight were poets and Congregationalist ministers from Connecticut, attended Yale, and served in the Revolutionary Army, but they had a falling out when Barlow moved to Europe and veered in what Dwight considered a dangerously deist direction. "I love thy Church, O God!" Dwight declared in his paraphrase of Psalm 137:

> If e'er to bless thy sons / My voice, or hands, deny
> These hands let useful skill forsake / This voice in silence die.
> If e'er my heart forget / Her welfare, or her woe,
> Let every joy this heart forsake / And every brief o'erflow.[25]

Like Billings, Barlow clearly had fresh memories of British oppression in mind when he paraphrased Psalm 137. In contrast, Dwight was concerned with the loss of authority of Connecticut's ecclesiastical establishment.[26]

After my conversation with Peggy Bendroth at the Congregational Library, I wander down the Boston Common to an old cemetery near the Boylston T entrance. A plaque on the fence stands in for a grave marker; no one knows exactly where Billings was buried, as he was destitute. Bendroth tells me that Billings fans—and there are many—periodically gather there to sing over (or at least near) his grave.

American Jeremiah

While American composers would continue to set the text during the first decades of the nineteenth century, the single most influential deployment of Psalm 137 would wait until the middle decade of the century, when Frederick Douglass would give it an entirely new, and lasting, political valence.

With the rhetoric of the Revolution ringing in my ears but Douglass on my mind, I navigate through Boston to its citadel of higher learning: Harvard Yard, specifically the office of John Stauffer, a leading authority on the great abolitionist. Directly across a courtyard from the Harvard Faculty Club, Baker Hall is a venerable old building that's been recently made over in state-of-the-art fashion. Its walls are tastefully punctuated with oil paintings and old plaques and reliefs assimilated into the new design of the building, which by the standards of higher education is stunningly posh. The office doors are closed, but nearly every plaque carries what for some field of the humanities is a household name.

Stauffer welcomes me cordially and quickly jumps up to grab a volume that ripples with yellow Post-its. I ask him if there any pages in the book that are not marked; he laughs. Stauffer is looking for passages from *My Bondage and My Freedom*, which he edited for Modern Library; in particular, the scene in which Douglass meditates on the double meaning of the spirituals he was singing as he plotted his first escape from slavery.

Was Douglass particularly well versed in the Hebrew psalms? I ask.

Stauffer replies that Douglass knew "many psalms," and "quoted frequently" from them, but never more dramatically than his use of Psalm 137 in "What to the Slave Is the Fourth of July," his famous 1852 oration. "I edited *My Bondage and My Freedom*, so all the quotes I traced back, and the one text he quotes from more than any other is the Bible. And within the text of the Bible, the Psalms are, if not the largest single book, one of the largest single books in the Bible that he quotes from."[27]

Douglass identified eloquently with a sense of exile. "The land of my birth welcomes me to her shores only as a slave, and spurns with contempt the idea of treating me differently," he wrote to his mentor, William Lloyd Garrison, on New Year's Day in 1846 while touring Ireland. "So that I am an outcast from the society of my childhood, and an outlaw in the land of my birth. 'I am a stranger with thee, and a sojourner as all my fathers were.' "[28]

Did Douglass have a particular interest in music, I wonder.

"Douglass loved music," Stauffer says. "Music was an important ritual and an important aspect of his abolitionism. He was a very good singer. Music is what first brought him together with [wife] Anna Murray. They fell in love—they were brought together because they were both connected to the Baltimore Mental Improvement Association, essentially this debating club. Douglass was the only slave. Anna loved music, and throughout their lives they would play duets together. Douglass had this rich baritone voice and he was evidently a very good singer; Anna would play the violin, and Douglass had learned the violin. Music, and hymns in general, were a very important part of his life . . . . For him to quote Psalm 137, to give it the kind of attention it has in 'What to the Slave Is the Fourth of July'—that's significant."

I ask Stauffer how Douglass came to deliver his renowned Rochester speech.

"The Ladies' Antislavery Society of Rochester invited him to give the keynote. He was already probably the most famous citizen of Rochester, and he was invited to give the keynote on July 5th rather than July 4th, and we're unsure exactly why. One reason would be that July 4th was on a Sunday or a Saturday and July 5th wasn't a day normally set aside for major events. The other reason was that New York blacks typically celebrated the 4th on the 5th, for two reasons: one, to highlight the hypocrisy of the Declaration vis-à-vis where the nation was going. The other, more practical, is that a lot of whites used the Fourth of July as an excuse to get drunk. If blacks celebrate on the 4th, and they're in the streets parading alongside of drunken whites, there could be trouble. So for reasons of safety, they celebrated on the 5th."

The oration was given in Corinthian Hall, completed just three years earlier in downtown Rochester. It was used for a variety of functions: lectures, orations, fairs, exhibitions, banquets, and suffrage meetings. Ralph Waldo Emerson, Daniel Webster, and Susan B. Anthony all spoke there. The same year as Douglass, Jenny Lind, the "Swedish Nightingale" and perhaps the nineteenth century's most celebrated diva, performed at Corinthian.[29]

Douglass challenged his audience with the blunt question: Why in the world should African Americans celebrate Independence Day? "The rich inheritance of justice, liberty, prosperity, and independence, bequeathed by your fathers, is shared by you, not by me," he said, addressing his primarily white audience. "The sunlight that brought life and healing to you, has brought stripes and death to me."[30] Why would an escaped slave celebrate the birthday of such a nation?

For an analogy, Douglass turns to Psalm 137, comparing the United States to another nation "whose crimes, towering up to heaven, were thrown down by the breath of the Almighty, burying that nation in irrecoverable ruin!" Introducing "the plaintive lament of a peeled and woe-smitten people," he cites verbatim the first six verses of Psalm 137. He then gets to the meat of his address:

> If I do forget, if I do not faithfully remember those bleeding children of sorrow this day, "may my right hand forget her cunning, and may my tongue cleave to the roof of my mouth!" To forget them, to pass lightly over their wrongs, and to chime in with the popular theme, would be reason most scandalous and shocking, and would make me a reproach before God and the world. My subject then, fellow-citizens, is AMERICAN SLAVERY.

He continues his withering indictment. "Standing there, identified with the American bondman, making his wrongs mine," Douglass states, "I do not hesitate to declare, with all my soul, that the character and conduct of this nation never looked blacker to me than on this Fourth of July. Whether we turn to the declarations of the past, or to the professions of the present, the conduct of the nation seems equally hideous and revolting. America is false to the past, false to the present, and solemnly binds herself to be false to the future."[31]

I ask Stauffer how this strong language went over.

"It was received very well," he replies. "Douglass spoke to very diverse kinds of audiences. This audience was a predominantly white middle-class audience, and a comparatively large number of women, because the Women's Antislavery Society sponsored it. And at this point Douglass was already embracing violence. He had already gone on record as saying the best solution for the Fugitive Slave Law—the best way to make the Fugitive

Slave Law a dead letter—is to, you know, kill a few more slave catchers. He said two years later, 'A slave owner has no right to live.' And there's a speech that he gave within a month of 'What to the Slave Is the Fourth of the July' which is profoundly militant—where he's basically saying: 'We are legitimate in killing slave-owners.'

"Yet there's no rhetoric of violence in 'What to the Slave Is the Fourth of July.' And I think that's in large part because Douglass was really, really brilliant about knowing his audience. The tone and the rhetoric of his speeches when it was a mostly black crowd at the A.M.E Zion church was very different than it was to a mostly white crowd. He was really subtle about that."

The speech was an immediate sensation. The audience of more than 600 people unanimously voted directly afterward to formally thank Douglass for his lecture. Two days later he apologized to his comrade Gerrit Smith for having been out of touch while he holed up to write the address: "You will readily think that the speech ought to be good that has required so much time," he wrote. "Well, some here think it was a good speech—foremost among those who think so, is my friend Julia. She tells me it was *excellent*! I hope you will think well of it." Quickly published in pamphlet form, it sold 700 copies. "I must tell you however that I really am desireous [sic] to make some money as well as do some good with that speech," he wrote Smith a week later. "I am intending to do considerable lecturing—and I must have something to carry with me to sell. I rely mainly on this method for the means of living and travelling."[32]

There is an intriguing ambiguity in the analogy Douglass draws between Babylon and the American slave power. It seems that Douglass wants to associate enslaved Africans with Judah, and to identify the United States with Babylon. But Judah itself was corrupt, according to the Hebrew Bible, its conquest by Nebuchadnezzar the result of its own sin. It's always risky to speculate how audiences hear particular points, especially without evidence of response. But it seems plausible that many whites in the audience would have identified with Judah: members of a people chosen by God, but badly corrupted by their nation's complicity in slavery, in danger of the sort of divine retribution that was inflicted on Jerusalem in 586 B.C.E.

There's another echo of Psalm 137 in Douglass's oration: the theme of mockery. "To drag a man in fetters into the grand illuminated temple of liberty, and call upon him to join you in joyous anthems, were inhuman mockery and sacrilegious irony," Douglass thunders. "Do you mean, citizens, to mock me by asking me to speak today? If so, there is a parallel to your conduct."[33]

Forcing enslaved Africans to perform music had been a notable feature of life under slavery. "Many observers were struck by the fact that as slaves departed for the South they were often singing," writes historian Walter Johnson. This may have been because slave traders sometimes used whips to make them sing. According to a slave narrative published in 1867, these songs were coerced to "prevent among the crowd of Negroes who usually gather on such occasions, any expression of sorrow for those who are being torn away from them."[34] Exile is doubled here: exile from the homeland, and from the familiar setting of the North to an unknown destination in the South.

Consider *Uncle Tom's Cabin*, to cite a famous example, published the same year as Douglass's Rochester oration. When Tom begins the final trudge to his Deep South plantation, Simon Legree orders his newly acquired slaves: "Strike up a song, boys,—come!" When Tom launches into a Protestant hymn, he explodes:

> "Shut up, you black cuss!" roared Legree; "did ye think I wanted any o'yer infernal old Methodism? I say, tune up, now, something real rowdy,—quick!"
>
> One of the other men struck up one of those unmeaning songs, common among the slaves.
>
> > "Mas'r see'd me cotch a coon,
> >   High boys, high! . . ."
>
> It was sung very boisterously, and with a forced attempt at merriment; but no wail of despair, no words of impassioned prayer, could have had such a depth of woe in them as the wild notes of the chorus . . . . There was a prayer in it, which Simon could not hear. He only heard the boys singing noisily, and was well pleased; he was making them "keep up their spirits."[35]

Such performances foreshadow blackface minstrelsy, which began its cultural ascent in the 1830s and was well established by 1852. "Slaves' performances were admittedly coerced," writes Ronald Radano, "frequently through degradation, whether by tossing coins to prompt dancers or when 'whiskey was handed out by the overseers, and the slaves becoming very merry, began to caper and sing more noisily than before.' But the slaves also profited from them, not only monetarily but also in accessing a form of cultural power." It is to the "commodified logic" of coerced performances by enslaved Americans that Eric Lott traces the blackface minstrel show.[36]

"Do you think Douglass knew what an impact this speech would have?" I ask Stauffer.

"When Douglass wrote 'What to the Slave Is the Fourth of July,' he under-stood that this was a significant speech. He labored intensely over it ... he felt proud of it." The oration "was an important kind of touchstone, or keynote, for how he understood himself and blacks within the context of the United States. And especially, the timing is important, because it's 1852. He had officially only become a political abolitionist for a year, and that's made clear in 'What to the Slave Is the Fourth of July.' So, it's his cultural kind of political critique of America that's very different than what it had been as a Garrisonian."

The year 1852 was also when *Uncle Tom's Cabin* was published; Solomon Northup's *Twelve Years a Slave* appeared the following year.

As our conversation winds down, I point to an impressively framed oil painting on Stauffer's office wall. "Oh, that's Charles Sumner," he says, referring to the great Massachusetts senator and abolitionist who was nearly caned to death in the Senate chamber by an irate pro-slavery congressman from South Carolina. It seems Harvard has more artworks than wall space to hang from; faculty can borrow them for their offices for a nominal fee. Stauffer explains a number of other artifacts on his walls, mainly nineteenth-century prints and daguerrotypes, including a rare one of John Brown.

Just before we part it finally occurs to me whom Stauffer resembles. I've been trying to place him. More than anyone I've met, Stauffer looks like Abraham Lincoln: the same tired dark eyes, ringed with black circles; craggy features; the same unruly black hair standing up in tufts. Stauffer has good reason to be haggard; he tells me he's been working feverishly to finish a cultural history of "Battle Hymn of the Republic" while teaching his classes. But I can't help wondering: how uncommon is it for biogra-phers to take on the appearance of their subjects?

Africa as New Israel

In the decades leading up to Douglass's Rochester speech, African Americans were finding fresh interpretations for the middle verses of Psalm 137. Noting increasing numbers of free blacks in the United States, leaders of both races began promoting the repatriation of free U.S. blacks to West Africa.

Motives were mixed. Some supporters of the American Colonization Society, founded in 1816, believed that African Americans would never escape race prejudice while living in North America, and would never be allowed to assimilate and achieve equality. Some white supporters of colonization considered free blacks to be inherently licentious and immoral, a societal burden who would drive down wages for white workers. While some abolitionists saw the movement as part of a campaign to eliminate slavery, a few slave owners supported the movement precisely because of their loyalty to the institution; they feared the existence of free blacks would incite slave rebellions. The issue of colonization was a major wedge between Abraham Lincoln, a famous proponent, and Douglass, who like many abolitionists resented and distrusted the motives of its supporters.

Here we remember a similar divergence of opinion among the people of Judah in the sixth century B.C.E. Despite Psalm 137's tone of nostalgic yearning, with its profession of loyalty to Jerusalem, many of the Judean exiles took the advice of Jeremiah and assimilated. Even when the Persian conquest of Babylon gave them the opportunity to return to Judah, they remained in the land of exile; that's where their lives were.

But there was no denying the appeal of an African homeland to many blacks. As early as 1774, the poet Phillis Wheatley, captured in Senegal before being pressed into servitude in Boston, took inspiration from Psalm 68: "Princes shall come out of Egypt; Ethiopia shall soon stretch out her hands unto God." As she wrote to Samuel Hopkins, the abolitionist minister and theologian who served a church in Newport, Rhode Island:

Methinks, Rev. Sir, this is the beginning of that happy period foretold by the Prophets, when all shall know the Lord from the least to the greatest, and that without the assistance of human Art of Eloquence . . . . I hope that which the divine royal Psalmist says by inspiration is now on the point of being accomplished, namely, Ethiopia shall soon stretch forth her hands unto God.[37]

We find a remarkable musical trace of this vision in the work of Newport Gardner. An uncanny doppelgänger to Billings—they were born the same year, 1746—Occramer Marycoo was captured in Africa and sold to a Newport sea captain named Caleb Gardner, who rechristened him. A prodigy, the teenager taught himself to read and compose music. Gardner helped form the African Union Society in 1780 and served as sexton in the First Congregational Church (Samuel Hopkins's church) before helping establish Newport's first African American congregation, the Colored Union Church, in 1824. He opened a singing school and also helped found and served as headmaster at a school for black children.

Meanwhile, he had obtained freedom for himself and his family from Gardner. All along he had retained an urge to return to his homeland, and late in 1825 he helped establish a church in Boston with the express purpose of emigrating to Liberia. The commissioning service closed with an anthem composed for the occasion by Gardner, who stitches together passages from Jeremiah 30 and the gospels of Matthew and Mark:

> For lo! the days come, saith the Lord, that I will bring again the captivity of my people Israel and Judah, saith the Lord; and I will cause them to return to the land that I gave to their fathers, and they shall possess it. . . . Hear the words of the Lord, O ye African race, hear the words of promise. . . . O African, trust in the Lord. Amen. Hallelujah. Praise the Lord.[38]

Five days later, the ship sailed for Monrovia, established a few years earlier as the capital of Liberia. With the eighty-year-old Gardner serving as deacon, the ship arrived a month later. Though the music has been lost, Gardner's anthem was reportedly still being performed at a church in Newport as late as 1940.[39]

Living in exile, or returning home from it—these alternatives continued to play out in the imagination of African Americans. The colonization movement never attracted enough support from free blacks or abolitionists, and faded from view after the Civil War. It was resuscitated in the 1920s by the Jamaican-born Marcus Garvey, founder of the United Negro Improvement Association (UNIA) and leader of the Back-to-Africa movement. Garvey's Pan-Africanism would inspire such later movements as the Nation of Islam and Rastafarianism, both of which claimed Garvey as a major prophet.

I have found no evidence that Garvey himself had a particular interest in the Babylonian Exile in general, or Psalm 137 in particular. The one indispensable biblical text, for Garvey and the UNIA, was the psalm invoked by Phillis Wheatley and African American church leaders since the eighteenth century: "Princes shall come forth from Egypt: Ethiopia shall soon stretch forth her hand to God" (68:31). The text was recited after the processional hymn in UNIA meetings and included in its catechism:

Q. What prediction made in the 68th Psalm and the 31st verse is now being fulfilled?
A. "Princes shall come out of Egypt, Ethiopia shall soon stretch forth her hands unto God."

Q. What does this verse prove?
A. That Negroes will set up their own government in Africa, with rulers of their own race.

Garvey even went so far as to say, "Otherwise I would not believe in God; but I am persuaded to believe in Him because He Himself said, 'Princes shall come out of Egypt and Ethiopia shall stretch forth her hands unto God.' "[40]

Putting aside Garvey's movement, Psalm 137 did begin attracting attention among African American intellectuals in the 1920s. For writers of the New Negro (or Harlem) Renaissance, the psalm served as a focal point for highlighting the ironies of black vernacular culture in white America. Author of the brilliant *Autobiography of an Ex-Colored Man*, James Weldon Johnson also wrote the hymn often dubbed the Negro National Anthem, "Lift Every Voice and Sing." In it we hear faint echoes of the middle verses of Psalm 137:

Keep us forever in the path, we pray.
Lest our feet stray from the places, our God, where we met Thee,
Lest, our hearts drunk with the wine of the world, we forget Thee.

In his preface to the groundbreaking *Book of American Negro Poetry* (1922), which he edited, Johnson blasts the "execrable versified version of the Psalms made by the New England divines," which frequently made its way into anthologies and textbooks. As proof he cites the tortured syntax of Psalm 137 as rendered by *The Bay Psalm Book*:

The Lord's song sing can we? being
in stranger's land, then let
lose her skill my right hand if I
Jerusalem forget.[41]

Johnson contrasts this with the unheralded genius of Phillis Wheatley, who arrived in Boston aboard a slave ship in 1761 as a girl of seven or eight. He points out that Wheatley received a thank-you letter from General George Washington, in his own hand, for a poem she dedicated to him; he later "received her with marked courtesy" when he was encamped near Boston.[42]

Johnson's important labors in documenting the extent and quality of African American literature and music were reinforced by the remarkable musical accomplishments of singer Roland Hayes (see Fig. 6). Not nearly as well remembered today as one would expect, Hayes was classical

FIGURE 6 Carl Van Vechten, *Portrait of Roland Hayes*, 1954. Courtesy of the Library of Congress Prints and Photographs Division [LC-USZ62-100858].

music's answer to Jackie Robinson, who broke the color line in Major League Baseball . During the 1920s Hayes blazed across Europe and North America, playing before royalty and garnering rave reviews in the finest concert halls in the world. Another comparison would be to the Fisk Jubilee Singers, who similarly took European royalty and cultural elites by storm fifty years earlier, a parallel Hayes himself draws in his memoir. Incredibly, no biography of Hayes has appeared since an account published in 1942 under the title, *Angel Mo' and Her Son, Roland Hayes.*

Hayes emerges from that volume as a lifelong outsider, the sort of existential exile discussed earlier in relation to African American Pentecostalism. Raised in rural Georgia and Tennessee, classically trained in Boston, Hayes described himself as deeply shaped by both a deep Holiness Piety absorbed from his mother and by his reading of Ralph Waldo Emerson. He got to know Booker T. Washington when hired to sing duets on lecture tours with Harry Burleigh, the pioneering classical singer, composer, and arranger.

"Some of us must advance beyond the rudiments, as Du Bois believes and teaches," Hayes explains; "but our racial culture ought to rest on the solid foundation of skill in factory and field. I may be old-fashioned, but I like to think that I am a better singer for having learned to plow a straight furrow when I was a boy in the Flatwoods."[43] It took Hayes a few years to sort out the various influences on his voice. Studying in Boston about 1918, he recounts:

> I had been working in a cloud of depression because my voice had not come out as "white" as, in the beginning, I must have hoped it would. Now I swore I would use the "rich purplish red" voice that Nature had given me. I felt a great release from nervous tension, and at the same time a kind of exaltation. I felt I could be what no white artist could ever be: I could be myself, sole, personal, unique.[44]

We get a sense of both the power of Hayes's artistry and the use to which he put Psalm 137 in the account of yet another luminary of the New Negro Renaissance. Sterling Allen Brown grew up in Washington, D.C., where his father (born a slave) was a minister and professor at Howard University and his mother was a public schoolteacher. Brown won a scholarship to Williams College, graduated Phi Beta Kappa, and earned a master's degree from Harvard. He eventually returned to Howard, where he taught literature and folklore for forty years, all the while writing poetry.

Brown's very first publication provides a perceptive eyewitness account of a recital by Roland Hayes before a racially mixed (though separately seated) audience at a somewhat shabby basketball gym in Washington, D.C., with backboards clearly visible. Brown's description of Hayes's encore, a piece by Antonin Dvořák, is worth recounting at length:

> Roland sings . . . .
> By the waters of Babylon—
> The whites start at the wild summoning of beautiful distress. Why is there arranging of them in a cantor's song—sung by a Negro? What histrionic ability in this man to so feign passionate despair?
>> We sat down and wept
>> Yea we wept
>> When we remembered Zion
> The Negroes brood; are stirred by something deep within, something as far away as all antiquity, as old as human wrong, as tragical as loss of worlds. What does he mean—and why are we so stirred—
>> . . . required of us a song
>> And they that wasted us
>> Required of us mirth.[45]

Here Brown connects Babylon's taunt to the exploitation of black vernacular culture, dating back to antebellum blackface minstrelsy but taking on new guises during the Harlem Renaissance:

> And a thousand of our girls prostitute their voices singing jazz for a decadent white and black craving, and a number of lyricists turn off cheap little well-made bits of musical bric-a-brac, and Mose, having trundled a white man's fertilizer, walks wearily home, strumming a guitar. And a street car conductor jogs a black bricklayer to hear a comic monlogue.
>> How shall we sing the Lord's song in a strange land?
>> Roland Hayes is singing with eyes closed, and head thrown back:
>>> If I forget thee, O Jerusalem
>>> If I forget thee, O Jerusalem
>>> Let my right hand forget her cunning.

What is it that he sees, this mystic seer clutched by the ferocity of the final phrases .... What is it that is denied to us .... That frightens us, nay, appals [*sic*]?

This is no pose, this tense attitude, this head flung haughtily back, these closed eyes ....

Many did not notice that he had left the stage.

Brown describes the audience response as tepid: whites uncomprehending, blacks feeling "somehow rebuked." But he turns to this particular number to close his essay. When Hayes sings—literally in that moment when his voice is reaching the ears of its audience—racial divisions dissolve. "Roland Hayes sings, and boundaries are but figments of imagination, and prejudice but insane mutterings," he writes. "And what is real is a great fellowship of all in pain, a fellowship in hope. Roland Hayes sings, and for that singing moment, however brief, the world forgets its tyranny and its submissiveness."[46]

Brown ends his essay quoting the first verse of Psalm 137.

Dvořák's Psalm

The piece whose performance made such an impact on that Washington gymnasium audience tells us something important about transnational flows of music during the fertile early decades of the twentieth century. It was composed by the great Czech composer Antonin Dvořák, who lived and worked in the United States for three productive years in the mid-1890s. He was deeply inspired by what we would now call the multicultural promise of American music. "It matters little whether the inspiration for the coming folk songs of America is derived from the Negro melodies, the songs of the creoles, the red man's chant, or the plaintive ditties of the homesick German or Norwegian," he declared. "Undoubtedly the germs for the best in music lie hidden among all the races that are commingled in this great country."[47]

In particular, Dvořák believed that "the future music of this country must be founded upon what are called the negro melodies ... the real foundation of any serious and original school of composition to be developed in the Unites States." In them Dvořák discerned "all that is needed for a great and noble school of music. They are pathetic, tender, passionate, melancholy, solemn, religious, bold, merry, gay or what you will."[48]

In *Angel Mo'*, Hayes recounts a story about Dvořák having learned the melody of the spiritual "Swing Low, Sweet Chariot" from a performance by Harry Burleigh in the 1890s; the melody then appears with minor modifications in the first movement of Dvořák's *New World Symphony*. "With Dvořák's encouragement, Burleigh had jotted down traditional musical settings for some of our Afro-American songs," Hayes recalled. "Traveling about with him, I felt close to the inspired sources of our native music."[49]

But the piece Sterling Brown watched Hayes sing at the gym in Washington was a different one: it was Dvořák's setting of Psalm 137 in *Biblical Songs*, Opus 99.

Dvořák composed the ten-part *Biblical Songs* during a time of serious emotional turmoil: he was grieving the recent loss of his friends Peter Tchaikovsky and the conductor Han von Bülow, and his own father was dying on the other side of the Atlantic. He was also torn over whether to continue in his position as director of the National Conservatory in New York City or to return to Prague.

Dvořák wrote the *Biblical Songs* quickly, in March 1894. But careful listening reveals complex and daring harmonic architecture. "The outline of primary key relationships ... reveals an intricate, religiously symbolic, series of keys derived from the Psalm texts themselves," writes musicologist Daniel Jacobson. "The key of F is the focal center and ultimate goal of the cycle, representing 'complete confidence in God.'" Other tonalities emerge which contrast sharply. "This symbolic dichotomy allowed Dvořák to create a wavelike design ... that vividly depicts his own struggle to understand God's actions at this moment of personal crisis."[50]

Jacobson continues, "The seventh song, "Pri rekách babylonskych" (By the Waters of Babylon) is one of the cycle's most remarkable settings. It begins and ends in different keys (C minor and E-flat), and its intricate rhythms and striking modulations vividly depict the desperate overtones of the text."[51] The piece opens in a dark mood with a pronounced pentatonic quality, ostinato figures supplied by the piano accompaniment. Sixteenth notes on the piano simulate the strumming of harps. The "jocular" central section suggests captives being taunted, then seems to brighten in response to the idea of singing. Rapid piano notes propel the vocal line, generating a sense of bravado that again falls off. We hear a cry of remembrance for Jerusalem. The vocal line climaxes with the word "O," which is followed by a very dissonant chord.[52]

The short piece finishes, leaving the sense that it is ultimately impossible to sustain the songs of Zion.

Dvořák's musical setting of Psalm 137 was inherited, so to speak, by the American who carried on Hayes's legacy to the classical concert stage: Paul Robeson.

A supremely talented athlete, intellectual, musician, and actor, Robeson's outspoken left politics led to him becoming an exile in his own land, where he was hounded by the U.S. government until his death in 1976. Early in his career Robeson was a great admirer of Roland Hayes, and studied his vocal art. He also hired Hayes's piano accompanist, Lawrence Brown, whom he named a major musical mentor and inspiration. In particular, Brown honed Robeson's appreciation for black vernacular music like church songs, work songs, and the blues.[53]

Robeson also made a close study of Hayes as a *race man*, a figure who modeled how one could achieve dignity and pride as an African American. "So today Roland Hayes is infinitely more a racial asset than many who 'talk' at great length," Robeson observed in 1924, about the time Hayes made such a powerful impression on the young Sterling Brown. "Thousands of people hear him, see him, are moved by him, and are brought to a clearer understanding of human values. If I can do something of a like nature, I shall be happy, I shall be happy. My early experiences give me much hope."[54]

Nearly thirty years later Robeson was asked to sing the psalm that had so impressed Sterling Brown on the basketball court. It was intended for use in a biopic on Dvořák produced in Czechoslovakia. The Hebrew psalms, Robeson averred, were "the searing outcry of an enslaved people against their oppressors, against *'those that carried us away captive.'*" He recounted the American meaning of the psalm in an article published in 1954 in the magazine *Jewish Life*.

> From ancient Judea these words of the 137th Psalm had crossed the vast reaches of time and distance to stir the hearts of the Negro slaves in our own southland; and the downfall of slave-holding Babylon was cited by our Frederick Douglass in his famous address
> . . . .
> Half a century later the gifted Dvorak came to our country, studied the melodies and lyrics of Negro song, and drew upon its richness for his own creations—and so, in this way, the words of this very song must have traveled back across the ocean with him; and I am told the song was especially popular among the

Czech people during their years of suffering under the terror of nazi occupation.

But history moves on: Hitler is gone; Prague lives and builds in a new people's democracy—and now I, an American Negro, sing for her this ancient Hebrew song in the language of the people of Huss and Dvorak, Fuchik and Gottwald:

> *Pri rekach babylonckych*
> *Tam jsme sedavali a plakavali.*[55]

About a decade later, sharp divisions began developing on the political left between Jews and African Americans over the state of Israel and a variety of domestic issues. Robeson's vision of the close links between African and Jewish Americans comes across as poignant, a road not taken. "The Hassidic Chant, for example," he wrote, "has a profound impact on the Negro listener not only for its content—a powerful protest against an age-old persecution—but also because of its form: the phrasing and rhythm have counterparts in traditional Negro sermon-song. And here, too, is a bond that can be traced back through the centuries to a common heritage."[56]

There is poignancy, too, in Robeson's life in those years and the decades to follow. Because of his outspoken support for the Communist Party USA and Soviet Union, his U.S. passport was revoked from 1950 to 1958. He was investigated by Senator Joseph McCarthy and summoned to testify by the House Committee on Un-American Activities. Robeson was pilloried in the press, both white and African American, making it difficult for him to perform onstage or in concert. He gradually succumbed to a number of physical and mental illnesses, including depression. During the last decade of his life Robeson became a recluse, living his final years at his sister's house in Philadelphia.

Just as Robeson was giving Dvořák's setting of Psalm 137 a transnational spin that built on Hayes's pioneering performances thirty years earlier, another leader, C. L. Franklin, gave the psalm a very different prod into public awareness. Born to a sharecropping family in Mississippi, Franklin made his way north through churches in Memphis, Tennessee, and Rochester, New York, and finally to Detroit, where he became pastor of the New Bethel Baptist Church.

Beginning in the 1950s, Franklin's charismatic "whooping" southern-style preaching (he was known as the "Million Dollar Voice") was building a national audience through radio broadcasts and recordings for Chess Records in Chicago. A confidant of Martin Luther King Jr. (who counted Franklin as his favorite preacher), and father of Aretha, Franklin played a major role in the political life of Detroit, his influence peaking during the civil rights movement.[57] Preaching one century after Douglass's famous Rochester oration, Franklin delivered a sermon, "Without a Song," based on Psalm 137. Because it was commercially released by Chess, we have the complete sermon in all its full-throated delivery.

"Here they were, these proud Hebrews, in Babylon," Franklin begins, "some of whom had been courtiers, government officials, rabbis, teachers, scholars, leaders in intellectual and religious thought, leaders in philosophical thought, sages." The Babylonians asked their Hebrew captives to sing, Franklin explains, because the music of Jerusalem was something unique; the captors had no need of scientists, scholars, philosophers, or politicians. "They had the great court of Hammurabi's that they could boast of, the wisdom of which has survived all the ages, and they weren't particularly worried about the Jews along that line," he preaches. Thinking the request "a bit disorderly and out of place," the Hebrews refused.[58]

"I take the position that they should have sung," Franklin preaches, warming to the sermon's thesis. "Yes, they were in a strange land; yes, they were among so-called heathens; yes, the situation in which they found themselves was an unfamiliar situation and possibly was not conducive to inspire them into spiritual expression. But even under adverse circumstances, you ought to sing sometimes. And not only sing, sing some of Zion's songs."[59]

Franklin then offers a series of illustrations of singers whose public performances had historic consequences for African Americans. There were the anonymous African Americans who created "Swing Low, Sweet Chariot," and "Steal Away" to help them survive the brutal tribulations of slavery; through their singing they found the strength to endure. Franklin recounts the story of an elderly black woman who heard Charles Wesley preaching "either in the Carolinas or in Georgia" and came into the sanctuary, only to be told to "Go and join some other church, some of your own churches"; a crowd of blacks gathered outside watching through the window broke into song: "Oh Mary, don't weep, don't mourn; Pharaoh's army got drownded."[60]

These heroes were anonymous; Franklin's third example was Roland Hayes.

The story Franklin recounted is one of the best known about Hayes, who told a similar version in his memoir; decades later he summarized it for a *New York Times* reporter. It concerns a recital at the venerable *Beethovensaal* in Berlin. "At the time," Franklin explains, "Nazism was arising and some of them did not want this Georgia Negro to come and stand on the stage where their great immortals had stood, and sing." Then comes this part, where we should imagine his incandescent preaching voice (I've heard it) doing justice to Hayes's own:

> And when he walked out on the stage, those who resented him and those who opposed him went into howls and hisses to make it impossible to sing. He stood there for a long time with his eyes closed and his arms folded, and then when apparently the noise would not subside, he just kept his eyes closed and his arms folded, and began singing in that great tenor voice, "Lord, thou art my peace, thou art my peace." And that great voice began to rise and soar above the noise, and search that great building, and then hisser and howler after howler began to get quiet and listen to that great voice. Eventually the whole house became quiet and listened, and was moved and thrilled and inspired by this great artist. And when he had finished, that same crowd that intended to make it impossible for him to sing, many of them ran to the stage and took him upon their shoulders and marched down the aisle, hailing and acclaiming him. I'm trying to tell you what can be done in a song.[61]

A master preacher, Franklin then brought his message home to his parishioners in Detroit and those who listened to his broadcasts and bought his records: "no matter how troublesome our situations become," we ought to sing. True, the Judeans may have remained silent, Franklin allows, but at that time they were still "hampered" by "nationalistic thinking," not yet "universal-minded." But Babylon itself would have been better off if the captives had sung, had shared the power and majesty of "Israel's God."[62]

Drawing closer to home, Franklin spoke of the tendency "of segregating certain communities and segregating certain peoples, and who act like their religion is too good to go certain places." But Jesus set another example, willing to appear "in the harlots' homes, in the publicans' homes, in sinners' homes, wherever people were." The point was to sing.[63]

Million Dollar Voice

On a hot day at the end of July I load up my iPad with google.maps and head to Detroit.

It's about time I see C. L. Franklin's stomping grounds and visit the New Bethel Baptist Church. Its current pastor, Reverend Robert Smith, and I converge like clockwork in front of the building, which sits on the corner of Linwood and West Philadelphia. Before Franklin moved his church there in 1963 the building housed the Oriole Theater. By mega-church standards it's not terribly large: block-shaped, without many windows, stained-glass or otherwise, and painted beige with coffee-colored trim, giving it a vaguely Tudor look. Four large wooden double doors mark the front entrance. Smith, a burly man dressed casually in black, invites me up to his office, exchanging brief remarks on the way up with a couple of neighborhood guys in need of care and direction; one has an injured foot and needs a ride. The office is festooned with photos and plaques, several of them featuring the illustrious C. L. Franklin. The bookshelves display books by Barack Obama, Bill Clinton, and Steve Jobs, which Smith recommends to me.

Smith only met Franklin once, he tells me, in New Orleans.

"And I asked him, you know, was he *the* Reverend Franklin. He said, 'I am.' He had a peculiar voice for a big man. The preachers of the 50's and 60's, like my seminarian teacher told me, they all had that *holy whine*. You know, they could talk in one voice like if you were talking about the King, and you'd be talking very ordinary, and they want to get up and say, 'I heard last night from some of my sick brothers.' They put that whine in there, and C. L. Franklin, he talked with that whine all the time, understand. He never came out of character. He used that preacher voice everywhere, understand, yeah, he put that whine on it."[64]

Franklin also had abundant charm and an amazing gift for connecting with people. "Anybody you talk to that connected to him in any way, I mean they melted all the way into him, he could do absolutely no wrong. People would be so crazy about him. The best thing he had, he knew how to make people feel very special. He really knew how to make the lowliest of person feel so super special. And I can go to Chicago, California, Dallas: Anybody that he had lunch with or met in any way, they would tell me how special he made them feel, you know. They would say, 'I was Reverend Franklin's close close friend. Reverend Franklin, you know, he did this; Reverend Franklin knew my name.'" Franklin would always greet people by name;

if he got the name wrong he would smoothly correct himself without the other person suspecting that Franklin had misfired.

Smith considers himself a very different type of pastor, more a missionary, really, than a preacher. He goes to Haiti about every six weeks, he tells me, and when he's in Detroit he emphasizes a ministry to the down-and-out population who live near the church: drug addicts, prostitutes, homeless people.

I ask Smith to tell me about Psalm 137; does he ever preach on the Psalm?

After thinking for a moment: no. He recalls hearing another sermon on the topic, by Sandy F. Ray, which he boils down to its core: Don't let your location and your situation obscure your destination. Smith mentions his son, also a minister, who has worked with the psalm. Before I know it, we're in a three-way conversation via iPhone with another Baptist preacher, a friend from Houston named Dr. Michael P. Williams. Smith introduces me over the speakerphone to Williams, who doesn't miss a beat. It turns out he has preached on the psalm, and promises to send me a copy of it.

Do you think Psalm 137 is still relevant to people? I ask Williams.

"Yeah, of course I do," he replies through the iPhone. "I described the psalm as being metaphorically about our joy. And that our happiness is connected to circumstances, but for the believer there's a reservoir of joy that is always under assault by the circumstances of life. It's been a long time since I preached it but that was basically the crux of the message. And how do we protect our joy in the midst of catastrophic and tragic circumstances? Israel found itself in the midst of a national catastrophe. And our own personal situations often seem as cataclysmic as Israel's exile."

An easy flow between the personal and the public, between private and communal affliction. Later I listen to Williams's sermon, in which the psalm becomes a metaphor for the trials of the individual.

Of which New Bethel has witnessed many. An article in the *Detroit News* painted a bleak picture of both the church and its neighborhood. Membership was down to 300 from a peak of 10,000 under Franklin in the 1960s. Ten church members had been killed in the past few years, and roughly thirty parishioners had lost family members to violence.[65] Plans for neighborhood revitalization had stalled; an apartment building across from the church that Smith had hoped would anchor local redevelopment was in danger of default.

The white flight of recent decades was being compounded by black working-class flight out of the downtown, he told me. "Some people want to go to church in a better neighborhood, where they aren't being asked for a quarter or a cigarette when they walk into the church," he told the *Detroit News*. "I'm afraid pretty soon I'll have a congregation of four people. But if we obey the Scripture, it's our job to stay here and try to make things better."[66] So the church does what it can: give away clothing and food from its pantry; weekly outdoor prayer services and neighborhood picnics; recreational outings to movies, waterparks, and Pistons games.

Which New Bethel has been known for since the beginning. The church had its origins in 1932 with a women's prayer band called "The Helping Hand Society," which put music near the center of its ministry. "But, now, it's always been a benevolent church," Smith told me. "Always. When people came from the South, during the hardship and Dust Bowl and Depression and civil rights struggle, this is where they came. And Reverend Franklin would raise offerings for them, help them get set up and started, you know. Always been benevolent."

Michael Williams underscores this. "The challenges have changed," he told me. "Dr. Franklin was preaching at a time when African American people were dealing with one particular form of marginalization and now we are dealing with another kind. The church he preached at and the people that he preached to were exiles, in a very real sense. They fled from the terrorism of the South, you know, to come up North. They had some of the same kind of challenges, but they were able to create free institutions. And the freest of all those institutions was the church.

"But now African American people are kind of confused about what our identity is and what our agenda is. The illusion of living in postracial America because of the election of President Obama: that balloon has burst quite a while ago. We are still dealing with the same kind of issues. So we need that kind of preaching again, and I'm not just necessarily saying stylistically—although that had a value too, because emotional release is very important. Because if you don't have a hole on the top of the tea kettle, it's gonna blow up. And that kind of preaching elicits an emotional response.

"I think that African American worship has become so cerebral and European in some ways that we don't have any way to let that stuff out. Those people didn't have access to Zoloft or Prozac. So they had to shout. They had to get that stuff off of them somehow."

I listen to Williams's sermon; he does let go. The recording isn't very good, but for the last several minutes he's shouting this and the band is playing that. C. L. Franklin followed that same rhetorical structure, going into his whooping for the final section of his sermon, "Without a Song."

Franklin's own life was tragically anticlimactic. After the roller-coaster extremes of the 1960s, when Franklin and New Bethel moved locations, grew exponentially, and were at the center of the political ferment of Detroit and the nation, the 1970s saw a decline. In 1979 Franklin was shot by a burglar in his home; he lingered in a coma for five years before passing away. Three years after the shooting, Robert Smith Jr. was called as pastor.

Smith guides me through New Bethel. We step into the History Room, full of plaques and photographs of Franklin and New Bethel in the glory days. I meet Franklin's longtime driver, still affiliated with the church. We walk through the sanctuary, not terribly large by contemporary standards, seating maybe 400 on the floor and 700 in the balcony. Smith and I pass through the small kitchen where the celebrities used to congregate. The church is gearing up for an appearance by Aretha in a few weeks. She gives free concerts there periodically, after many years of being estranged from Smith. "The last five years, I would say, she's really just in a give-back kinda thing," he tells me.

Smith is the author of what is probably the most self-effacing book I've ever read: *In the Shadow of C. L. Franklin*. Its main thrust is to convey the extreme difficulty of following a legendary preacher like Franklin, let alone one with a daughter like Aretha. Despite the myriad setbacks and disappointments he's encountered from the Franklin family and those in the church who remain eternally loyal to his predecessor, there's no bitterness in Smith's account. "I have always lived in a *shadow*," Smith writes matter-of-factly. "First, the *shadow* of my father, and now, the *shadow* of C. L. Franklin. Once a stranger at an airport approached me and prophesied that I would be the next pastor of New Bethel Baptist Church. I laughed and replied that whoever replaced Reverend Franklin would be a fool for he would have to live in C. L. Franklin's shadow for the next fifty years."[67]

For Smith, it's now been over thirty years in New Bethel's pulpit.

After our conversation I drive over to see the mansion where Aretha came of age, metamorphosed from ultratalented local gospel singer in her father's church to the Queen of Soul. It's a few blocks east of the church, past a small park that bears Franklin's name. Many of the back streets have that bombed-out quality that Detroit is known for. Some people find such extreme urban blight strangely fascinating: "ruin porn." The self-evident quality of so many of the homes never fails to astonish me. Some men working on a house next door point out some bullet holes in Franklin's

home and tell me its previous owner was a "Caucasian gentleman."
Driving up Linwood I see a large urban farm, one of the more hopeful
innovations that Detroit has embraced in the past decade. It's a huge city
with almost unlimited arable land.

Moses or Jeremiah

Driving six hours west across Michigan on I-94 brings you to another
great Midwestern metropolis, one whose fortunes have diverged dramatically from Detroit. If the Motor City struggles mightily to reinvent itself
against steep handicaps in the postindustrial age, Chicago—at least the
public face of that city, its most visible neighborhoods—has prospered
mightily. Chicago was home to someone who for a time was the most
famous—some would say infamous—African American preacher in
America. And given that the twenty-first century, with its twenty-four-hour
news cycle and hyperactive digital ecology, supplies a media environment
nearly unrecognizable from the one that Franklin faced, the nature of this
fame was dramatically different.

The pastor was an ex-Marine named Jeremiah Wright, graduate
of Howard University and the University of Chicago Divinity School,
holder of a Doctor of Ministry degree, longtime senior minister at
Trinity United Church of Christ in Chicago. If Franklin's sermon was an
extended affirmative answer to the question, *How can we sing the Lord's
song in a strange land?* Wright's is an elaborate analogy between the
experience of the exiled Judeans in Babylonia and the exiled Africans in
America. Wright, who as a student at Howard University studied with
Sterling Brown, begins his sermon by quoting Psalm 137, but then interprets the African American experience through the account given in
Daniel 6.

First, like Daniel and his three fellow captives, Africans are robbed of
their names: "The empire stripped the exiles of their names and imposed
its own names upon them so that five or six generations later the original
names were lost to memory," Wright asserts. Second, the oppressors strip
the Africans of their history and their culture: "The empire tells them that
they have no history prior to the Babylonians introducing them to civilization; the empire tells them outright lies and blatant distortions so that they
will disown any linkage that they once had with Africa, and they become
more Babylonian than the Babylonians," Wright states. "In a foreign land

there is the deliberate and devious attempt to take away the exile's heritage and replace it with a fabricated 'Babylonian' heritage that distorts truths and tells outright lies."[68]

And in many cases this seems to work: "You will have African exiles who think that unless the Babylonians said it, it ain't true; unless Babylonians wrote it, it ain't right; unless the Babylonians made it, it ain't gonna work." But the oppressors ultimately overplay their hand. And it leads them to ruin. When they try to strip Daniel of his faith, he refuses to renounce Yahweh, and God protects him.

> You see, they had taken away his history and his name and had called him Belteshazzar. They had taken away his heritage and taught him Babylonian literature, language and philosophy. But when they tried the ultimate take-away—when they tried to take away his religion—they did what all oppressors do: they tried to take away his hope.

"But Daniel had"—and here Wright uses a phrase that will resonate in the writings of one of his church members—"But Daniel had *the audacity to hope*."[69]

Did Barack Obama hear Wright preach that sermon? He certainly could have. Obama was baptized at Trinity in 1988. Three years later he graduated from Harvard Law School and was writing his first memoir, *Dreams of My Father*, during the year Wright's book of sermons was published. Obama went on to use the phrase in the speech at the 2004 Democratic Convention that suddenly catapulted him into the ranks of future presidential candidates. And of course it became the title of his second book.

We know that Jeremiah Wright ended up coming closer to the plight of his biblical namesake than anyone could have predicted. During the run-up to the 2008 presidential election, clips of footage from Wright's incendiary sermons hit the news cycle, causing a near meltdown of the Obama campaign. Especially damaging were clips from a sermon Wright gave in April 2003, in which he intones, "Not God bless America. God *damn* America." The candidate was forced to distance himself from Wright and, eventually, to deliver, at the National Constitution Center in Philadelphia, a speech on race in America that turned out to be a defining moment of the 2008 campaign.

Wright, nearing retirement after building Trinity into a huge church and making huge contributions to Chicago, faced a fate not dissimilar

to the biblical Jeremiah. At the time Obama delivered his race speech
Wright was on what he would call a Caribbean "cruise from hell" with his
wife, children, and grandchildren. As Obama biographer David Remnick
reports, clips of Wright's sermons were looping constantly on cable news.

> "Many of the white passengers on the boat were livid with me, say-
> ing ugly things to me and around me," Wright said after the elec-
> tion. "'You're unpatriotic, you oughta go back to Africa.'" Some
> people at the dining table next to Wright's asked to be moved. "I
> started staying in my cabin most of the time," Wright recalled,
> "except for dinner at night with my family, because to be out was
> going to invite comments that I didn't want my grandkids to hear."
> When the ship docked in Puerto Rico, Wright picked up a copy of
> the New York *Times* in which Maureen Dowd called him, indelibly,
> a "wackadoodle."[70]

Such are the perils of delivering prophetic jeremiads in an age in which
nothing can be forgotten; all is visible for anyone with eyes to see and a
wifi connection.

For his onetime parishioner and protégé, however, this high-stakes
experience marked the transformation of Obama into a postmodern
Frederick Douglass. The scholar Henry Louis Gates Jr. asserts that both
men have functioned as mythical "trickster" figures who mediate and rec-
oncile social opposites:

> Frederick Douglass is the figure of mediation in nineteenth-
> century American literature; he, the mulatto, mediates between
> white and black, slave and free, between "animal" and "man."
> Obama, as mulatto, as reconciler, self-consciously performs the
> same function in our time, remarkably self-consciously. And the
> comparisons don't stop there; they both launched their careers
> with speeches and their first books were autobiographies. They
> spoke and wrote themselves into being: tall, elegant, eloquent
> figures of mediation, conciliation, and compromise. Douglass
> launched his career as a radical no-holds-barred combatant against
> slavery. As he aged, however, he grew more conservative. He cer-
> tainly believed in the basic class structure of American capitalism;
> and he believed in a natural aristocracy and that he was a member
> of it—just like Obama.

Gates adds, "The only thing radical about Obama is that he wanted to be the first black President."[71]

To compare Obama to Frederick Douglass opens up even more venerable analogies.

Remnick begins his biography with the speech Obama delivered at Selma, Alabama, in March 2007, only one month into his presidential campaign, as he was beginning to methodically peel away African American voters from his rival, Hillary Clinton. Obama's goal in Selma was to retell his own story, a man with mixed ancestry who had grown up mainly in Hawaii, in the context of the heroic sacrifices of the civil rights movement. He did so, in part, as Martin Luther King Jr. and innumerable others over the generations had done, by invoking Moses and the Exodus.

"They took them across the sea that folks thought could not be parted," Obama said, referring to King's generation. "They wandered through a desert but always knowing that God was with them and that, if they maintained that trust in God, that they would be all right. And it's because they marched that the next generation hasn't been bloodied so much."[72]

Representatives of that generation were present in the historic A.M.E. sanctuary where Obama was speaking—John Lewis, Joseph Lowery, C. T. Vivian—but he was speaking as, and to, the next generation, the generation of Joshua, who unlike Moses actually made it into the Promised Land. Obama worried that his generation, the Joshua generation, had become too complacent, too willing to accept the sacrifices of their parents without being willing to add their exertions:

> That's what the Moses generation teaches us. Take off your bedroom slippers. Put on your marching shoes. Go do some politics. Change this country!. . .
>
> Joshua said, "You know, I'm scared. I'm not sure that I am up to the challenge." The Lord said to him, "Every place that the sole of your foot will tread upon, I have given you. Be strong and have courage, for I am with you wherever you go." Be strong and have courage. It's a prayer for a journey. A prayer that kept a woman in her seat when the bus driver told her to get up, a prayer that led nine children through the doors of the Little Rock school, a prayer that carried our brothers and sisters over a bridge right here in Selma, Alabama. Be strong and have courage . . . .
>
> That bridge outside was crossed by blacks and whites, northerners and southerners, teenagers and children, the beloved community

of God's children. They wanted to take those steps together, but it was left to the Joshuas to finish the journey Moses had begun, and today we're called to be the Joshuas of our time, to be the generation that finds our way across the river.[73]

Joshua inaugurated what the Bible counts as the golden age of ancient Israel: the conquest of Canaan, the unification of the kingdom under David, Solomon's glory, erecting the Jerusalem Temple. All of which came to a crashing halt with the Babylonian conquest.

Exodus or Exile

Moses and Jeremiah, Exodus and Exile: the two critical watersheds in the formation of Judaism, and both crucial narratives for North Americans, as movements and communities. The Exodus story, with Moses in the starring role, has been celebrated and echoed in American popular culture and by many of its most prominent leaders: George Washington, Frederick Douglass, Martin Luther King Jr. The Exile story, far less so, and by spokespeople farther from centers of power.

We can readily see how the Exodus lends itself to popular culture—Hollywood, for example—in ways that the Exile doesn't. The Exodus has a strong central character, Moses, who though not without flaws is undeniably cut from heroic cloth. By contrast the Exile features a shifting cast of characters, none of whom seem quite heroic. There are two malcontents, Jeremiah and Ezekiel, who alienate nearly everyone around them and die on what seems the losing side of history. Daniel rises far in Babylon but doesn't himself lead the Judeans to the promised land. There is no triumphant entry into the Promised Land in the Exile; some of the Judeans slowly drift back to Judah after Babylonia is conquered by the Persians, and eventually the Temple is rebuilt.

Given these manifest differences in the emotional impact of the Exodus and Exile stories, it's revealing to see them fused in a Jewish ritual like this lament for *Tisha B'av*, which commemorates the destruction of the first and second Jerusalem Temples:

A fire kindles within me as I recall—*when I left Egypt,*
But I raise laments as I remember—*when I left Jerusalem.*

Moses sang a song that would never be forgotten—*when I left Egypt,*
Jeremiah mourned and cried out in grief—*when I left Jerusalem.*
The sea-waves pounded but stood up like a wall—*when I left Egypt,*
That waters overflowed and ran over my head—*when I left Jerusalem.*
Moses led me and Aaron guided me—*when I left Egypt,*
Nebuchadnezzar and the Emperor Hadrian—*when I left Jerusalem.*[74]

Yerushalmi directs our attention to the "antiphony of the hammering refrain" of this lament, memories of the two watershed events reinforcing and heightening each other, as well as to the lack of historical detail. "That which is remembered here transcends the recollection of any particular episode in an ancient catastrophe," he writes. "It is rather the realization of a structural contrast in Jewish historical experience, built around the dramatic polarity of two great historical 'departures' (Egypt/Jerusalem—Exodus/Exile), each with its obvious though unstated clusters of meanings and implications."[75]

Exodus and Exile are frequently intermingled by African Americans as well. Jewish studies scholar Jonathan Boyarin cites Bob Marley's "Exodus," which juxtaposes the assertion "We're leaving Babylon" with the petition to "Send us another brother Moses ... from across the Red Sea." "The Exodus model of liberation and mass movement is certainly more dramatic a model than the gradual and partial return from Babylon," he notes. "Yet the Rastafarians focus on Babylon as a model of captivity, partly because of its reputation for corruption and partly because it is more explicitly depicted as a place of Exile, such as in Psalm 137."[76]

Newport Gardner's commissioning anthem, sung just prior to setting sail for Liberia, discussed earlier, includes that same fusing of the two narratives: "For lo! The days come, saith the Lord, that I will bring again the captivity of my people Israel and Judah, saith the Lord; and I will cause them to return to the land that I gave to their fathers, and they shall possess it."[77]

In *Exodus and Revolution*, social philosopher Michael Walzer reminds us that it is a mistake to read the Exodus story as some sort of unalloyed triumph. Moses and the Israelites face continuous struggles right up to entering the Promised Land of Canaan, which Moses himself doesn't enter (and which simply sets in motion further ordeals for the Israelites; there's no living happily ever after). But by all accounts the Exodus narrative does follow a linear plot with a beginning, middle, and end; for all its unfinished character, by the end of Exodus, the Hebrews are poised to achieve an undeniable improvement in their collective standing.[78]

There's no denying that Moses has heroic stature, and accomplishes far more than any character of the Exile. He does see Yahweh face-to-face and receive the Ten Commandments; he does defy Pharaoh and lead his people through innumerable obstacles to the Promised Land, even if he doesn't himself cross over. And his life story and accomplishments are so much more vividly recounted than those of any single figure in the Exile story. The narrative density of characters and subplots exceeds anything the Bible conveys about the Exile.

Hence the zeal of such Exodus celebrants as Walzer and, more dramatically, best-selling author Bruce Feiler. "From Christopher Columbus to Martin Luther King, from the age of Gutenberg to the era of Google, Moses helped shape the American dream," Feiler writes toward the end of *America's Prophet*. "He is our true founding father. His face belongs on Mount Rushmore."[79] Feiler continues to pour on hyperbole:

[Not] only did he provide a common cultural language, and not only did he command attention and mobilize resources, Moses actually helped shape American history and values, helped define the American dream, and helped create America. Moses was more important to the Puritans, more meaningful in the Revolution, more impactful during the Civil War, and more inspiring to the immigrant rights, civil rights, and women's rights movements of the last century than Jesus. Beyond that, Moses had more influence on American history than any other figure from the Bible or antiquity. Also, while certain intellectuals might have had a greater impact on particular periods of American life, no single thinker has had more sustained influence on American history over a longer period than Moses—and that includes Plato, Aristotle, Locke, Hobbes, Montesquieu, Marx, Darwin, Freud, and Einstein.

Moses, he concludes, "is a looking glass into our soul," the figure helps give American history a coherent shape.[80]

No one would make that assertion about the Exile, at least not in the broad sense of "our soul" (meaning the American character, or some such construction). Who would claim that Jeremiah, or Ezekiel, provides a looking glass into our soul? The Exile is simply a much less heroic narrative. Not all of the displaced Judeans even return to Jerusalem; many remain in Babylonia and drop out of the history recounted in the Hebrew Bible. The line of divine kingship established by David comes to an end, not to be reestablished. Israel itself never achieves the power of influence it is reported to have commanded under David and Solomon.

All this helps explain why the Exile hasn't captured the popular imagination in the way the Exodus has. It is not a story that lends itself to a sense of triumphant destiny of either nation or of people struggling for respect within the nation. Precisely for this reason, its trajectory of exile and return fits the diasporic sensibility of so many ethnic and racial communities in North America. Some groups did immigrate regarding North America as a Promised Land or New Jerusalem, but many others imagined themselves as temporary sojourners, never forgetting the links that bound them to a homeland.

The Exodus does have its modern-day critics, however. They make the case, with passion, that the overwhelming emphasis placed on Moses leads people to ignore the exclusionary, imperialist thrust of the Exodus story and to overlook the ethical or political lessons that might be drawn from the Babylonian captivity. In *The Curse of Cain*, Regina Schwartz shows how biblical notions of collective identity based on covenant, exclusion, and a logic of scarcity have contaminated much of the history of the West. In the Hebrew Bible, and the history that has unfolded in its wake, liberation and domination are inseparably yoked; the Yahweh of deliverance is the Yahweh of conquest.[81]

"With what voice will we, the Canaanites of the world, say, 'Let my people go and leave my people alone?'" asks Robert Allen Warrior. "And, with what ears will followers of alien gods who have wooed us (Christians, Jews, Marxists, capitalists), listen to us? The indigenous people of this hemisphere have endured a subjugation now a hundred years longer than the sojourn of Israel in Egypt. Is there a god, a spirit, who will hear us and stand with us in the Amazon, Osage County, and Wounded Knee? Is there a god, a spirit, able to move among the pain and anger of the Nablus, Gaza, and Soweto of 1989? Perhaps. But we, the wretched of the earth, may be well advised this time not to listen to outsiders with their promises of liberation and deliverance."[82]

Edward Said's scorching critique of *Exodus and Revolution* likewise takes aim at "the injunction laid on the Jews by God to exterminate their opponents, an injunction that somewhat takes away the aura of progressive national liberation which Walzer is bent on giving to Exodus." The Exodus is greatly overrated as a founding document for liberation movements and theories. "For not only does Exodus seem to blind its intellectuals to the rights of others," Said writes, "it permits them to believe that history—the world of societies and nations, made by men and women—vouchsafes certain peoples the extremely problematic gift of 'Redemption.'" And Redemption inevitably leads human beings to claim divine inspiration and to lose any sense of responsibility to "unredeemed" others.[83]

Some are turned off by the triumphalism and chauvinism of the Exodus; others find a more humane and usable past in the story of the Exile.

A Protestant minister I met shared a memory from the Iran hostage crisis of 1980. He was pastoring a small Congregationalist church in Putnam, Connecticut, a minor mill city. Nearly every Sunday for a year, during the worship service, his congregation sang a hymn based on Psalm 137. "I'm sure that we were identifying the captives [American hostages] with the exiles of the psalm," he told me. "I don't think we particularly identified the Iranian captors with the Babylonian empire. I don't remember pushing the image that far. Rather, I think, we were expressing our disbelief that such an event could happen. (The world was certainly different then!)"[84] Needless to say, that crisis turned out to be a harbinger of many such episodes to come involving Americans in the Middle East. The version they sung, incidentally was the setting found most often in American hymnals, its text set to a Latvian folk tune "Kas Djiedaja," known in English as "Captivity."

Of course, American citizens as captives, in exile, is highly uncommon, the exception that proves the rule. But many immigrants have imagined themselves as exiles. As we've seen, Cubans remain caught between a homeland that has driven them out and a powerful northern neighbor that has used them for its own geopolitical interests. "The exodus, however, is not the rubric exilic Cubans use to read the scriptures," De La Torre explains. "It is the second exodus, narrating the Babylonian Captivity, that resonates within our very being. Like the Psalmist (Psalm 137), we sit by the streams of this country, singing about our inability to sing God's songs."[85] Members of Irish and Korean diasporas in America, likewise, have felt more like exiles from their homeland, either temporary or long-term, rather than as people escaping from conditions of slavery in a land that is, like Egypt for the Israelites, in no sense their homeland.

These distinctions shade into what we might regard as more theological differences between the Exodus and the Exile. For one, a theology based exclusively on the Exodus that fails to take into account the trauma of the Exile, suffered centuries later, is an incomplete one. "The way in which Israel conceived herself and her God as bound by an everlasting covenant did not remain unchallenged," writes Anne-Mareike Wetter, "and the biblical writers made it very clear that without the Exile as a counterpart of the Exodus, the faith of Israel would be overly optimistic to the point of arrogance."[86] The formative events narrated in Exodus are fundamentally modified by the painful lessons of the Exile: namely, that the penalty for violating the commandments handed down by Yahweh was to be subject to ruination by a foreign power.

So the Exile both completes and complicates the story of Yahweh's covenant with the children of Israel.

From a Christian perspective, social and political movements have been far too eager to appropriate the Exodus for their politics du jour, argues John H. Yoder, the influential Mennonite theologian. Writing toward the end of the Vietnam War, Yoder challenges what he considers a too-facile appropriation of the Exodus story for the purposes of justifying political action in the twentieth century. He points out three distinct sets of problems.

First, depending on the Exodus as a model for politics produces a distorted selective reading of the Bible that dispenses with other important themes of biblical witness: "exile, captivity, cross, the giving of the law, the taking of the land, the scattering of the faithful." Second, it leads to theology that simply mimics what people in the broader culture are advocating, rather than developing biblical critiques that transcend the common sense of the moment. Finally, the Exodus story doesn't provide clear criteria for evaluating real, on-the-ground political movements of our own time. Writing at a time when liberation theology was modish in progressive church circles, Yoder questions whether "particular guerilla efforts which call themselves liberation fronts" may simply be "a new form of cultural colonialism" just as alien, oppressive, and violent as what they seek to overthrow.[87]

In contrast to a theology based on "leaving Egypt and destroying Pharaoh on the way," Yoder offers a theology based on Jeremiah's advice to his exiled compatriots: "Seek the welfare of the city where I have sent you into exile, and pray to the Lord on its behalf." "'You'll be in Babylon a long time,'" Yoder paraphrases the prophet. "'Seek the peace of that city. Identify your welfare with theirs. Abandon the vision of statehood.'" Exodus occurs only once, but Jeremiah's advice is echoed repeatedly throughout the Hebrew Bible:

This advice of Jeremiah was given in the age of the exile after the
defeat of Josiah: but we have the same stance taken by Joseph in
Egypt, by Daniel under Nebuchadnezzar, and by Mordecai in Persia
and even in a sense by Jonah in Nineveh. Far from destroying
the pagan oppressor, the function of the insightful Hebrew is to
improve that pagan order so as to make it a resource of protection
for the people and viable as a government. He does this in ways
which force the pagan power to renounce its self-mythologizing
religious claims and to recognize the higher sovereignty that is pro-
claimed by the Hebrew Monotheist.[88]

This approach, rather than anything Moses enacts, is more characteristic of the Hebrew Bible—and more relevant to situations in which moderns
are likely to find themselves. "The complement to the Exodus of the counter
community is not a coup d'etat by the righteous oppressed," Yoder insists,
"but rather the saving message of the resident minority." He cites historical
examples: the early church during the Roman Empire; Jews in medieval
Europe; the Pennsylvania Dutch in early America; Indians in East Africa;
Chinese in South Asia; "unmeltable ethnics" in the modern United States.[89]

Yoder was a Mennonite pacifist best known for his book *The Politics
of Jesus*. Interestingly, his preference for Exile over Exodus is echoed by
Cheryl Sanders, the scholar/practitioner of the African American Holiness
tradition. "Liberation theology emphasizes the moral obligation of the
oppressor to set the oppressed free," she writes. This approach underscores polarities that surely exist in the world but tend to concentrate
agency with those who already control power. By contrast, "An 'exilic' theology would equally obligate the entire community of faith, inclusive of
exiles and elites, to offer authentic liturgies of welcome and memory that
enable the experience of liberation as homecoming."[90] It's no coincidence
that music and song are so central to Holiness worship, and that Yoder
explicitly endorses singing over politicking.

Whether celebrated (Walzer, Feiler) or critiqued (Yoder, Said), a key point
of contention regarding the Exodus narrative is its role in underpinning
Zionism, an ideology that for generations has convulsed the geopolitics of
the Middle East and beyond. There are many reasons to perceive Exodus
as "the blueprint for Zionism," Boyarin acknowledges. But a Zionism that
paid more attention to the Exile would be healthier. Actually, this was true of
early Zionism of the late nineteenth through the early twentieth centuries,
Boyarin writes, "when the Balfour Declaration was explicitly analogized to

that made by the Persian King Cyrus—the role of Cyrus in permitting the Return to Zion was prominent in Jewish 'historical memory.' "[91]

The Exile analogy fit early Zionism for a number of reasons. It provided a "myth of the empty land" that justified Israeli colonial settlement in the "desolate" landscape of Palestine (although the vision of creating a "land of milk and honey" was also prominent). The settling of Palestine by displaced Jews could be imagined as a return to a homeland. Unlike Australia and many other settler societies where Europeans "had to transform space that to them was initially 'raw' into space that was marked by and within their culture," Boyarin writes, "Palestine was already an 'occupied territory of the Jewish imagination.' " Finally, the Exile better captures the ambivalent relationship of Zionism to European and U.S. imperial support. While the Exodus represented a "complete divorce" from an oppressive imperial power (Egypt), the Exile involves a more ambivalent and ongoing relationship with Babylon. This provides an opening, Boyarin observes, for right-wing Zionists to strategically deploy anticolonial rhetoric against the very power (the United States) that provides them the military and economic support without which their project would have been unable to succeed.[92]

It made perfect sense, then, for Yitzhak Shamir, prime minister of Israel, to open a session of Middle East peace talks with the central verses of Psalm 137: "If I forget thee, O Jerusalem, let my right hand forget its cunning," adding: "I stand before you today in yet another quest for peace, not only on behalf of the State of Israel, but in the name of the entire Jewish people, that has maintained an unbreakable bond with the Land of Israel for almost 4,000 years."[93]

A journalist named Ari Shavit published a powerful meditation on the small city of Lydda, now known by its biblical name, Lod, situated 20 kilometers southeast of Tel Aviv. Only 40 kilometers west of Rahmallah and Jerusalem—"the very epicenter of the Arab-Israeli conflict." Lydda was the site of Ben Shemen, a utopian Zionist "youth village" created by a Jewish German philanthropist in 1927 for Jewish orphans. Twenty-one years later, the year Israel was created, Lydda was evacuated of its Arab citizens after a burst of violence: 250 Palestinians, including women, children, and the elderly, were massacred by Israeli soldiers. Shavit interviewed Shmarya Gutman, who was named military governor after Lydda was occupied by the Israeli army. Gutman climbed the minaret of the Great Mosque to watch the exodus of Lydda's Palestinians, who were given an hour and a half to gather belongings and evacuate:

From the top, he watched chaos engulf the town. People grabbed anything they could: bread, vegetables, dates, and figs; sacks of flour, sugar, wheat, and barley; silverware, copperware, jewelry; blankets, mattresses. They carried suitcases bursting at the seams, improvised packs made from sheets and pillowcases. Everything was loaded onto horse-drawn wagons, donkeys, mules.

Gutman descended from the minaret and walked to the eastern edge of town, overlooking Ben Shemen. The procession of civilians had assembled into a long Biblical-looking column of thousands. As he watched the faces of the people marching into exile, he wondered if there was a Jeremiah among them to lament their calamity and disgrace. Suddenly, he felt an urge to join them. For one long moment, he who was their Nebuchadnezzar wished to be their Jeremiah.

Mula Cohen [the Israeli brigade commander], standing by the command car, also watched the people of Lydda depart, carrying on their backs heavy sacks made of blankets and sheets. Gradually, they cast aside the sacks; they couldn't carry them any farther. Old men and women, suffering from terrible thirst in the heavy heat, collapse. Like the ancient Jews, the people of Lydda went into exile.[94]

Jewish exodus and Palestinian exile, fused as in the *Tisha B'av* litany.

The Exile will never rival the Exodus as a narrative model and rhetorical resource for describing and mobilizing political movements. As the use of the two stories in Jewish liturgy and some popular music attests, it's best to regard the two narratives as symbiotically linked; the Exile is always embedded in a full understanding of the Exodus, and vice versa. They exist together in collective memory, where stories are much more apt to jostle and mix together than in the sharply delineated pages of the Bible.

Which brings us back, finally, to verses five and six of Psalm 137, with their call to remember Jerusalem, under penalty of physical incapacity. What can we observe about the various forms of memory operating within the psalm?

Memory Coerced

As we've seen, Psalm 137's middle verses, with their oath of remembrance, has been adopted by musicians and by speakers who wish to mobilize their own zeal for a cause and, by example, those around them. But what does it mean to force memory in this way? If the psalmist has to take an oath to remember Jerusalem, what does that say about the quality—the authenticity, we might say—of that memory? Why should the psalmist threaten himself with corporal punishment if he fails to remember Yahweh and the people of Israel, when presumably those attachments should inspire sufficient loyalty? And how should this loyalty be demonstrated? What is entailed in the oath to remember Jerusalem?

All clues within the text point to the psalmist being a temple musician. The first section of the psalm focuses on the inflammatory request by the captors to sing a song of Zion, which would make most sense if addressed to musicians. "How shall we sing the Lord's song in a strange land?" sounds like the sort of question a musician might ask. And both of the penalties, of the right hand losing its cunning and the tongue cleaving to the roof of the mouth, would strike a musician as particularly onerous. We might speculate, then, that taking an oath to remember Jerusalem would entail remembering the songs of Zion that embody most directly the psalmist's affiliation with Yahweh and Israel. If this is true, memory is not some abstract image conjured up in the mind's eye but a form of embodied action.

We've noted the prevalence of the verb *zakhar* in the Hebrew Bible. To fully unpack the exhortation to remember in Psalm 137, we need to consider some of the inflections and associations of memory in the Western tradition in which Psalm 137 has been interpreted and assimilated. The nature of memory was greatly intriguing and puzzling to Plato and Aristotle, and has remained so into the present century through philosophers like Paul Ricœur. Conveniently for my own thinking about Psalm 137, Ricœur published a formidable treatise investigating memory and its relation to history and amnesia shortly before his death.

In their ingenious efforts to theorize memory, the ancient Greek philosophers drew a distinction between *mneme*, an unexpected unbidden popping into mind of a concrete memory, and *anamnesis*, the intentional recall by which the mind carries out an active search for something in the past. *Mneme* was understood as an affection, a pathos; *anamnesis* was a disciplined activity of the mind.[95]

Something of this distinction carried over into French, in the language of great modern theorists of memory like Henri Bergson. The French language distinguishes between *mémoire souvenir*, memory as a pointed recollection, and *mémoire habitude*, memory as a habit. What English language terms *memory* can refer to either the thing intended, *le souvenir*, or to the intention itself, *la mémoire*. The first meaning of memory focuses on the content of the memory; the second emphasizes action—the who that is doing the remembering, and how.[96]

Returning to the psalm, we find both forms of memory operating. The opening verses, with the scene of captives mourning beside a waterway, exemplify memory as *souvenir* or *mneme*, with its pathos, its characteristic emotional affect of longing and loss. It's a memory not directly tied to any individual; it evokes that sense of a collective memory likely perceived by the group. The second section of the psalm, with its inward turn toward the first person, suggests memory in the second sense, of *mémoire* or *anamnesis*: an act of intentional recall, of disciplined effort. This sense jibes well with the scenario of the temple musician not simply conjuring up a sensual memory of Jerusalem—a visual image, olfactory association, even a sonic recollection—but the muscle memory involved in remembering not just the sound of a song of Zion but the embodied skill required to execute that song.

The more than two-millennia-long effort to theorize the mystery of memory has produced another distinction useful in unpacking the senses of memory present in Psalm 137. And this one was implicit in the previous paragraph: the distinction we draw between ordinary memory, thought of us individual, and what we sometimes label collective memory. Though Plato and Aristotle were concerned with probing the enigma of memory—the presence of the absent—Ricœur traces the familiar notion of memory as essentially private back to Augustine, with his emphasis on subjective inwardness. In this understanding of memory, nothing is more private, individual, and personal than memory.[97]

With all due credit to Descartes' cogito ("I think, therefore I am"), John Locke represents the next great advance in positing the centrality of memory. He argues that memory actually constitutes our sense of self—that the self is essentially coterminous with its memories. Bergson and later Husserl probe with enormous subtlety the intricate cognitive mechanics of memory and self.[98]

In this lineage, the notion of collective memory is necessarily a metaphor, a fiction; how could the images and mental habits so fundamentally yoked to the self have a social component? People might share memories, of course, but they share them as individuals whose memory-lives are irreducibly private.

Analyzing the *Tisha B'av* litany cited above, with its alternating lines about the Exodus and the Exile, Yerushalmi notes the way in which the litany specifically invokes the *I* rather than the *we* that might be expected. "For whatever memories were unleashed by the commemorative rituals and liturgies were surely not a matter of intellection, but of evocation and identification," he writes. "There are sufficient cues to indicate that what was suddenly drawn up from the past was not a series of facts to be contemplated at a distance, but a series of situations into which one could somehow be existentially drawn."

Yerushalmi finds in the Passover Seder a quintessential expression of Jewish memory, "not so much a leap of memory as a fusion of past and present." This idea is expressed most vigorously in a Talmudic dictum applied to the Passover Haggadah: "In each and every generation let each person regard himself as though *he* had emerged from Egypt," as a Talmudic dictum phrases it. "Memory here is no longer recollection, which still preserves a sense of distance, but reactualization. It is this quality that impels the 'I' in the Tish'ab be'Ab lament as well."[99]

And, we might add, impels the "I" in the second section of Psalm 137, as we move from communal mourning by the river to a private vow of memory.

Having said all this, there is another, fundamentally different way to think about memory. Challenging the dominant view of private memory articulated so persuasively by Bergson, French sociologist Maurice Halbwachs argued that memory is fundamentally social rather than individual. We obviously can't and don't remember everything, so all memory is necessarily highly selective. Of the flux of experience available to our memory, Halbwachs asserts, we retain only those images and experiences that are reinforced by the people around us, initially our families but eventually larger communities. Memories are kept alive through conversations, rituals, reminiscences, artifacts. How much of our childhood would we remember without the stories told by parents and siblings, without the prompts provided by photo albums and cherished toys? Our social networks are what sustain memory, and memories that cease to live can't be said to exist; like nearly everything we experience they are lost in the flux of time. So rather than collective memory being a metaphorical extension of genuine memory, which is inherently private, collective memory is primary—ontologically prior—the fund from which our personal memories are drawn.[100]

If this theory of memory is correct, perhaps the first-person singular "I" of the psalmist is not as significant as Yerushalmi makes it out to be. Being "existentially drawn" into the powerful forms of "evocation and identification" triggered by the Exile may be experienced as a private emotion but can only be activated by being part of the collective whole, the Judeans who experienced captivity and forced labor. The act of remembering Jerusalem can be meaningful only through the public actions of being part of a ritual of prayer and music making. To "remember Jerusalem" is to act in a public role that defines one primarily in terms of one's role in the community and only secondarily as an individual.

Something akin to what Svetlana Boym labels "reflective nostalgia" comes into play here. "One becomes aware of the collective framework of memories when one distances oneself from one's community or when that community itself enters the moment of twilight," she observes. "Reflective nostalgia has elements of both mourning and melancholia. While its loss is never completely recalled, it has some connection to the loss of collective frameworks of memory. Reflective nostalgia is a form of deep mourning that performs a labor or grief both through pondering pain and through play that points to the future."[101]

Boym links its emergence to the ascendance of Romanticism in the nineteenth century, which happen to be decades when the Babylonian Exile was of particular interest to artists: painters like Eugène Delacroix (1798–1863), Ferdinand von Olivier (1785–1841), Eduard Bendemann (1811–1889), and Carl Wilhelm Friedrich Österlev (1805–1891); composers like Giuseppe Verdi, whose early opera, *Nabucco* (a shortened Italian name for Nebuchadnezzar), helped launch his career when it premiered in 1842 and contains one of his most beloved choruses, "Va pensiero," sung by a chorus of "Hebrew Slaves" on the banks of the Euphrates; poets like Lord Byron, who wrote loose psalm translations, including 137, in collaboration with the English composer Isaac Nathan for an 1815 collection, *Hebrew Melodies*, supposedly elaborated from ancient Jewish tunes, and Wilhelm Müller, who collaborated with Franz Schubert on the song cycle *Die Schöne Müllerin* (1824).[102]

The question remains as to why the biblical psalmist would need to gird himself so resolutely to remember. We could infer that the coercive pressures from Babylon to forget are substantial, or that the appeal of embracing the host society might be strong. There might be penalties for remembering as well as rewards for forgetting. The condition of exile is not free of ambiguity; as we have seen, Jeremiah 29 makes a strong case for dropping any resistance to Babylon. In any event, it would seem that the threat to memory is real.

This begs the question: What kind of memory is it that needs to be coerced under penalty of corporal punishment? If collective memory/cultural affiliation needs to be self-coerced so vigilantly, how genuine and rooted is that collective identity/affiliation? Again, we are talking here about memory as an intentional faculty of mind rather than as a passive screen into which memories float.

Literary critic Walter Benn Michaels highlights the paradox of forcing cultural affiliation. "The fact ... that something belongs to our culture cannot count as a motive for our doing it," he argues, "since, if it does belong to our culture, we already do it and if we don't do it (if we've stopped or haven't yet started doing it), it doesn't belong to our culture." Michaels is arguing that the sort of memory advocated by the psalmist is self-defeating. "It is only if we think that our culture is not whatever beliefs and practices we actually happen to have but is instead the beliefs and practices that should properly go with the sort of people we happen to be that the fact of something belonging to our culture can count as a reason for doing it."[103]

However plausible Michaels's argument might be for a highly diverse pluralistic society like the United States (and it is certainly open to challenge), his argument points to the vast difference between our own world and the world of the psalmist. Michaels offers as an example the debates over what works of literature to teach in the public schools. "It makes no sense, for example," he asserts, "to claim that we shouldn't teach Shakespeare because he isn't part of our culture since to teach him will immediately make him part of our culture, but it also makes no sense to claim that we should teach him because he is part of our culture since, if we stop teaching him, he won't be any longer."[104]

The difference between thinking we should teach Shakespeare in the public schools because he is integral to the culture we think we belong to and the psalmist thinking he should remember the songs of Zion is vast. Michaels points out that the aspirational view of culture he is critiquing requires an "appeal to something that must be beyond culture and that cannot be derived from culture precisely because our sense of which culture is properly ours must be derived from it. This has been the function of race .... It is this idea also that makes it possible to think of people as losing their culture or, more dramatically, having it stolen from them."[105]

But the identity of the psalmist is precisely one that lies beyond culture, and from which an idea of Judean culture is derived: the idea of a chosen people in covenant with Yahweh. Obviously this is nothing like the modern ideology of race applied at the time of the Exile, or the composition of the Hebrew Bible, but the sense of distinct peoplehood among the Judeans was just as strong. The psalmist's concern about forgetting his collective memory—or having it stolen by the captors—was perfectly legitimate.

This helps account for why the rhetoric of the middle section of Psalm 137 has been a favorite text of many African American speakers and preachers exhorting communal solidarity—Douglass, Franklin, Wright, among others—but sounds a bit odd coming from the likes of a British American like William Billings. (Maybe that reflects the possibility that Billings lived through an atypical historical moment during which a white male from Boston could feel oppressed.)

For Ricœur, collective memory is inextricably bound up with the pursuit of justice. He considers a number of examples of artificial memory, feats of memorizing, *ars memoria*, that in his view represent an "abuse" of memory. With the horrors of the European twentieth century rather than the ancient world in mind, Ricœur writes: "Extracting the exemplary value from traumatic memories, it is justice that turns memory into a project; and it is this same project of justice that gives the form of the future and of the imperative to the duty of memory."[106] Coercing the memory is justified only for the sake of justice, Ricoeur believes, and justice hinges on the ability to remember.

"Memory-project" is a good description of what Psalm 137 is about. It is also an apt name for historical research.

Though historians can be among the most solitary of scholars, the writing of history is fundamentally social. For Ricœur, history-writing begins with an individual's testimony: *I was there; believe me; if you don't believe me, ask someone else.* Only when testimony is inscribed and collected in some sort of archive does the writing of history become possible: "The moment of the archive is the moment of the entry into writing of the historiographical operation. Testimony is by origin oral. It is listened to, heard. The archive is written. It is examined. In archives the professional historian is a reader."[107] And both the inscribing of testimony and the establishing of archives are social activities. Out of the virtually infinite snatches of speech spoken every day, only a very few are ever regarded as testimony; out of the vast quantities of testimony that are committed to paper, only a miniscule amount are ever deemed worthy, by somebody, of inclusion in an archive.

Like jurists, historians depend on the social practices that convert testimony into archived traces, and depend on other social processes to test and evaluate those traces. "I have said that we have nothing better than our memory to assure ourselves of the reality of our memories— we have nothing better than testimony and criticism of testimony to accredit the historian's representation of the past."[108] Like judges, historians seek to achieve some manner of justice through their work, more or less directly. Memory-projects are carried out in academic settings as well as judicial ones.

The challenge of Psalm 137 is that while it appears as a trace, a form of testimony transformed into a historical source, its own sources are obscure: we don't know who originally uttered the testimony that constitutes the psalm, or when or where that testimony was first inscribed. It is written in such a way as to convey the authority of an eyewitness participant, but the history of history-writing is of course replete with examples of forged documents. The great majority of Jews and Christians over the millennia assumed the psalmist to be King David, even though he was known by the evidence of the Bible itself to have lived many generations earlier. In some traditions, we have seen, authorship was attributed to Jeremiah. The documentary traces that would allow us to resolve the question of authorship are long gone; the earliest extant manuscripts of the Hebrew Bible, the Dead Sea Scrolls, date only to the third century B.C.E.[109]

So Psalm 137 is just one tiny artifact in the endless and fascinating project of determining the time and place in which the Bible was transformed from testimony to written text. And the most plausible evidence points to the decades of the Exile, and the cosmopolitan milieu of Babylon, as the most likely setting in which this could have transpired.

"Wood Street"

On every Saturday or Sunday of the year, if you know where to go, you will find people in the United States, Canada, even Europe singing from an oblong red-brown book called *The Sacred Harp*. During a July heat wave I ventured to Kalamazoo, Michigan, where nearly two hundred singers have assembled for the annual Sacred Harp singing convention. The singings usually run from 9:30 a.m. to 3 p.m. or so, with an hour for "dinner on the grounds" and periodic breaks to relax, stretch, and rehydrate.

Mid-morning, a woman from Chicago named Judy Hauff walks into the steamy basement, running late. As serendipity would have it, the assembled singers are in the middle of singing one of Hauff's own songs, "Granville."

Judy Hauff is in unusual company in having three of her compositions in the latest edition of *The Sacred Harp* (1991), most of whose songs date back to the eighteenth and nineteenth centuries. Even more unusual, she is the only one of the living composers whose songs have fully entered the mainstream of the canon. I've never been to a singing where at least one of them wasn't

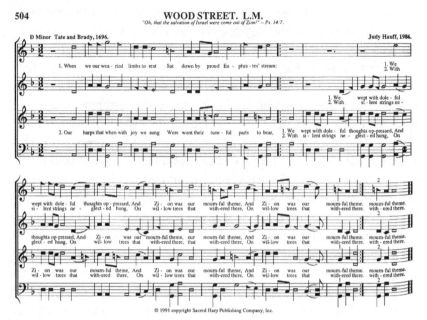

FIGURE 7 "Wood Street." Used with the permission of the Sacred Harp Publishing Company, Inc., Carrollton, Georgia, publisher of *The Sacred Harp, 1991 Edition.*

called by a song leader. (Part of the Sacred Harp tradition is that everyone who attends the singing and wants to can choose and lead at least one song.) After the closing benediction, while the Kalamazoo people are moving chairs and packing up leftover food, we talk in a side room. I'm interested in a particular song of hers called "Wood Street," which begins: "When we our wearied limbs to rest / Sat down by proud Euphrates' stream (Figure 7)."

The text is attributed to the Tate and Brady psalter of 1696, Hauff's tune to 1986. The piece is memorable in several ways. It has a powerful rhythmic drive to it, a tangible groove, produced by the counterpoint of the voices in the chorus, with its repeated lines: *And Zion was our mournful theme ....* *On willow trees that withered there.* I mention this propulsive quality to her.

"Yes, I had heard that I could have put it in a duple time, but I thought no, I want that kind of relentless [Hauff makes rhythmic beating noises]. It just seemed to fit. It seemed to fit the words and the mood of—what do I want to say?—that their grief was unassuageable. It was something that they had to go through; they couldn't go around it, they couldn't skip it. They had to go through this step, this diaspora, this punishment for whatever reason it was. So there's no stopping and breaking in the song, it just keeps going. I like that kind of inexorable feeling about it."[110]

There's also a strong modal sound to the song, I point out, something that sets it apart from most other songs in the collection.

"Oh yeah, I'm the big Dorian mode freak in *The Sacred Harp*; they're like 'Oh Judy, she's gotta have the raised sixth.' But I find that it makes a song so incredibly distinctive, it sounds like a different piece of music to me. Maybe not to other people—maybe they don't even hear the difference— but I hear it strongly. It has a strong effect on me.

"And when I heard some of the older Southern singers doing it, naturally, they didn't know they were doing it of course, but when I first went down in the mid-eighties and heard these older Southern people doing it I thought, Oh, my God. That book by George Pullen Jackson where he talks about it, and I thought, Really? And then I heard it firsthand, and I thought, Oh wow.

"Well, 'Granville' [another of her *Sacred Harp* songs] didn't mean to have it, 'Agatite' does, and so does this. I just said, I'm gonna write it in. And I thought, if I don't mark it all, the Yankees will flat it, and the Southerners will probably sing it correctly. But if I mark the accidental, I will force everybody north of the South to do it and I'll just tell the Southerners not to pay any attention to the natural sign, just sing it. But I think everybody pretty much does it now with the raised sixth. I don't know how to describe it, you know. I don't know how it affects you, I just know how it affects me. It would sound terrible without it to me."

I ask Hauff why she named the song "Wood Street."

"All the tunes in the book are place names," she explains, "because the tunes are separate from the words in this literature. So, at the time I wrote this, there were like seven Sacred Harp singers in Chicago who lived on Wood Street. I myself live on Granville, and other friends of mine live on Agatite. So I thought, well, if you can name things 'Wells,' and 'Abbeyville,' and all these other place names, I'll just, you know, I can't name them 'Chicago,' but I can do different streets. So that was it. Ted Mercer still lives on Wood Street," she says, referring to another venerable Chicago singer who also has a composition in *The Sacred Harp*.

Why was she drawn to the text of Psalm 137?

"I was raised as a Roman Catholic so I really did not know a good history of the Jews," Hauff says. "I just didn't. I'm not a scholar at all! And being Roman Catholic I certainly never studied the Bible and learned verses, because they're like, 'We'll teach you what that means!' So I was comparatively ignorant next to all the other people that I've been singing with that grew up studying the Bible closely. So I was just borrowing from other tune books, you know, I'd just look through for texts that I liked. So sometime in my thirties or forties I just started in reading books about the history of the Jews, the Diaspora, and it just seemed a dreadful story, such a loss of glory, totally annihilated. So it struck me: the sense of loss they must have felt, certainly, expressed in these words."

"So was your interest in the psalm mainly historical, or were you interested how the psalm resonates with people today?"

"Well, it was more historical. I thought, Gee, if I could go back in time and see what really happened . . . . I mean, obviously the Bible is tremendously slanted for sympathy to the Jewish people. It's like: Oh, those Canaanites, they're just a bunch of idol-worshippers, get 'em out of here, right? But the same thing is going on today: Oh, those Palestinians, get 'em out of here. It's like they were depersonalized in the Bible, the Canaanites. They were nobody, they were nothing. They were not chosen people, certainly.

"And I wonder if it was kind of like it is today, where one group is trying to push the other out. In the old days, you know, we won. Our side won, the Jewish people won. Nowadays they are not having such luck, you know, they aren't having the same kind of luck. So, I find those echoes very interesting: that really nothing's been solved. Nothing's been solved. The old enmities are there."

I ask Hauff about how people have responded to "Wood Street." She admits occasional misgivings over donating the song to *The Sacred Harp* rather than selling it to a publisher; she would have been receiving royalties from it for some twenty-five years.

"People love this song like I cannot tell you. I was stunned at the reaction to this song. I mean, I liked it, it satisfied me, but then, you know, there's other things I have written that have satisfied me. But people came back to me—not the people in the South; they were not particularly interested in it, they could take it or leave it—but the people in the North, the new singers, the twenty-somethings, thirty-somethings, forty-somethings. People from Seattle to Maine to California and everybody in between just come swarming up to me: *Sign my book. It's my favorite song in the book. Favorite song in the book.*

"I'm like, well, thanks—I've certainly hit a nerve with it. And I was very surprised and very pleased. I don't exactly know what the nerve was, but it obviously. . . . That howling and misery, I think, reached people, and they thought: Yes, that's the way it is. You know—something."

PART THREE

Forgetting

*Remember, O LORD, the children of Edom in the day of
Jerusalem; who said, Rase it, rase it,
even to the foundation thereof.*

*O daughter of Babylon, who art to be destroyed;
happy shall he be,*

that rewardeth thee as thou hast served us.

*Happy shall he be, that taketh and dasheth thy little ones
against the stones.*

(Psalm 137:7–9)

EVEN IN A brutal century's particularly savage decade, it's hard to wrap
our minds around an episode that occurred in Poland in 1941.

That summer, in the Polish town of Jedwabne, the entire Jewish
population—sixteen hundred men, women, and children—was rounded
up, taunted, beaten, and incinerated in a barn. By neighbors with whom
they had coexisted for generations. The atrocity was described four years
later in a deposition taken from a Pole who witnessed the slaughter.

> Beards of old Jews were burned, newborn babies were killed at
> their mothers' breasts, people were beaten murderously and forced
> to sing and dance. In the end they proceeded in the main action—
> the burning. The entire town was surrounded by guards so that
> nobody could escape; then Jews were ordered to line up in a col-
> umn, four in a row . . . and all were ordered to sing and were chased
> into the barn. Hooligans bestially beat them up on the way. Near
> the gate a few hooligans were standing, playing various instru-
> ments in order to drown the screams of horrified citizens. Some
> tried to defend themselves, but they were defenseless. Bloodied

and wounded, they were pushed into the barn. Then the barn was doused with kerosene and lit, and the bandits went around to search Jewish homes, to look for the remaining sick and children.[1]

In this one horrifying episode we find enacted both verse three and verse nine of Psalm 137: Jews are both forced to sing and also, in effect, to have their own children dashed against the rocks: "*and as for the little children,*" the testimony continues, "*they roped a few together by their legs and carried them on their backs, then put them on pitchforks and threw them onto smolder-ing coals.*"[2]

I learned about this episode in an article by Dutch scholar Athalya Brenner, who draws an explicit comparison to the violent finale of Psalm 137. How was it possible for neighbor to commit such atrocities against neighbor? The Polish Catholics who committed the massacre felt victim-ized themselves; they had been invaded first by Soviet Communists, then again within a few months by German Nazis. But that hardly begins to explain the savagery committed by the townspeople of Jedwabne, which they undertook willingly, apparently with little or no coercion from the Nazis.[3]

Brenner is well aware of the potential of language like the final lines of Psalm 137 to incite physical violence, but points out: "There is a great dif-ference between expressing a sentiment and 'dashing the infants'—as, in a reversal of roles, the Poles were happy to turn verbal threats and plans into action and dash the Jewish children into the fire."[4] Rather than recoiling from the unseemly spirit of violent retribution against innocents, she rea-sons that it is better to *think* such actions than to carry them out. To release such emotions through language can be therapeutic—and possibly reduce the likelihood of actually committing physical violence.

Brenner's larger point about the psalm is that we avoid moral supe-riority: "The dialogic condition of being perpetrator as well as victim is a distinct human condition … together with the knowledge that every monotheistic religion, especially if missionary or elitist, is inherently vio-lent, and thus potentially fosters perpetration/victimization."[5]

In effect, everyone is potentially Judean, potentially Babylonian; poten-tially a victim, potentially a perpetrator. Sometimes both at the same time.

Virtually no one sings the strange, final three verses of Psalm 137.

They are silenced. Or forgotten. Or perhaps forgotten because we have silenced them. Moving through the three sections of the psalm, we have seen musical interpreters of the psalm bail out along the way. As the scene shifts from river bank to the interior self of memory and self-admonition, the psalm loses a few passengers.

Patrick McCreless, a longtime church organist and choir director (as well as a professor of music at Yale), remembers conducting an anthem based on Psalm 137, which included verse nine. One of the choir members was adamant that the final verse not be sung. The choir, and its director, were equally adamant that the piece needed to be performed in its entirety. The choir member finally quit the choir rather than sing the offending verse.[6]

The fact is that in recent centuries, very few religious people, Jewish or Christian, include the final lines of Psalm 137 in their liturgies or musical settings. Among composers, only Salamone Rossi of Renaissance Mantua, to my knowledge, included the verses in his musical setting. At present, Orthodox Jews are among the few who intone them. Ashkenazic Jews (who emerged in Eastern Europe) traditionally recite the full psalm on weekdays at the beginning of the *Birkat Hamazon* (Blessing of the Meal/ Blessing for Food), which is offered after the meal. Orthodox Sephardic communities, who trace their ancestry through Spain, recite the entire psalm as part of *Tisha B'av* (Ninth of Ab) liturgy observances, a ceremony that takes place in July to commemorate the destruction of both the first and the second Jerusalem Temples, the first by the Babylonians, the second by the Romans.

On the other hand, Conservative, Liberal, and Reform Jewish prayer books for more than a century and a half have made Psalm 137 optional for both weekday prayers and *Tisha B'av*. In either case, only the first six verses are used; the vengeful final verses are simply expunged from prayers and services.[7]

"Psalm 137 in its full version may not be the most appropriate text for contemporary spirituality," admits Jonathan Magonet, "but it does provide us with a reminder that there are dimensions of our personal and collective lives that do evoke anger and the desire for revenge, and that these cannot simply be wished away or ignored."[8] Magonet quotes the great founding figure of Liberal Judaism in the United Kingdom, Claude Montefiore, from an 1899 book for Jewish parents on reading the Bible with their children:

It would be tempting to omit the third stanza. But in a Psalm so famous as this it would be historically unfair. Doubtless the Psalmist had seen and heard of many deeds of heartless cruelty, which partly palliates the cruelty of his own heart's desire. For us, however, the close of the Psalm destroys the beauty of its opening. Realizing as we do that tit for tat is not the highest moral law, the vengeance cry of the Psalmist belongs for us to a lower and superseded religious plane. Yet it is not for us to forget that it is not *our* wisdom and piety which enable us to detect the religious deficiencies of our ancestors. Rather it is the sifted piety and purified wisdom of the past which enable the present to start at a higher moral and religious level. As the old saying goes, "Dwarfs on giants' shoulders see further than giants."[9]

Revisiting a Vanished World

A quiet August afternoon in Michigan. I'm on the deck with the composer Marjan Helms, talking with her about a choral work she wrote: *Voices of a Vanished World.* Sung by a children's choir, it evokes the experience of the Holocaust from a child's point of view.[10]

The first piece, "Fire Upon the Ocean," begins this way: "Do you know what it means to say goodbye forever? / To watch your people dragged away to die? / Do you know how it feels to grind your heart / Against a truth more bitter than lies?" The libretto is not unremittingly bleak, however. It includes more whimsical lines and images: a rabbi teaching children the alphabet, a droll complaint about a steady diet of potatoes, a lullaby, a celebration of the daily routines of manual work, cooking, studying, "shmoozin' with your neighbors."

I'm particularly interested in the song "Babylon." We sit together listening, and Helms comments on the six-minute piece. It opens with a few measures of haunting modal chords on the piano.

"This is supposed to suggest some kind of watery background," Helms says. "A little echo there, different rivulets coming together." The children's voices enter:

By the rivers of Babylon, there we sat and wept
For Zion, fairest Zion

"There is a watery idea going on," she says about the piano part. "The pedal helps create part of the effect. And then the voices enter with the basic line from the poem. Babylon obviously is a place of captivity and darkness. The worst of the worst revisited in the camps.[11]

"So, I'm working largely with images, and the picture that I have is just the impossibility of what children, especially, might have thought in this perplexing, bewildering, incomprehensible situation.

"I like using the word Zion instead of any other translation. It is something that is other: a mystical place, almost, with the same kind of connotations as Jerusalem would have through the ages. I love that language, and the music blossoms at that point. There is a faraway kind of almost fairy-tale romanticism about it. But then, after the first blossoming of the voices it comes back to the minor tone of what had preceded it. And then you're back to the river idea."

> *For our captors required of us:*
> *"Sing for us, sing for us a Yiddish song!"*
> *But how could we sing a song of our God*
> *'Mid ice and mud, lice and mud?*
> *How could we sing a song of our God?*
> *How could we sing at all?*

"I use dissonance when there is anything that is obviously forced—like, our captives asked us to sing. And in the question, *How can we sing?* the voices are higher. And it takes on—for children's voices at least, and with the piano accompaniment—it has a boldness about it. The intervals are larger. They're strong. And that's the character of defiance, in a way: How can we sing in this horrible situation?"

"And there's a tenderness with, *We sing a song of our God.* When that first comes in, the interval is intimate and sweet. And then all the questions that follow, the things that I made up: the ice and mud and lice and mud. The line keeps lowering, lowering, until it dissolves back into the mire of the background ugliness of the camps."

Helms draws attention to something in the piano accompaniment. "That little note is a kind of Eastern European klezmer thing built into the language of Chopin. So it's got a refinement as well. There's your little watery thing: *dee da dee da.*"

> *When the rivers ran salty from the land to the sea,*
> *Why were they salty? Why did they bleed?*
> *Salt pours a blessing to savor our lives.*
> *But this salt was poison, our tears black as night.*

"What I thought was a good thing, salt, that blesses our lives. Savory. But then, *this salt was poison.* It's very pointed. The high note. Echo. Poison. Poison. Dissonance. Questioning part in the piano. *Our tears black as night.*"

"I come back to an octave or unison oftentimes. It's like a settling idea. You think it's resolved but it's really not resolved. It's just left there as a bare question."

> *But how could we sing a song of our God?*
> *In stench and shame, the sacred Name?*

"Name is a big deal in Judaism. Listen. Name. You can't lock it in. The harmony itself is not fixed; it's soft around the edges. It's a dissonant cluster that's left there, not particularly related to anything else. And so it's kind of a comment on naming the unnamable. It's a questioning, troubled, not understanding, very vulnerable, reverence. How are you reverent in the middle of something that is so unimaginable?"

"The blending to nothing," she says, listening to the voices fade.

"Rivers keep running through the whole thing."

> *When the rivers rose swiftly to flood toward the sea,*
> *Bearing within them what precious debris,*
> *Chalk on the waters, our lives ground to dust,*
> *O rivers of ashes, remember us.*

"Imagine it going out, and then this silence. Ashes falling on ashes, ashes, ashes. Ghostlike. At least the rivers will remember us. And that final interval is a sixth. It's not the octave or the unison. It stays with a sweet poignancy because of the kind of interval. It's a softer sound. The water just disappears. It gets right to the edge of silence, where you can't tell where it ends."

I ask Helms how she happened to choose this particular psalm for her piece on children caught up in the Holocaust.

"After the fact I could probably make up all kinds of stories about it, but when I'm in the process of creating—especially a theatrical work like that—whatever comes, comes. And I think I really was working from the image of ashes on the water from the crematoria, because I read accounts of that some place—I'm not sure where, I didn't document it, but more than once I ran into that. The image was so strong and brutal."

Helms might have been recalling a passage from a memoir by a man named Norbert Troller, who survived an extended stay in the Nazi concentration camp, Theresienstadt. Dumping ashes from the crematorium into the river as part of a work assignment, he joked darkly about the rabidly anti-Semitic Sudetan Germans living downstream, blithely drinking the ashes of Jews.[12]

"The Psalms are a backdrop to pretty much my entire life," Helms continued, "because I grew up in a religious home; I have gone through Protestant, Catholic and Jewish incarnations as I moved along."

"There's also a huge vocabulary, lifetime vocabulary, of sounds and musical gestures or nuances. The flowing idea, the water idea, and then playing with the light and shadow elements, the darkness, the blood, the tears, and all of that, and then the 'Zion, fairest Zion'—it just kind of opens up into something more transcendent and tender at the same time. So, those opposites."

"So the language just merged, you know. The imagery was there and it was just subliminal, basically; it came up and then I played with it. And the irony of it, I could play back and forth. The idea of remembrance I kind of turned on its head a little bit in this because instead of, you know, remembering Jerusalem, it's like—there is Jerusalem, asking to be remembered."

"The challenge in that piece and all the others would be to try and maintain some kind of balance so that you don't step into sentimentality or cheap effects, that there's still dignity."

"That's basically how that came about, just the grotesque image of ashes on the water."

Why do the rivers run salty? I ask.

"Tears. The bitterness, the tears. The whole program just has these strains that run through it, and if you isolate one movement you can look at it, but if you hear it as a whole then you find them even in the musical language."

"Also, there were many accounts where there was just torment in the streets or actually in the camps, where Jews were asked to perform, to sing, to dance, to do whatever. Especially at Theresienstadt, for instance, they had the whole false program that they had to put on, musicals and concerts and everything. So that when the Red Cross would come in, they could pretend that this was what was going on there all the time. And then when the Red Cross was gone they'd close it down and go back to business."

"Did you have a strong awareness of the Holocaust as a young person?" I ask her. "I mean, was any of this part of your childhood, a sense of vicariously experiencing this sort of trauma?"

"I discovered it when I was thirteen years old. I had never heard of anything like that. Jews were something I heard about in church, but the Holocaust I just discovered, and then it became .... People nowadays like to use the word 'passion,' and I really hate that, but I do believe in looking for it in the students that I teach and trying to encourage whatever crazy thing they're coming up with, if it seems like it is from some deeper source, and that was it for me. I was ... not *obsessed* with the Holocaust, but so drawn to it. And I still can't explain that."

It was at roughly that age that Marie, in Norway, developed her own fascination with the Holocaust, which contributed to her obsession with Psalm 137. With the Holocaust in mind, I ask her how she would answer the psalm's central question: How should we sing the Lord's song in a strange land? As her own piece "Babylon" puts it: "But how could we sing a song of our God? / In stench and shame, the sacred Name?"

"Well, there were certainly countless instances of prayer and some kind of devotion," she begins, "make-do liturgies for Passover, or Yom Kippur, or whatever. There were people, you know, thousands of people who died singing the *Shema*, the core prayer of Judaism, singing it in groups. I think if you think of singing as resistance, there's a point for that. If it's a tool for individual or group survival, there's a reason for that. I think different people responded differently."

"I mean, even if you branch out of the idea of some kind of explicitly sacred singing, you had the Theresienstadt model. Or at Auschwitz, where you had the little makeshift orchestra that was put together to try to distract people when they were being kicked off the trains, you know. Here the prisoners happened to play Beethoven and Mozart. I mean, that's a sacrilege too."

Music was everywhere in the Holocaust, it turns out, when one listens for it.

"I know that in the darkest times of my own life," Helms told me, "I couldn't bear music. You know, some people put it on as background, and I couldn't. The truly darkest moments of my life I could not stand music. Especially music that sounded like it was all together, like Mozart; I was like, Don't give me that."

"And when I finally got to a point where I could, it was listening to high church choral music, like Duruflé, things like that. That eased my way back in. But I think for me, music has a way of just gradually dissolving all the protections, and you're left with raw feeling against raw reality, and sometimes you just need some kind of buffer there."

Going back to the psalm's central question, I ask Helms: Should the exiles sing the Lord's song?

She pauses. "I should think hard about this, though. I have kind of a core image of my own that is . . . . I had a dream once where I was running at night in the face of a tornado, and it was like, the ugliest, darkest, scariest face of what He is. And I knew somehow that that was, it represented the divine to me, and I was singing at the top of my lungs and I was singing the *Hallelujah Chorus*. It was like daring God to be God."

"So I guess my most honest answer is that I *would* sing. Singing may be different; it's very different from listening to music. Your question was more about singing, so, yes, I would pick singing. Which is why I would write this piece, to begin with. And it comes to music at that point, and my hope for the whole program was that through music, people would be able to—in the company of others—go where they wouldn't go on their own, and get closer to that raw, horrible, horrible reality. So, that's about listening and singing, but obviously—and that was the balance—how do you do something that is almost unbearable?"

"But yeah, I do believe in singing."

Helms tells me she was raised Methodist in northwest Florida. She grew up singing hymns, even occasionally shape-note songs. But from about the time she developed an interest in the Holocaust she was drawn to another tradition.

"I wanted to convert to Judaism in my teens," Helms says, "but did not feel that I was worthy of it. That's kind of a personal, very personal statement, but I felt that the Jewish people had suffered too much and there was no way that I could come into that and have any right to it. And so I stayed at a distance and converted to Catholicism, largely because of the sense of history that went back farther. I did that in my early twenties, and was very active in that. I have a degree in liturgy from Notre Dame, so I pursued it. I was in religious life ever so briefly. I had prayed psalms all my life, but you could, you know, be assured of it there in a monastic kind of setting."

"And then, after I finished this piece, I felt finally that I had immersed myself enough in Jewish life and Jewish suffering that I could bear to convert to Judaism, and I did."

I remember very well when I first heard *Voices of a Vanished World*. It was at the world premiere of the piece; my daughter was singing second soprano in the choir. I can't listen to the recording now without thinking of that performance, on a sunny May evening in a synagogue in Michigan.

Like every musical setting of Psalm 137 of past centuries that I've come across, except Rossi's, *Voices of a Vanished World* expunges the final lines of the psalm. What could be less appropriate than a children's choir singing about dashing little ones against the stones? Especially in a work commemorating the horrors of the Holocaust. Musically speaking, then, the final section of the psalm gives us little to work with. But perhaps what is unsung holds as much significance as what is sung.

First, though, we should take a closer look at what these lines actually say.

Parsing the Unspeakable

The final verses of Psalm 137 feature a number of shifts of tone and register. If the first section of the psalm paints a memory-picture of exiles languishing beside a canal, and the second turns inward to swear loyalty to Jerusalem, the final section directly addresses a third party: first Yahweh, then Babylon herself. The conditional voice of part two—"If I forget thee, if I do not remember"—gives way to a declarative voice: Remember! And the psalm completes the move from memory in the first part to prophecy in the last. Babylon will be destroyed, and some unspecified parties will be happy that vengeance will be visited against the enemies of Israel. Babylon will be treated as it treated Judah, its children massacred as it massacred (we surmise) the children of Judah.

An omniscient Yahweh presumably doesn't need to be reminded to remember; She will remember how Her chosen people were treated. But in reminding Yahweh, the psalmist is able to pivot from the accomplices of its destruction, the Edomites, to the real perpetrators, the Babylonians. Edom isn't addressed, even if only directed to remember, but Babylon is. The psalmist goes over the head of Edom, to Yahweh, but Babylon warrants a direct warning.

> *Remember, O* LORD, *the children of Edom in the day of Jerusalem; who said, Rase it, rase it, even to the foundation thereof.*
> *O daughter of Babylon, who art to be destroyed; happy shall he be,*

that rewardeth thee as thou hast served us.

Happy shall he be, that taketh and dasheth thy little ones against the
stones.

Stepping back to better appraise the ethical complexity of the situation, a reader might ask: Why should Yahweh punish Babylon for its conquest and oppression of Israel, when Yahweh specifically used Babylon
to punish Israel for its wrongdoing? Wasn't Babylon simply carrying out
Yahweh's mission? And for that matter, what became of the advice offered
by Jeremiah in his letter to the Judean exiles in Babylon? What about building houses, planting gardens, taking wives, and bearing children, seeking
Babylon and praying for it, "for in its peace you will have peace?"

Jewish and Christian commentators, no surprise, have been working
over such ethical conundrums for nearly two millennia, and these questions will no doubt remain unresolved. As a prophet, Jeremiah was not
expected to be reliably consistent; despite his irenic letter to the captives,
the Book of Jeremiah blasts Babylon in no uncertain terms in chapter fifty,
prophesying in vivid detail exactly the sort of destruction invoked in Psalm
137. (The same radical shifts in tone occur in the Book of Isaiah.) And in
fairness to Jeremiah, the conditions of the first Exile, when he wrote his
letter to the captives, were very different than they would be a decade later.
After the first Exile Babylon simply took the Judean elite into captivity;
with the second Exile they destroyed the Jerusalem Temple, blinded King
Zedekiah, and put to death the royal inner circle.

While searching for some ethical purchase on the psalm's final lines,
we might wish to distinguish between vowing to carry out violent retribution, petitioning Yahweh to allow such vengeance to be carried out, and
appearing to bless (*Happy shall he be*) the agent of such retribution. There
is also a distinction to be drawn between sinful thoughts and actions. As
David Noel Freedman points out, all of the Ten Commandments except
one proscribe actions (worshipping other gods, taking the Lord's name
in vain, killing, lying, stealing, committing adultery, and so on). Only
the final commandment proscribes thoughts: Do not covet another's wife
or property.[13] In the gospels, of course, Jesus Christ challenges the com-
fortable distinction, emphasizing that sinful thoughts count as much as
actions: looking at a woman with lust, he teaches, is tantamount to committing adultery.

Leaving aside these thorny theological questions about holding human
agents responsible for divine providence, there is still the question of the

final verse. After all, verse eight simply promises to repay Babylon in kind for what it did to Judah. Since the Bible doesn't specify a great number of atrocities committed against Judah, there's no reason to expect that a proportional response would involve atrocities against Babylon—let alone dashing little ones against the stones.

Hebrew Bible scholars point out that the brutal killing of noncombatants, including women and children, was the norm in biblical times; it's a recurring biblical trope. Isaiah, for example, delivers this prophecy against Babylon: "All who are found will be stabbed, all who are taken will fall by the sword; their infants will be dashed to the ground before their eyes, their houses rifled and their wives ravished" (13:16). Hosea warns Israel, "Because you have trusted in your chariots, in the number of your warriors, the tumult of war shall arise against your people, and all your fortresses shall be razed as Shalman razed Beth-arbel in the day of battle, dashing the mother to the ground with her babes" (10:13–14). And Nahum on Nineveh: "She too became an exile and went into captivity, her infants too were dashed to the ground at every street-corner, her nobles were shared out by lot, all her great men were thrown into chains" (3:10). A note in the *New English Bible* comments simply, "In ancient warfare children were often cruelly killed."

In short, "Unyielding hatred of her foes was the correlate of intense love for Zion," writes an eminent psalm scholar in the *Anchor Bible*. "To the psalmist the law of retaliation for cruelty seems only just, and the shocking form in which he expresses his desire for the extermination of his country's destroyer must be judged in the light of customs prevailing in his age." As C. S. Lewis reminds us, "We live—at least, in some countries we still live—in a milder age. These poets lived in a world of savage punishments, of massacre and violence, of blood sacrifice in all countries and human sacrifice in many. And of course, too, we are far more subtle than they in disguising our ill will from others and from ourselves."[14]

Others observe that verse nine doesn't actually advocate violent action, or directly petition Yahweh to take such action; it is more akin to a revenge fantasy. "No personal vendetta is authorized, no pouring sugar in the gas tank, no picking up a gun or hiring one," writes Ellen Davis. "On the contrary, the validity of any punishing action that may occur depends entirely on its being God's action, not ours. And readers of the Bible recognize that this is in fact a severely limiting condition."[15]

The language actually asserts that whoever does take this action will be *happy*. Brenner argues that rather than the word "happy," with its connotation of gleeful joy in slaughtering infants, a more felicitous translation might be "praised" or "blessed." A soldier might be praised for performing a tough but necessary job without subjectively taking anything like pleasure in it. Translation is a tricky business, though. Magonet argues that the Hebrew word usually translated as "happy" is actually intended to be deliberately shocking and jarring, since in the Hebrew Bible it is nearly always used in reference to the satisfaction of trusting in, learning from, and being forgiven by Yahweh.[16]

Peggy Bendroth offered another suggestion for interpreting the final line.

"As a historian, one of the things I was interested in was the history of childhood, and how people theologize about childhood. And so dashing infants against a stone might mean something different, you know, in one age, and certainly by the nineteenth century it's pretty awful, because they're innocent. But children aren't always innocent in Christian tradition." In other words, the modern sense that babies are the most innocent of bystanders and therefore off-limits to warfare is a relatively recent moral innovation. For most readers over the past 2,500 years, verse nine would not have stood out as violating some sort of taboo.

The American theologian and pastor Jonathan Edwards, for example, one of North America's most brilliant intellectuals, cites verse nine of Psalm 137 for exactly this purpose. In his treatise, *Original Sin*, Edwards develops a detailed argument for why even newborn babies are not to be considered innocent, but rather are already tainted by Adam's sin. He cites a number of instances in Scripture where children and infants were not spared, and with God's explicit or implicit approval: during the destruction of Sodom and Gomorrah; of the human race during the flood; of the Canaanites, the Midianites, and the Amalekites. For his knowledge of the historical context Edwards relied on Henry Prideaux, who asserted that when Babylon was besieged by Persia, "the Babylonians took 'the most desperate and barbarous' measures to stay alive by killing 'all unnecessary Mouths,' 'whether wives, sisters, daughters, or young children useless for the wars.' "[17]

To this litany of slaughter Edwards adduces without comment the final verse of Psalm 137: "Happy shall he be that shall take thy little ones, and dash them against the stones." Edwards then cites the anecdote from Ezekiel 9, where Yahweh commanded invaders to slaughter every inhabitant of Jerusalem—"utterly old and young, both maids and little children"—all except those who had been marked as having resisted the "abominations of the city." His point seems clear: "We may well argue that from these things, that infants are not looked down upon by God as sinless, but that they are by nature children of wrath, seeing this terrible evil comes so heavily on mankind in infancy."[18] Yahweh has never given infants a pass when it comes to the burden of sin, so why should we, in our supposedly enlightened times, expect to now?

It would be a mistake to oversimplify Edwards's position on the imprecatory psalms like Psalm 137. David Barshinger notes that Edwards is careful to emphasize "that the psalmist does not use them for personal vengeance but speaks as head of the church and as a prophet to highlight God's response of justice to sin, recognizing the limits of salvation as he speaks against God's enemies and pleads for the safety of the church against its enemies while looking toward the final fulfillment of these curses in the eschaton," that is, the End Times.[19]

Even so, it's hard to imagine a church in which Edwards' theology on this point would get a sympathetic exposition. But more than a few commentators resist jettisoning the kernel of the final verse without facing it unflinchingly. "You may have not heard these words in church," Ellen Davis writes. "Sunday lectionaries omit psalms like this altogether, or they include them in highly expurgated form. But by clapping our hand over the psalmists' mouth in that way, we lose something the Bible intends us to have. By refusing to listen to that anger and even take it on our lips, we lose an opportunity to bring our anger into the context of our relationship with God."[20]

Perhaps reflecting the ascendance of therapeutic models in the work of the church, theologians advocate owning up to emotions of violent rage rather than rejecting them as unworthy. At any given moment the world witnesses myriads of crimes against individuals and communities—pick up a newspaper on any given day—that can and probably should trigger nearly murderous rage. In the face of intolerable injustice—the gunning down of nine members of a historic black church in South Carolina by a white supremacist, for example—it's better to acknowledge and articulate rather than repress that rage, but then—and this is the key theological move—*submit that anger to God* rather than act on it. In other words, the faithful believer leaves it to God to punish iniquity in Her own way, at Her own time. As Babylon was in fact punished—brought down by Yahweh—about fifty years after it destroyed the Jerusalem Temple.

Theologian and Hebrew Bible scholar Walter Brueggemann complains that most contemporary churchgoers know only a handful of psalms, and usually read them "in the flattest, most reassuring kind of way." Instead, as he told an interviewer:

If you can read a few verses of a psalm and those are verses you couldn't imagine anyone in this congregation ever saying—they wouldn't do that—just ask the interpretive question, who would you imagine could talk like that? Do you know anybody who would talk like that, or have you seen anybody in the news lately that you could imagine talking like that? If you take an angry psalm . . . you can imagine that it's a Palestinian mother who is picking up the pieces of her exploded son, or something like that, and has to talk like that.

Brueggemann calls this "being in extremis," those (hopefully) rare moments when "what we know almost immediately is that our safe, conventional language doesn't quite work." He reminds us that these are the times we need to be open to authoritative voices from our tradition who "speak faith in ways other than the way we speak faith."[21]

Ellen Davis recommends this thought experiment involving a radical displacement of self and other: "The ancient rabbis said of scripture: 'Turn it and turn it, for everything is in it.' If you have the courage (and it will take some), try turning the psalm a full 180 degrees, until it is directed at yourself, and ask: Is there any one in the community of God's people who might want to say this to God about me—or maybe, about us?"[22]

There's some irony here: a psalm centrally concerned with memory—that commands memory and warns against forgetting—has itself been partially suppressed because it expresses ideas that we would rather not remember. So, one strategy for making sense of that final verse is to remind ourselves how many people justifiably feel a kind of violent rage in the present—the kind that each of us has likely experienced and probably will again. Road rage, anyone?

The Christian tradition includes a more radical way of responding to these "cursing" scriptures. For psalms scholar William Holladay, the question of how Christians should use the psalms is deadly serious: "The crucial question then is: With regard to their enemies, what are Christians to wish for and pray for?"

He lists some possibilities: a change of heart; recognition they are wrong; to cease their oppression. Getting closer to the specifics of Psalm 137, Holladay acknowledges, "It is difficult to say whether it is legitimate for Christians to wish for commensurate hurt on their enemies, whether that hurt be exercised by the psalmist empowered by God . . . or by God alone . . . . Commensurate hurt on one's enemy is certainly one kind of parity, but it may not be the best kind; the removal of power from one's enemies may be preferable." He concludes, "It follows from what has been said that it is not legitimate for Christians to wish death on their enemies." Holladay specifically cites Psalm 137:9 as being "excluded for Christians, unless one's notion of the identification of one's 'enemies' is drastically transformed."[23]

Allegorical Answers

In fact, the Christian tradition offers examples of such drastic transformations going back at least to Augustine. One approach has been to radically allegorize the psalms, as Augustine does with the curses uttered in Psalm 137. Unlike Jews and Christians before him, Augustine didn't equate Rome with Babylon; by his time Rome itself was threatened by the Visigoths, and Rome's pagan citizens accused Christians of helping bring about the sacking of their city. In *Dei Civitate Dei*, Augustine offers Babylon as an archetype of the earthly city, contrasting it to Jerusalem, which symbolizes the City of God and which will ultimately triumph in the fullness of time.

A decade before writing this masterwork Augustine had developed extensive psalm commentaries, including a lengthy sermon on Psalm 137 that he preached in Carthage on New Year's Eve, 412. He advances allegorical readings of nearly every verse. "The rivers of Babylon are all the things which people love in this world but which flow away from us," he writes, while the willow trees are nonbelievers unprepared to accept the Gospel of Christ. "Do not be too ready to answer a person of this type: he is a willow, a sterile tree, so do not try to strike your harp for him; just hang it up. He may insist, 'Tell me, sing to me, explain to me. Don't you want me to learn?' "[24]

But Augustine warns his readers not to be taken in by such voices. "He does not ask in order to learn but only to find something he can sneer at. So I am not going to talk to you. I will simply hang up my harp."[25] In considering this interpretation, we should bear in mind the animus against musical instruments that pertained in the early church (and in Judaism after the destruction of the Second Temple), so that all references to musical instruments (and Psalm 150 famously is full of them) needed to be understood figuratively.[26]

Each individual stands in relation to Christ and Satan as Judah stood in relation to Jerusalem and Babylon, according to Augustine. "The newborn child is potentially a citizen of Jerusalem—indeed, by God's predestination a citizen already—but for the time being he or she is a prisoner," he writes. "What can a child learn to love except what his parents whisper to him . . . . In this sense Babylon persecuted us when we were still little tiny children, but as we grew up God gave us some knowledge of himself, and so we learned not to copy the mistakes of our parents."[27]

Therefore, Augustine concludes: "It will be the turn of Babylon's little ones to be choked now; or rather, its infants will in their turn be dashed to pieces and killed. Who are these little ones in Babylon?" he asks. "Evil desires newly come to birth. Some people have to fight against inveterate desires, but you can do better than that. When evil desire is born, before your bad habits reinforce it, while it is still in its infancy and has not yet fortified itself by alliance with depraved custom, dash it to pieces. It is only a baby still. But make sure it does not survive your violent treatment: dash it on the rock. *And the rock is Christ* (1 Cor. 10:4)."[28]

This allegorical interpretation was not original to Augustine, who died in 430. Chances are it originated with Origen of Alexandria, who lived two centuries earlier; and versions of it appear in Latin writings by Hilary, Jerome, Ambrose (who baptized Augustine), and Cassian. But such a reading of the psalm and others like it was practically inevitable. "Since the desire that real Babylonian babies be smashed on real rocks was both historically no longer relevant and hardly consistent with the teaching of Jesus," according to Timothy Fry, "it was obvious to the Patristic interpreter that the verse must have a 'spiritual' meaning. There were spiritual rocks readily available in the New Testament; it remained only to spiritualize the babies into wrongful thoughts. It must also be remembered that for Christians the focus of the struggle between good and evil was no longer against the powers and principalities of this world but within the individual soul."[29]

Nowhere did this interpretive strategy make more of a lasting impact than in the Rule of Saint Benedict. Compiled a century after the death of Augustine, Benedict's directive established a sequence for reciting the daily office in monastic communities. The entire psalter would be recited in its biblical sequence, in eight daily times of prayer or "offices," over the course of a week: the Vigil (or Nocturn) at midnight; Laud at daybreak; Prime at 7 a.m.; Terce at 9 a.m.; Sext at noon; None at 3 p.m.; Vespers in the evening; and, at bedtime, Compline. According to the Catholic Church's liturgical calendar for Divine Office in effect as the Reformation commenced, Psalm 137 was to be chanted once a week, on Thursday, at Vespers.[30] As the psalms were chanted to the plainsong melodies out of which Western music evolved, the musical impact of these practices was also immense.

The resulting scheme of regular prayer through the psalms, according to Holladay, "was so sensible that it stimulated similar but more rigorous rules," not just for monasteries but also for parish priests. "And the Divine Office was recited not only by priests, monks, and nuns but by some lay people as well, particularly pious monarchs and nobility who had the leisure and the impulse to do so (and who had the learning as well; for the office, we must remember, was only in Latin)." Alfred the Great (849–899), for example, who successfully led English resistance to the Viking occupation, was described as "frequent in psalm-singing and prayer, at the hours both of the day and night," and carried a breviary listing all the psalms and prayers.[31]

As a kind of medieval Christian lingua franca, then, any mention of Psalm 137 in the Rule of Saint Benedict would have had a substantial influence in Europe at a time when the availability of biblical interpretations, let alone the literacy required to read them, was extremely limited. It's significant that Benedict's Prologue, in exhorting its readers to a life of obedience and good deeds, cites the example of Psalm 137: "He has foiled the evil one, the devil, at every turn, flinging both him and his promptings far from the sight of his heart. *While these temptations were still young, he caught hold of them and dashed them against Christ.*" And later Benedict exhorts: "Hour by hour keep careful watch over all you do, aware that God's gaze is upon you, wherever you may be. As soon as wrongful thoughts come into your heart, dash them against Christ and disclose them to your spiritual father."[32]

The Reformation Turn

Interesting, then, that the Reformation witnessed an acceptance of more literal and therefore more bloodthirsty renderings of verse nine. Babylon was still understood metaphorically by Protestants, not as the long-gone Mesopotamian empire but as a spiritual Babylon: the Roman Catholic Church.

Martin Luther, we recall, borrowed the language of Psalm 137 for his savage polemic against Rome, *The Babylonian Captivity of the Church*. It was the second of three treatises he wrote in 1520 expostulating his irreconcilable differences with the Church of Rome. This was a dramatic season. Luther wrote the text in the same month he received a papal bull giving him sixty days to recant or be declared a heretic. The first of his treatises published that fall, *To the Christian Nobility of the German Nation*, had ended with this defiant foreshadowing of his next broadside:

> In the past I have made frequent overtures of peace to my enemies, but as I see it, God has compelled me through them to keep on opening my mouth wider and wider and to give them enough to say, bark, shout, and write because they have nothing else to do. Well, I know another little song about Rome and the Romanists. If their ears are itching to hear it, I will sing that one to them, too—and pitch it in the highest key! You understand what I mean, dear Rome.[33]

Two months later appeared *The Babylonian Captivity*, which has been described as "a deadly dagger aimed at the very heart of sacramentalism and clericalism and monasticism . . . . The most devastating assault Luther had yet undertaken against Roman teaching and practice."[34] His target was the system of sacraments by which the Church structured the lives of European Christians. Disappointingly, Luther doesn't develop an analogy between the captivity of the Judeans and the situation of sixteenth-century European Christians; he uses the captivity as a metaphor. Written in Latin, the treatise is a theological work aimed at fellow intellectuals (though its tone is unmistakably combative).

The closest Luther comes to developing an analogy appears a few pages from the end, completing his discussion of the Eucharist. "Not content with these things," he writes, "*this Babylon of ours has so completely extinguished faith* that it insolently *denies its necessity in this sacrament*. Indeed, with the wickedness of Antichrist it brands it as heresy for anyone to assert that faith is necessary. What more could this tyranny do than it has done. Truly, 'by the waters of Babylon we sit down and weep, when we remember thee, O Zion. On the willows there we hang up our lyres.' May the Lord curse the barren willows of those streams! Amen."[35]

Though he no doubt had a premonition of the violence and vengeance likely to engulf Europe, Luther doesn't engage the final verses of Psalm 137 in *The Babylonian Captivity*. Years later, as Wars of Religion were engulfing Europe, John Calvin was more direct in his literal interpretation of the psalm's closing verse. "It may seem to savor of cruelty," he wrote in a commentary, "that he should wish the tender and innocent infants to be dashed and mangled upon the stones, but he does not speak under the impulse of personal feeling, and only employs words which God had himself authorized, so that this is but the declaration of a just judgment, as when our Lord says, 'With what measure ye mete, it shall be measured to you again' (Matthew 7:2.)."[36]

Calvin's acceptance of this harsh image might have something to do with his theology of predestination, which, like that of his theological descendant Jonathan Edwards, did not conceive of infants as innocent and sin-free. And it may also be attributed to his theology of earthly life as "perpetual warfare," reflecting his harrowing experience of religious and political violence in mid-sixteenth-century France.

"The French Civil Wars, like the English, may have inured their participants and victims to a level of violence otherwise unacceptable to Christian readers of the Psalms," writes literary scholar Hannibal Hamlin. A minister in England could therefore preach approvingly of the violent death of "little ones." "It is an interesting case of the broad influence of the Psalms that both sides in the Civil War turned to the same psalm for solace or support," he notes. "Any conditions of alienation or estrangement could be interpreted as exile, and 'Babylon,' as noted above, could be applied to any convenient enemy and oppressor." As Calvin wrote, "In our own day under the Papacy . . . whether Frenchmen, Englishmen, or Italians, who love and practice the true religion, even their native country is a foreign clime when they live under that tyranny."[37]

Even well before the Reformation, we find Psalm 137 being deployed in England in a bitter controversy that pitted the English Church and Crown against the Lollards, religious dissenters influenced by the reformer John Wycliffe (later declared a heretic), who anticipated many of the theological positions taken by Reformation Protestants. In his poem, *Defence of Holy Church*, the prolific poet John Lydgate begins by drawing an analogy between the English Church, threatened by Lollard dissenters, and the Judeans taken captive by Babylon: "on the floodis of fell Babiloun, / Al solitaire and trist in compleynyng, / Sat with hire children aboute hir euerichoun, / Almost fordrowynd with teerys in weeping." The English monarch, Henry V, is compared to the Psalmist, David, and implicitly urged to stand firm against heresy. He did in fact put down the uprising, driving Lollardy underground until it appeared to emerge a century later during the Reformation. "Although Lydgate does not directly paraphrase the cursing verses at the close of Psalm [137] in the Defence," writes Michael Kuczynski, "their tone informs his bitter description of the spiritually blind and crippled, and his self-assured identification with the prophet Samuel, who butchered Agag when Saul would not."[38]

Certainly English poets in the early modern period did not shy away from the vengeful climax of the psalm. Several psalm translations "simply wallow in the gore," with the final verse rendered: "With dasht-out brains the crying stones to feed" (Sandys); "Thy brats 'gainst rocks, to wash thy bloudie stones / With thine own bloud, and pave thee with thy bones" (Fletcher); "'Gainst the walls shall dash their bones, / Ruthless stones / With their braines and blood besmearing" (Davison).[39]

Or the 119-line travesty published by John Oldman in 1676, which Donald Davie describes as "the most horrible of psalm-versions in English, and among the most risible." What the Hebrew and King James cover in three verses, Oldham extends for twenty-two overwrought lines:

> A day will come (oh might I see't ere long)
> That shall revenge our mighty Wrong.
> Then best, for ever blest be he,
> Whoever shall return't on thee,
> And grave it deep, and pay't with bloody Usury.
> May neither Aged Groans, nor Infant-Cries
> Nor piteous Mother's Tears, nor ravish'd Virgin's Sighs
> Soften thy unrelenting Enemies.
> Let them, as thou to us, inexorable prove,
> Nor Age nor Sex their deaf Compassion move.
> Rapes, Murders, Slaughters, Funerals,
> And all thou durst attempt within our Sion's Walls,
> Mayst thou endure and more, till joyful we
> Confess thyself outdone in artful Cruelty.
> Bless, yea thrice-blessed by that barbarous Hand
> (Oh Grief! that I such dire Revenge commend)
> Who tears out Infants from their Mother's Womb,
> And hurls 'em yet unborn unto their Tomb.
> Blest he, who plucks 'em from their Parents' Arms,
> That Sanctuary from all common Harms;
> Who with their Skulls and Bones shall pave they Streets all o'er
> And fill thy glutted Channels with their scatter'd Brains & Gore.[40]

Philosopher Stephen Toulmin makes an important argument about unexpected consequences of the Thirty Years War (1618–1648) and other conflicts generated within Christianity. "The intellectual debate between Protestant Reformers and their Counter-Reformation opponents had collapsed, and there was no alternative to the sword and the torch," he writes. "Yet, the more brutal the warfare became, the more firmly convinced the proponents of each religious system were that their doctrines *must be* proved correct and that their opponents were stupid, malicious, or both .... All that mattered, by this stage, was for supporters of Religious Truth to believe, devoutly, in *belief itself*."[41]

For a handful of philosophers and scientists, the horrific bloodshed triggered by disagreement over the proper interpretation of the Bible and the practice of Christianity spurred efforts to find more rational, universal methods for adjudicating truth claims. In France, for example, the playful skepticism of a figure like Montaigne was replaced by the foundational aspirations of Descartes, who wanted to find an Archimedean point on which to ground all knowledge. The reasoned intellectual world of Descartes, Galileo, Hobbes, and Newton—which would dominate intellectual life in the West for three centuries—obviously had much to commend itself, following the clash of incommensurable differences typical of the Wars of Religion.[42]

Given the religious and political context that produced the slew of gory English psalm translations, the approach taken by Isaac Watts (born around the time Oldham composed his blood-spattered translation) offers a refreshing contrast—up to a point. Watts excluded Psalm 137 from his influential 1719 collection, judging it "almost opposite to the Spirit of the Gospel ... foreign to the State of the New-Testament, and widely different from the present Circumstances of Christians."[43] But he did include it in a collection of fugitive writings published near the end of his life.

"This particular *Psalm* could not well be converted into *Christianity* and accordingly it appears here in its *Jewish* Form," he wrote in the 1734 volume: "The Vengeance denounced against *Babylon*, in the Close of it, shall be executed (said a great Divine) upon *Anti-christian Rome*; but he was persuaded the *Turks* must do it, for *Protestant* Hearts, said he, have too much Compassion in them to embrue their Hands in such a bloody and terrible Execution." Managing to be both anti-Semitic and anti-Muslim, and rather piously Protestant (who were equally capable of violent excesses), Watts renders the final verses with admirable concision:

> VIII
> 'Twas Edom bid the conquering Foe,
> *Down with thy Tow'rs, and raze thy Walls:*
> Requite her, Lord: But *Babel*, know
> Thy Guilt for fiercer Vengeance calls.

IX

As thou hast spar'd nor Sex nor Age,
Deaf to our Infants' dying Groans,
May some bless'd Hand, inspir'd with Rage,
Dash thy young Babes, and tinge the Stones.[44]

This is still a long way from the pacifistic revision of eighteenth-century poet Christopher Smart, who wrote not long after Watts:

But he is greatest and the best,
Who spares his enemies profest,
And Christian mildness owns;
Who gives his captives back their lives,
Their helpless infants, weeping wives,
And for his sin atones.[45]

As the example of Watts suggests, whole-hearted embrace of Psalm 137's vengeful finale finds significantly less expression in the eighteenth century than in the seventeenth.

Who was the "great Divine" whom, Watts informs us, had prophesied vengeance by Turks against "Anti-christian Rome?" It's doubtful he had in mind the younger Jonathan Edwards; he may have been referring to Matthew Poole or Matthew Henry, English Protestant theologians not reticent about hurling vituperations at Rome (and major intellectual influences on Edwards). Luther himself addressed the issue in a pamphlet titled *On War against the Turk*, published shortly before the Turks laid siege to Vienna, damning both sides in that conflict in typically unequivocal terms:

I and my followers keep and teach peace; the pope along with his followers, wages war, commits murder, and robs not only his enemies, but he also burns, condemns, and persecutes the innocent, the pious, the orthodox, as a true Antichrist. And he does this while sitting, in the temple of God (2 Thess. 2:4), as head of the Church; the Turk does not do that. But just as the pope is Antichrist, so the Turk is the very devil incarnate. The prayer of Christendom against both is that they shall go down to hell, even though it may take the Last Day to send them there; and I hope that day will not be far off.[46]

Writing more than a century later from the relative peace and tranquil-
ity of New England, Edwards shared this dim view of the Catholic Church:

> The dashing the "little ones" of Babylon "against the stones" prob-
> ably was fulfilled in some degrees when Cyrus took the city, but
> it had its greatest fulfillment afterwards, when that prophecy was
> fulfilled (*Isaiah 47:9*) . . . . It was God's pleasure to show the event to
> be agreeable to his will by giving those that did it external prosperity.
> But the prophecy seems to look beyond the destruction of the literal
> Babylon to that of the spiritual Babylon. *They indeed will do God's*
> *work, and will perform a good work, who shall be God's instruments of*
> *the utter overthrow of the Church of Rome with all her superstitions, and*
> *heathenish ceremonies, and other cursed fruits of her spiritual whore-*
> *doms, as it were without having any mercy upon them.*[47]

Edwards may shift the focus from "literal Babylon" to the Roman Catholic
Church, but the threat of vengeance seems material, not spiritual. Coming
so soon after the Wars of Religion it's hard to imagine the "utter overthrow" of the Church being anything like bloodless.

American Vengeance

Regardless of what pious Calvinist poets and theologians were writing, of
course, the American people have been as prone to revenge fantasies as
any other nationality. No living scholar of American history and culture has
explored the material and symbolic consequences of American violence
more thoroughly than Richard Slotkin. In his massive trilogy, *Regeneration*
through Violence, *The Fatal Environment*, and *Gunfighter Nation*, Slotkin
documents how the mythology of the frontier—taming the natural landscape and exterminating Native peoples—shaped the ideology of nation
building and imperial expansion from the period of European settlement
through the end of the twentieth century.[48]

I asked Slotkin if he thought that Psalm 137 reflected something important about the American experience. "It certainly captures the vengefulness of the Puritans with respect to the Indians," was his reply.[49]

He alerted me to two references, both responses to King Philip's
War that pitted English colonists in Massachusetts, along with some
Amerindian allies, against a confederation of Indians led by Metacom

(dubbed Prince Philip by the English). The fourteenth-month-long war that began in 1675 was the greatest calamity experienced by the British settlers during their first century in North America. It destroyed or severely damaged half its towns, wrecked the colonial economy, and nearly bankrupted the colonial treasury. In proportion of population, King Philip's War was for colonists the most deadly American conflict; it was even more so for Native peoples. It permanently altered the climate of Indian-white relations across the region. And the psychological and spiritual impact of the war was as devastating as the casualties and material losses. For Puritans, the analogy between the war and the Babylonian conquest of Judah was unmistakable.[50]

Psalm 137 surfaces in a long "history-sermon" published in 1676 by yet another "great Divine," Increase Mather (Cotton's father). Mather interprets scripture to allow the New England Puritans to make sense of the devastating war in terms of Divine Providence. Mather cites the psalm toward the end of his sermon as a kind of warning: "*In the last place,*" he writes, "*let me assume the boldness to speak to any in other parts of the world, into whose hands this may come.* Let not those that bear us ill-will say in their hearts *Aha* so would we have it. Will not the Lord remember the children of Edom, who in the day of Jerusalems Calamity said *rase it, rase it to the foundation thereof?*" New England may have sinned and fallen short, Mather acknowledges, but its enemies, perhaps especially those in England, should not look on its plight with gloating: "For if this be done to *Immanuels Land,* what may other Lands expect ere long?"[51]

Slotkin explained to me that Mather's sermon "functions as one of many texts which represent the Indian attack on New England as an attack on the New Jerusalem, Puritan sufferings as rebuke for sins, and which also call for merciless war against the Indians, who are likened to the Edomites in Psalm 137, but more frequently to the Amalekites," another enemy of ancient Israel. "These texts represent a turn in the Puritan relation to the Indians, from an ambivalent toleration toward prospective converts (and trading partners) to exterminationist anger."

He offers another example, this one from probably the most widely read work of early American literature: the *Narrative of the Captivity and Restoration of Mrs. Mary Rowlandson* (1682). The first and perhaps finest captivity narrative, according to Slotkin, Rowlandson's account "became part of the basic vocabulary of American writers and historians, offering a symbolic key to the drama of American history: a white woman, symbolizing the values of Christianity and American civilization, is captured and

FIGURE 8 Mary Rowlandson in captivity. Wood engraving from *Harper's Weekly*, 1857. Courtesy of the Library of Congress Prints and Photographs Division [LC-USZ62-113682].

threatened by a racial enemy and must be rescued by the grace of God (or, after the Puritan times, by an American hero)."[52] Again, echoes of the Babylonian Exile are striking.

Rowlandson was in her "eighth remove" (change of camp) when she and her captors made their way to the banks of the Connecticut River, intending to meet Metacom. Alarmed by something, the Indians moved north up the river; at noon they rested, and Rowlandson read psalms with her son. The next day they again came to the river and crossed by canoe (see Fig. 8). At which point transpires an almost biblical scene:

> When I came ashore, they gathered all about me, I was sitting alone in the midst: I observed they asked one another questions, and laughed, and rejoiced over their gains and victories. Then my heart began to fail: and I fell a-weeping which was the first time to my remembrance, that I wept before them. Although I had met with so much affliction, and my heart was many times ready to break, yet could I not shed one tear in their sight: but rather had been all this while in a maze, and like one astonished: but now I may say as, Psalm 137. I. *By the rivers of Babylon, there we sat down: yea, we wept when we remembered Zion.* There one of them asked me, why I wept, I could hardly tell what to say: yet I answered, they would kill

me: No, said he, none will hurt you. Then came one of them and gave me two spoonfuls of meal to comfort me, and another gave me half a pint of peas; which was more worth than many bushels at another time.

Then comes an audience with Metacom himself, who invites Rowlandson to sit and offers her a pipe: "a usual compliment nowadays amongst saints and sinners." Rowlandson admits she used to smoke tobacco but had given it up in her captivity: "surely there are many who may be better employed than to lie sucking a stinking tobacco pipe."[53] The juxtaposing of Rowland's terror with the unexpected kindness and hospitality by the captors is what makes the encounter so extraordinary.

I mention to Slotkin that the final verses of the psalm are usually glossed over. "Do you think of vengeance as being a particularly American response," I ask, "then or now?"

"I think the 'turn' I described above, with respect to the Puritans," he replies, "characterized white/Native relations throughout the period of expansion and colonization. Initial periods of friendship and even cultural interchange gave way to violence aimed at destroying or displacing the Natives—violence usually justified as revenge for an attack on the colony or settlement, always figuratively a New Jerusalem or Promised Land.

"With this in mind, I find the 'repression' of the last six verses very interesting," Slotkin continues. "It would seem apt for justifying Indian-killing in biblical terms, yet it isn't used. One problem with the text is: 'dashing little ones against the stones.' It is too frank and explicit in describing just what the white man's revenge entails. Once we get into the nineteenth century, there are even scandals when white troops or militias massacre Indian women and children. The earliest such that I recall involves the 'Paxton Boys' in prerevolutionary Pennsylvania, but the most infamous is probably Sand Creek, in 1864.

"Then too," he tells me, "once we get beyond the Puritans there is a gradual shift in emphasis from the Old to the New Testament in the religious references used to interpret current events. Less pure-white tribalism, more mercy. Rereading these texts, I'm struck by the imbalance between Old and New Testament references, even in Mrs. Rowlandson's narrative—she is in desperate need of comfort, but finds it more often in Psalms than in the Christian gospels."

The subject of violence had come up when I talked with John Stauffer about Frederick Douglass and the run-up to the Civil War, nearly two centuries after King Philip's War. "What about that thread of vengeance in American history?" I start—and Stauffer finishes my sentence:

"—is very much part of the Radical Abolition Party. And Douglass, in rhetorically violent states, reflected this quest for vengeance. The best example is after Douglass learns that Charles Sumner has been almost killed on the Senate floor. He gives an address at the second annual convention of the Radical Abolition Party, and he basically says—and I can give you the exact quote—he calls for, as an act of vengeance, to slash the throats of slave owners. That's his term. In his *Life and Times*, he even then acknowledges that this is an appropriate act of vengeance—this is how we have to fight these people.[54]

"And it was consistent with Brown's own view. Brown was a member of the Radical Abolition Party, and their understanding was that we're already, you know, we're peacemakers. Slavery is a state of war, and these inhuman, barbarous people are leading the Civil War, and we need to vanquish them. We need to respond with vengeance in order to end this war and preserve the peace. That was their understanding.

"So, Douglass definitely was someone who believed in the biblical idea of vengeance, in certain circumstances. He was very different than Brown in that he was always what I would call a prudent revolutionary.

"There is another example of a hymn or story I was going to use. Brown, at the very first Radical Abolition convention, in front of Douglass, in front of everyone, quotes Hebrew 22: 'Without the shedding of blood, there can be no remission of sins.' And no one blinks. It's like, Yeah, that's right. And that was Hebrews? It's kind of a weird biblical text in terms of attribution, but that was widely quoted then. You never hear that quoted now, or rarely."

"Were the abolitionists unusual in their vengefulness," I ask, "or was this the ethos of the time?"

"That was prevailing. In fact they were less so than, I would say, most other people. It was a culture of honor, certainly in the South but even in the North. Lincoln displayed that with his political opponents. I mean, Lincoln almost gets in a duel. The difference is that—and you especially see it in the whole kind of mob activity—the mobs are organized then by 'gentlemen of property and standing' is what they were called. Whether it's against abolitionists or another group, the mob riots are viewed, and people acknowledged at the time, these are acts of retaliation or vengeance.

"So the emphasis on the Old Testament notion of vengeance is much more profound than it would become in the twentieth century," Stauffer says. "So I would say abolitionists, they were *less* vengeful. I mean, the worst were Southerners, in terms of their proclivity toward violence. Southerners—and a number of people agree on this—they would, if they felt slighted at all, they would just slash someone's throat. They'd challenge them to a duel. They'd get in a fight.

"There's a 700-page diary by this African American William Johnson who was a black barber and actually a slave owner. He documents life in Natchez every day from 1831 to 1851. Virtually no one has analyzed it. But *the* most prominent cultural fact of life in Natchez is violence, and mostly it's revenge. People get in an argument and that immediately escalates because, you know: You dissed me, so I'm going to kill you. And people loved it—they would gather round and watch."

I mention having recently heard Steven Pinker lecture, and his argument that over history, human violence has been declining statistically, dramatically so in the past two hundred years.

"Yeah, it is. And part of it is the rise of liberalism and the move away from Old Testament toward New Testament, but I concur on that point. The one difference is: soldiers in war, if their buddy gets killed in Iraq, they're still going to seek vengeance."

"Yes, we have seen that."

"But out among the civilian population it's much different. It's much different."

I mention that this is reflected in the expunging of verse nine in uses of Psalm 137.

Stauffer agrees. "I was actually really surprised in the 'Battle Hymn of the Republic,' at how popular it has remained. Because that's a hymn that certainly calls for vengeance, for retribution. Now people, in recording or live performances, rarely sing all five stanzas, and they delete the ones that are the most vengeful. But at the time people did sing all five stanzas. And some liberal Protestant churches have excised the 'Battle Hymn' from the hymnbook because of its militancy. And so that gives a sense of the times."

The principle of retaliation—"happy shall he be that rewardeth thee as thou has served us," in the psalmist's words—is, of course, a bedrock principle of statecraft for the United States (and other nations). The war on Iraq launched by President Bush in 2003 was justified at times as payback for 9/11. The U.S. destruction of the Taliban in Afghanistan that began shortly after September 11 was unequivocally so. The use of unmanned drone strikes by the Obama administration to take out enemies of the state in Pakistan is a form of retaliation against those deemed complicit in terrorist actions against the United States or its allies. There were jubilant celebrations outside the White House when it was announced that U.S. forces had killed Osama Bin Laden. Or nearly a decade earlier, the glee when military forces captured the modern-day king of Babylon, Saddam Hussein, after which he was quickly executed. The slogan occasionally seen after 9/11: "Kill 'em all and let God sort 'em out."

A group of Christian leaders gathered in New Jersey the day after the attack on the World Trade Center. They invited people in the audience to share Scripture to help them make sense of the still unfathomable attacks of the day before. A wide range of selections were offered. "And then," recalled Christopher Hays, "a woman raised up her voice and haltingly read the end of Psalm 137: 'Happy shall they be who pay you back what you have done to us! Happy shall they be who take your little ones and dash them against the rock!' A longer-than-usual pause followed." No doubt, her selection captured the mood of the American body politic through much of the decade that followed.[55]

In the Middle East, for decades the predictable pattern of hostilities between the state of Israel, its Palestinian population, and its territorial neighbors has been governed by endless cycles of violent retribution. Rockets are fired, air strikes (sometimes invasions) follow, and so on. Oftentimes the killing strikes observers as reckless, with children and other noncombatants too frequently ending up as casualties. The invasion of Gaza in the summer of 2014 was only the most recent of these episodes: 2,251 Palestinians killed, including 1,462 civilians; 18,000 homes destroyed; 115 children and 50 women killed by Israeli precision-guided weapons. From the Palestinian side, 4,881 rockets and 1,753 mortars were shot at Israel, many targeting civilians.[56]

Popular culture has enthusiastically embraced this principle of retaliation. Where would Hollywood's most profitable action movies be, for example, without predictable sequences of violent retribution? Yet organized religion in the United States, with its hymns and liturgies, mainly steers clear of the language of imprecation sounded in cursing psalms like Psalm 137.

We get a musical echo of these geopolitics in Steve Reich's *Daniel Variations* (2006), a piece animated by the savage aftermath of the 2003 U.S. invasion of Iraq. The four movements alternate short, gnomic texts taken from the Book of Daniel with fragments of comments made by Daniel Pearl, a young reporter for the *Wall Street Journal* who was captured, held hostage by the Taliban in Pakistan, and beheaded.[57]

The first passage Reich sets to music is spoken to Daniel by Nebuchadnezzar; this is one of the scenes that mark Daniel's success as an interpreter of dreams: "I saw a dream. Images upon my bed & visions in my head frightened me" (4:5). As Reich comments in the liner notes, referring to the events that inspired *Daniel Variations*, "it is unfortunately possible to feel a chill of identification with these words." The second text comes from a terse statement Pearl made on videotape for his Taliban captors: "My name is Daniel Pearl." The third movement is based on a biblical text; Daniel's response to Nebuchadnezzar after the king shares yet another puzzling dream: "Let the dream fall back on the dreaded."

The final text comes from another comment by Pearl, this time to a friend during a bicycle trip on the Potomac River: "I sure hope Gabriel likes my music, when the day is done" (the last phrase an addition by Reich). Reich explains that because Pearl was a fiddle player who favored jazz and bluegrass, he wrote the second and fourth movements to feature stringed instruments playing the lead.

Daniel Variations opens with jagged dissonant chords played by the four pianos, followed by the chilling words, "I saw a dream," sung in ominous voicings. Reich explains his tonal logic: the piece "has two related harmonic ground plans—one for the first and third movements using four minor dominant chords a minor third apart in E minor, G minor, B-flat minor, and C-sharp minor. The other harmonic plan is for the second and fourth movements using four major dominant chords in the relative major keys, G, B-flat, D-flat, and E. This gives a darker chromatic harmony to the first and third movements and a more affirmative underpinning to the second and fourth," something readily apparent to the casual listener.[58]

Daniel Variations gives us alternating voices, alternating cosmic worldviews, alternating musical moods. The notes include a photograph of Pearl playing the fiddle, accompanied by a remark made by his father: "For a glimpse into the spirit of Reich's, *Daniel Variations*, just contemplate Danny's face in the picture left, and ask yourself: where does human civilization acquire its calm, almost humorous confidence that, when the day is done, Bach will triumph over Nebuchadnezzar."

Interestingly, Daniel Pearl's father's first name is Judea.

Our Better Angels

No contemporary scholar has worked more ambitiously to historicize human violence than Steven Pinker, author of the best-selling study, *The Better Angels of Our Nature: Why Violence Has Declined*. His book opens with a catalog of biblical bloodshed, culminating in the episode in which Solomon offers to cut a baby in half with his sword so that the two women who claim to be its mother can share it. Pinker's account doesn't quite get to the Babylonian invasion, except to mention it as the period in which the Hebrew Bible was first committed to writing. His point is to illustrate how extreme and routine warfare and violence were in the ancient world.

"The Bible depicts a world that, seen through modern eyes, is staggering in its savagery," he writes. "People enslave, rape, and murder members of their immediate families. Warlords slaughter civilians indiscriminately, including the children. Women are bought, sold, and plundered like sex toys. And Yahweh tortures and massacres people by the hundreds of thousands for trivial disobedience or for no reason at all. These atrocities are neither isolated not obscure. They implicate all the major characters of the Old Testament, the ones that Sunday-school children draw with crayons."[59]

"The good news, of course, is that most of it never happened," he writes of biblical slaughter. "Not only is there no evidence that Yahweh inundated the planet and incinerated its cities, but the patriarchs, exodus, conquest and Jewish empire are almost certainly fictions." Scholarship has established that the Bible is actually a wiki, he says, "compiled over half a millennium from writers with different styles, dialects, character names, and conceptions of God, and it was subjected to haphazard editing that left it with many contradictions, duplications, and non sequiturs." So the actual warfare that undoubtedly took place was not as horrific and one-sided as the Bible reports.[60]

"Though the historical accounts in the Old Testament are fictitious (or at best artistic reconstructions, like Shakespeare's historical dramas)," Pinker writes, "they offer a window into the lives and values of Near Eastern civilizations in the mid-first millennium B.C.E. Whether or not the Israelites actually engaged in genocide, they certainly thought it was a good idea. The possibility that a woman had a legitimate interest in not being raped or acquired as sexual property did not seem to register in anyone's mind. The writers of the Bible saw nothing wrong with slavery or with cruel punishments like blinding, stoning, and hacking someone to pieces. Human life held no value in comparison with unthinking obedience to custom and authority."[61]

I caught up with Pinker after a public lecture. When I mention my work on Psalm 137 he shoots me a wry look: "That's the verse that gets bowdlerized out of the Bible, isn't it?" Raised Jewish in Montreal, now an atheist, Pinker tells me that he always associated the vignette about the Judeans mourning beside the river not with the Psalms but with the Book of Lamentations.[62]

If you trace the evolution of world religions, Pinker explains, you find that religion is subject to the same humanizing forces as other areas of social life: "So religion itself is a kind of moving target." Even among observant Jews and Christians there is, fortunately, a good deal of hypocrisy; people pay lip service to the Bible but seldom take it as a literal guide to action. "How is it that the Bible has become a kind of talisman for people," he wonders, "rather than an actual guide to moral behavior?"

Which is more good news, in Pinker's view. Thanks to this process, "even the most hard-core fundamentalist Christian in the U.S. wouldn't publicly call for persecution of heretics." We see this moderating tendency in the world religions over the last couple of centuries. "The big question is"—another mischievous smile—"when is this going to happen with Islam?"

Pinker's book is rigorously framed, exhaustively documented, elegantly argued, apparently irrefutable. Still, it has to overcome the bloody burden of the twentieth century. Given the immense slaughter of the past century, how could it possibly be true that our better angels are winning out when it comes to violence? Perhaps in terms of casualties as proportion of the total world population—but can evil be quantified in quite so straightforward a manner?

Philosopher Emmanuel Levinas articulates the more widely held view that violence and the suffering it produces have spiraled beyond reckoning. He challenges the notion of theodicy: theories that explain evil in terms of some larger divine plan. "Perhaps the most revolutionary fact of our twentieth-century consciousness—but it is also an event in Sacred History—is that of the destruction of all balance between Western thought's explicit and implicit theodicy and the forms that suffering and its evil are taking on in the very unfolding of this century," he writes. After all, "This is the century that in thirty years has known two world wars, the totalitarianisms of right and left, Hitlerism and Stalinism, Hiroshima, the Gulag, and the genocides of Auschwitz and Cambodia."[63]

Pinker clearly puts no stock in theodicy. But he has evidence, reams of it, and sophisticated analytical models, and they are exhaustive. Counterintuitive though it seems, Pinker makes a convincing case that the horrors of the twentieth century are, in effect, the exceptions that prove the rule that human violence is declining. But big exceptions they are.

When it comes to measuring human violence, don't *absolute* numbers of deaths make a difference, even if in proportional terms they may not overwhelm earlier epochs of violence? And can the style of violence make a difference—the Holocaust's eerie melding of bureaucratic efficiency combined with the totalizing and deliberate humiliation imposed on a massive scale on its victims? Isn't there more to evil than death tolls and body counts?

What does any of this have to do with music, or with Psalm 137, for that matter? We wouldn't expect to find genocide and music in the same sentence, paragraph, or even the same section of the bookstore. But, to take that paradigmatic genocide, the Holocaust, music was all around, if one listened for it. Having written a book about big-band jazz, I know something about Nazi attempts to root out jazz as "Judeonegroid" cultural expression unworthy of Aryans, inimical to the Third Reich. Marjan Helms first brought to my attention the extraordinary range of musical activity being produced in the concentration camps.

Several books have been written about the concentration camp/ghetto in Terezin, Czechoslovakia (in German, Theresienstadt), where the Third Reich warehoused Jews who were too prominent or accomplished simply to deport to the death camps. A Czech musician named Jǒza Karas wrote an entire book about music in Terezin between 1941 and 1945, documenting the extraordinary labors of musicians, conductors, and composers who staged concerts, recitals, cabarets, operas, revues, and musical theater under the most nerve-wracking conditions between 1941 and 1945. The relatively optimistic mood of the camp's early days was reflected by a piece called "The Terezin March," one of more than fifty works known to have been composed there by residents:

> Hey! Tomorrow life starts over,
> And with it the time is approaching
> When we'll fold our knapsacks
> And return home again.
> Where there is a will, there is a way,
> Let us join hands
> And one day on the ruins of the ghetto
> We shall laugh.[64]

Prisoners at Terezin organized a jazz band, called the Ghetto Swingers. Though not an extermination camp, many Jews were murdered there and tens of thousands deported to the death camps further east. Less than one-sixth of the 154,000 who passed through Terezin survived.[65] The threat of selection for deportation and "the gas" hung constantly in the air; these selections were used as punishment by the SS for even minor offenses.

"Music was functional for the Nazis and permitted in service of Nazi goals: marching, departing, arriving, moving, staying or moving together," Ken Waltzer, a social historian who researches the Holocaust, told me. "But music was also a form of resistance, a means of sustaining or raising spirits, a way of sustaining humanity amidst the destruction of the human. Singing was also a form of sustaining spirits. Music should be thought of in the camps in this double-visioned way. Nazis also liked music. Music was played at annual Christmas observances. Nazis also attended performances by musicians. Crazy world." He mentioned Perec Brand, the former concertmaster of the Riga Symphony Orchestra, who while a prisoner at Buchenwald played violin in the children's block and in prisoner ensembles, along with command performances for Buchenwald's commandant, Herman Pfister.[66]

Staggering cultural contradictions played out daily in the camps. Terezin's inmates, for example, were ordered to perform Verdi's *Requiem* for their guards and camp officials. "No doubt the listeners enjoyed both the musical beauty of the event and the sadistic irony of having some of Europe's top Jewish musicians sing their own mass for the dead before they were sent to Auschwitz to be murdered," writes historian Doris Bergen. "There is no record of those privileged auditors objecting that the performers they heard were Jews and the composer of the work Italian. Anti-semites in the audience also managed to overlook the fact that the text of the 'Dies Irae,' the Day of Wrath, was largely derived from the Old Testament, in particular the Book of Daniel:

> Lo the book exactly worded,
> Wherein all hath been recorded,
> Thence shall judgment be awarded.

"One cannot know how the Germans present experienced the event," Bergen observes. "Did they observe with discomfort the degradation of their nation—the self-proclaimed 'people of music'—or feel reinvigorated by the excellence of the musical performance?"[67]

A French cabaret singer named Fania Goldstein (who later took the name Fénelon) wrote a bleak, harrowing memoir of her years in Auschwitz and Bergen-Belsen. She was a member of the young women's orchestra authorized by the SS to play both for inmates headed to their interminable work details and to the gas chambers and for private recitals for SS officers themselves, who at times served almost as patrons. "Our main function was to go to the Main Gate every morning and every evening and play marches for the thousands of prisoners who worked outside the camp, at places like I. G. Farben, inter alia," wrote Anita Lasker-Wallfisch, another member of the Auschwitz ensemble. "It was imperative that these columns of prisoners should march neatly and in step, and we provided the music to achieve this. We sat out there in all weathers, sometimes in subzero temperatures, scantily dressed, and we played. In this uniquely strategic position we witnessed all sorts of things (Figure 9)."[68]

"Regularly, they were compelled to work during the obligatory tattooing of new inmates, but often their job was even more gruesome than that," writes historian Michael Kater of these ensembles. "When men were carted by on lorries to be hanged, they had to play, as well as during the actual executions, or processions of entire phalanxes of emaciated inmates to the gas chambers. And they had friends who performed in idle gas chambers for SS men frolicking there with SS women, straight out of Dante's Hell."[69] Auschwitz even had a jazz combo, known as The Merry Five; so did Buchenwald.

Reading these accounts, it's difficult not to be reminded of the opening tableau of Psalm 137: exiles in a work camp remembering their lost lives, their hidden god, facing the taunts of their captors. The parallels could be uncanny. "In camps such as Auschwitz or Buchenwald," Kater writes, "Jews were permitted and sometimes ordered to perform 'Jewish' music as a sport for the SS." Imprisoned at Lemburg concentration camp, Wiesenthal recalled, "In the early mornings, when the prisoners left the camp to go to work, the band played them out, the SS insisting that we march in time to the music. When we passed the gate we began to sing."[70]

Non-Jewish Poles, Czechs, Hungarians, and others frequently served as camp kapos, accomplices to the German Nazis, analogous to the Edomites of Psalm 137, who assisted the Babylonians in the destruction of Jerusalem. Sometimes the SS recruited Russian deserters or

FIGURE 9 Gate at Auschwitz concentration camp, Poland. © Ventura (Shutterstock).

prisoners, whom they called *askari*, to assist in the camps. Wiesenthal writes:

Strangely enough the askaris were extremely keen on singing: music in general played an important part in camp life. There was even a band. Its members included some of the best musicians in and around Lemberg. Richard Rokita, the SS lieutenant who had been a violinist in a Silesian café, was mad about "his" band. This man, who daily slaughtered prisoners from sheer lust for killing, had at the same time only one ambition—to lead a band. He arranged special accommodation for his musicians and pampered them in other ways, but they were never allowed out of camp. In the evenings they played works of Bach and Wagner and Grieg. One day Rokita brought along a songwriter called Zygmunt Schlechter and ordered him to compose a "death tango." And whenever the band played this tune, the sadistic monster Rokita had wet eyes.[71]

Very rarely, music appears in survivors' memoirs as something other than coerced. Leon Szalet, who survived eight months in Sachsenhausen before being released, recalled spending the Day of Atonement in the concentration camp. His account is worth quoting at length.

Pain and the fear . . . kept us awake. A cloudless sky, thickly set with glittering stars, looked in upon our grief-filled prison. The moon shone through the window. Its light was dazzling that night and gave the pale, wasted faces of the prisoners a ghostly appearance. It was as if all the life had ebbed out of them. I shuddered with dread, for it suddenly occurred to me that I was the only living man among corpses.

All at once the oppressive silence was broken by a mournful tune. It was the plaintive tone of the ancient "Kol Nidre" prayer. I raised myself up to see whence it came. There, close to the wall, the moonlight caught the uplifted face of an old man, who, in self-forgetful, pious absorption, was singing softly to himself the sorrowful melody with the familiar, deeply moving words. . . .

The man who prayed was an orthodox believer whom we revered for his unfailing piety. The manner in which he accepted the misfortunes that had fallen upon us won our astonished admiration . . . . It was not strange, then, that by reciting aloud the "Kol Nidre" prayer he instantly recalled us to the mournful, devout mood that belongs to the Day of Atonement. His prayer brought the ghostly group of seemingly insensible human beings back to life. Little by little, they all roused themselves and all eyes were fixed on the moonlight-flooded face.

We sat up very quietly, so as not to disturb the old man, and he did not notice that we were listening. As if transported into another world, he chanted the prayer to the end, so softly that the words were scarcely distinguishable to those who did not know them by heart. His old, quavering voice held us in a spell. When at last he was silent, there was exaltation among us, an exaltation which men can experience only when they have fallen as low as we had fallen and then, through the mystic power of a deathless prayer, have awakened once more to the world of the spirit.[72]

All the themes of Psalm 137—the coerced performance, the challenge to remember Jerusalem, the question of how (whether) to sing in a strange land, the struggle of memory against forgetting, the contest between justice and the visceral hunger for vengeance—all played out in the concentration camps. These experiences lodged in the memories of the infinitesimal remnant who survived the camps and found the courage to write or speak about their ordeals.

Homecoming after forced migration evokes a complicated set of emotions. Abraham Cohen urges us to think of the psalmist of 137 "as an exile recently back from Babylon, viewing with horror the havoc wrought in the city he dearly loved." He offers a modern analogy: "Refugees from Europe, when they returned and saw how their native cities had been turned into masses of rubble by the Germans, surely shared this mood."[73]

Not surprisingly, a desire for revenge could help galvanize the will to survive. Interviewed for the documentary *Hell on Earth*, for example, a Czechoslovakian Jew named Jan Salus recounted an emotion straight out of Psalm 137: "The way I survived such horrible circumstances was by harboring an utterly insane hatred and a desire for vengeance. I was imagining I would survive and one day I would get into some little German town and when I would see a mother with a baby in her stroller I would go to her, take the child by its leg [pause] . . . and smash the child's head on the sidewalk."[74]

After liberation, Salus was hospitalized, likely for the typhus that was endemic to the camps; he describes a more playful form of revenge. "When the diarrhea cramps began, I peacefully defecated in the bed," he recalled. "I yelled at the German woman, 'Mrs. Schmidt, I shit in my bed!' And she came, picked up the dirty sheets and clothes, washed my Jewish bottom, oiled it nicely and powdered it. I rolled another cigarette, lit it up, smoked it in bed, and waited almost impatiently for the next cramp so I could scream again, 'Mrs. Schmidt, I shit in my bed!' "[75]

This form of expiation turned out to be adequate, according to Salus. "I felt no hatred anymore," he said. "I got rid of it through my diarrhea."

Given the pervasive concentration camp use by Nazis of what Terrence Des Pres has labeled "excremental assault"—allowing their victims to wallow in their own waste in order to attempt to break down any remaining sense of dignity and self-worth before actually murdering them—it seems fitting that Salus achieved some measure of justice in this way.[76]

As survivors' testimonies make clear, memory was the only resource European Jews had by which to imagine some small measure of cosmic justice against the Nazis and others who terrorized them. This was especially the case when the SS specifically taunted their victims with the prediction that this history would be erased—that no one would believe what had actually happened in the camps. Fénelon said she began her book exactly thirty years to the day after Bergen-Belsen was liberated in April 1945. "After thirty years of silence during which I tried to forget the unforgettable, I saw that it was impossible," she said. "What I had to do was exorcise the orchestra"—membership in which she admits kept her alive in conditions of unimaginable hardship for more than a year.[77]

However much music was made, against all odds, by Jewish musicians inside the death camps, we should remember the obverse. What vast numbers of works of music—and literature, and art, scholarship, science, any manner of other cultural productions—simply *did not come into existence*, because its creators were killed or otherwise silenced by the Nazis and their allies.

Sepulchers of Memory

In 2010, the BBC aired a new opera, *The Wandering Jew*, by British composer Robert Saxton.[78] The work traces the peregrinations of the "wandering Jew" of medieval legend who, as punishment for mocking Jesus on his way to Golgotha and the crucifixion, is condemned to wander the earth until Judgment Day. The opera unfolds in eight scenes scattered across time and space: Jerusalem after the destruction of the Second Temple in 70 c.e., a synagogue in eleventh-century Cordoba, sixteenth-century Leipzig, eighteenth-century Venice. Along the way, the Wandering Jew meets and interacts with a variety of characters, ordinary and mythological: Roman soldiers, beggars, carnival revelers, a young widow, Faust, Mephistopheles, the Norse god Odin. And Jesus.

A Nazi death camp is where *The Wandering Jew* begins and ends. The narrator intones:

> After nearly two thousand years of wandering, here, now, in this
>   camp of death, I see total destruction.
> The innocent about to die.
> In my undying state, I cannot help them, but can only witness . . .

The first vocal music heard in the opera is the chorus of prisoners singing, in angular melody, the opening verses of Psalm 137:

> By the rivers, by the rivers of Babylon
> We sat down and we wept when we remembered Sion
> We hung our harps upon the willows in the midst thereof.
> How shall we sing the Lord's song in a strange land?

We hear a guard berating an old, weakened prisoner, then dragging a protesting inmate to her death. The prisoners again sing the psalm's opening verses, then:

> Five thousand years of belief,
> The Light will shine forth.
> The Covenant, illumined by faith, in this dark time.
> Our spirits will live on down the ages.
> Lord, into your hands we commend our spirits.

The Wandering Jew, as narrator, comments, "I could not save them, as I could not two thousand years ago, when the Temple burned in Jerusalem."

The opera's penultimate scene returns to the death camp, now denuded of all living beings; the prisoners persist as a chorus of spirits. With one exception: the Wandering Jew recognizes a beggar he befriended in an earlier scene, bringing him bread and wine; he turns out to be Jesus. The two, Jesus and the Wandering Jew, achieve a sort of reconciliation. The beggar/Jesus sings:

> We are one, You and I, through all eternity.
> You are my brother, friend, my witness on earth.
> We stand here, amongst the victims of Eden's Sin

Warmed by Sarah and Abram's journey,
Jacob's dream, the Red Sea crossed.
Moses Sinai,
My pain is your pain.

The Wandering Jew's CD cover features a famous painting by Marc Chagall, *White Crucifixion*, said to be the favorite painting of Pope Francis. The work was completed in 1938, in response to the Nazi campaign of terror against Jews that culminated in Kristallnacht, when Nazis smashed Jewish businesses and synagogues across Germany on November 9–10. *White Crucifixion* depicts a very Jewish Jesus on the cross: he wears a prayer shawl as loincloth and a head covering rather than a crown of thorns. Instead of angels, he is surrounded by biblical patriarchs in Jewish garb. Around the cross are scenes of fiery pogroms: a mob brandishing weapons, a village in flames, a pillaged synagogue and Torah Ark. Refugees flee on foot and by boat, while a mother comforts a child. A mysterious figure dressed in a green robe and carrying a bundle crosses the painting, perhaps suggesting Elijah, perhaps a wandering Jew.[79]

White Crucifixion was a perfect choice for Saxton's opera. Both artists were Jewish, and both were interested in using Jesus as an icon, or interlocutor, to meditate on the often-traumatic history of Judaism. "Throughout his career," writes Aaron Rosen, "the figure of Jesus oscillates in Chagall's imagination between, in his words, 'the true type of the Jewish martyr' and, as he asserts elsewhere, the 'great poet whose poetical teaching had been forgotten by the modern world.' In the 1930s and 1940s, as the events of the Shoah unfolded, it was the agony of the Crucifixion which compelled Chagall above all else." He said:

> For me, Christ has always symbolized the true type of the Jewish martyr. That is how I understood him in 1908 when I used this figure for the first time . . . . It was under the influence of the pogroms. Then I painted and drew him in pictures about ghettos, surrounded by Jewish troubles, by Jewish mothers, running terrified with little children in their arms.

In addition to their timely political message, these paintings allowed the artist to "grapple with his place within the Western canon, painting himself into dialogue with all the great artists who have treated the theme in the past, from Grünewald to Picasso."[80]

Only once did Chagall portray the Babylonian Exile, but where he did so is significant.

In the 1960s Chagall was commissioned to create art for the State Hall of the Knesset in Tel Aviv. Chagall produced four colorful wall tapestries exploring themes of Jewish diaspora, along with floor mosaics. He also created one large wall mosaic depicting a stylized imagining of Psalm 137 (see Fig. 10). Like most modern visual renderings of the psalm, Chagall's is far from literal; a casual viewer would have difficulty recognizing the details of the psalm amid the visual substitutions and displacements. The

FIGURE 10 Marc Chagall mosaic for the State Hall of the Knesset, Tel Aviv. © 2015 Artists Rights Society (ARS), New York/ADAGP, Paris.

mosaic is dominated by a large lighted menorah at its center, above which appears an angel. Psalm scholar Susan Gillingham describes the mosaic:

> The setting here is of prayers at the Western Wall (still under Jordanian control at the time of completion in 1966), with the Old City and Tower of David in the background. In the centre of the muted blues and greens a lighted Menorah hangs in space, a modern symbol of the harps which once hung unused on the trees, but the gold flames evoke light and hope. Above the golden light is an angel with a Shofar, calling the people below to return to Zion: this echoes the tradition about the angels who curse Edom and Babylon on behalf of Israel in the Targum and *Midrash Tehillim*. There are further hints of Messianic hope in the star of David, set in the heavens to bring the people home.[81]

In Part 2, I referred to Psalm 137 as a biblical memory-project. For Paul Ricœur, the quest for justice serves as memory's highest imperative. "Extracting the exemplary value from traumatic memories, it is justice that turns memory into a project," he writes, with victims of the Holocaust very much in mind; "and it is this same project of justice that gives the form of the future and of the imperative to the duty of memory."[82] An *act of sepulcher*: this is what Ricœur names the transformation of memory into written history.

> Sepulcher, indeed, is not only a place set apart in our cities, the place we call a cemetery and in which we depose the remains of the living who return to dust. It is an act, the act of burying. This gesture is not punctual; it is not limited to the moment of burial. The sepulcher remains because the gesture of burying remains; its path is the very path of mourning that transforms the physical absence of the lost object into an inner presence. The sepulcher as the material place thus becomes the enduring mark of mourning, the memory-aid of the act of sepulcher.[83]

It is one mark of the age in which we live that the memory-project of responding to mass atrocity has produced numerous sepulchers since the discovery of the Nazi death camps in 1945. The Nuremberg trials and Tokyo War Crimes Tribunal came first, immediately following World War II. In recent decades, countries as diverse as East Timor, Rwanda, the Czech Republic, Chile, Argentina, Poland, El Salvador, and the former East

Germany and Yugoslavia have witnessed a variety of collective national responses to mass atrocities: truth and reconciliation commissions, war crimes trials, collective apologies, reparations policies, and amnesty programs.

Often these initiatives have taken on a religious aura, a sometimes uneasy blending of church and state. This has something to do with the sort of individuals recruited to contribute to the project of memory. "In countries like South Africa, Sierra Leone, and Northern Ireland, religious leaders and organizations have been related to state-sponsored truth commissions and faith-based diplomacy, and ideals and practices of forgiveness, reconciliation and commemoration have become part of current political discourse and practice," write two scholars who have analyzed the phenomenon. "On the basis of his influence in the South African truth commission, Archbishop Emeritus Desmond Tutu has become a global icon of the potential of religious leaders and religious language and values in relation to societal endeavors to civilize the barbarous space that exists after atrocity."[84]

More than simply a matter of who has served on these commissions, there is a striking affinity between mass atrocity and religious language. Survivors often choose words with religious connotations—sacred, martyr, living hell, pure evil, the demonic—to describe their experiences. Jennifer Geddes writes of the "double-bind" that characterizes attempts to describe atrocities like the Holocaust: "that it is *necessary* to speak about what happened, but *impossible* to do so adequately."[85] She locates this idea in the writings of notable Holocaust survivors Primo Levi, Elie Wiesel, and philosopher Sarah Kofman, a French Jew, who poses the question this way:

> How is it possible to speak when you feel a "frenzied desire" to perform an impossible task—to convey the experience just as it was, to explain everything to the other, when you are seized by a veritable delirium of words—and yet, at the same time, it is impossible for you to speak. Impossible, without *choking* . . . a strange *double bind*: an infinite claim to speak, *a duty to speak infinitely*, imposing itself with irresistible force, and at the same time, an almost physical impossibility to speak, a *choking* feeling.[86]

A similar sense of double-bind holds true for descriptions of religious experience. People who have such encounters sense that language is inadequate to capture the core experience, that words can only provide gestures or metaphors for truths that lie outside the realm of ordinary communication. Music and art are two types of response that allow one to sidestep the limitations of verbal language.

The pioneering scholar of religion Rudolph Otto proposed the term *numinous* to describe such experiences, which he thought grounded all religions, captured in the Latin phrase *mysterium tremendum et fascinans*— the human encounter with the wholly other, transcendent, beyond comprehension; typically generating responses of terror, dread, and awe, but a kind of magnetic fascination as well.[87] Many of us recognize these emotions in the uncanny fascination we may feel about the most horrific forms of human violence and cruelty.

This sacralization of state-sponsored remembrance has not come without criticism. The very ability of religious language to articulate the inexpressible carries its own dangers. With its engrained impulse toward the seeking of redemption, religious language can potentially "contain, tame, and frame the atrocity" in ways that interfere with the pursuit of justice." God talk lends itself to "simple theodicies that explain the atrocity in terms of a greater good; comforting clichés; calls for forgiving and forgetting and moving on," Geddes writes. "Redemptive religious language can be used to cover over in vaguely evocative language that which requires accurate reporting, the full force of justice, and the persistence of anger." Alternately, speaking of perpetrators as monsters or demons—essentially dehumanizing them—removes them from a category that can be held morally responsible for their actions. And by regarding victims as martyrs, we imply that they chose their fate, that their deaths may have had a higher moral purpose.[88]

The necessity for forgiveness, highlighted by Archbishop Tutu during the Truth and Reconciliation Commission, raises particular concerns. One line of argument charges that the emphasis on forgiveness places a burden on victims who may be unable or unwilling to forgive. These victims are in a sense being punished twice: once by the original atrocity, a second time by expectation that they will grant forgiveness that they are unable or unwilling to offer.

Cynthia Ozick has written, "Forgiveness is pitiless. It forgets the victim. It negates the right of the victim to his own life. It blurs over suffering and death. It drowns the past. It cultivates sensitiveness toward the murderer at the price of insensitiveness toward the victim . . . . It is forgiveness that is relentless. The face of forgiveness is mild, but how stony to the slaughtered." In place of forgiveness, Ozick advocates vengeance, but not in the form of eye-for-an-eye retaliation: "What we call 'vengeance' is the act of bringing public justice to evil—not by repeating the evil, not by imitating the evil, not by initiating a new evil, but by making certain never to condone the old one; never even appearing to condone it."[89]

Ozick's comments come in an essay she wrote for Book Two of *The Sunflower: On the Possibilities and Limits of Forgiveness*, a book by celebrated Nazi-hunter Simon Wiesenthal that collects dozens of responses to an experience Wiesenthal had as a young man imprisoned in a Lemberg concentration camp in 1943. The book's focal point, emblazoned on the cover, is this question: "You are a prisoner in a concentration camp. A dying Nazi soldier asks for your forgiveness. What would you do?"

The responses, gathered from leading writers, theologians, activists, and genocide survivors, span the gamut. Self-identified Christians are more sympathetic to granting forgiveness than Jews, Buddhists even more than Christians. Expressing the view of many, Abraham Joshua Heschel writes, "No one can forgive crimes committed against other people. It is therefore preposterous to assume that anybody alive can extend forgiveness for the suffering of any one of the six million people who perished." He adds, "According to Jewish tradition, even God Himself can only forgive sins committed against Himself, not against man."[90]

Desmond Tutu writes, "It is clear that if we look only to retributive justice, then we could just as well close up shop. Forgiveness is not some nebulous thing. It is practical politics. Without forgiveness, there is no future." The Dalai Lama concurred: "I believe one should forgive the person or persons who have committed atrocities against oneself and mankind. But this does not necessarily mean one should forget about the atrocities committed."[91] (Not a particularly cogent point, as none of the book's fifty-three respondents even come close to advocating forgetting the crimes of the Holocaust.)

Thomas Brudholm has further elaborated the ways in which forgiveness in the wake of mass atrocity—or better, the expectation that victims will forgive—is problematic. That expectation can foreclose the middle ground between vengeance and forgiveness, such as punitive justice; hurries victims prematurely past their anger and resentment; unfairly judges those incapable or unwilling to forgive; oversimplifies the very complex question of who has the right to forgive whom. Valorizing forgiveness may even project an expectation of Christian belief about forgiveness on victims from other faiths or those of no faith at all.[92]

These tensions played out in real time during the decade after World War II ended, with the Nuremberg and Tokyo trials, and when the recently created State of Israel struggled with the question of whether to accept reparations from West Germany. Many in Israel considered that remuneration from West Germany would amount to blood money. A young Menachem Begin, who three decades later would found the right-wing Likud Party, be elected prime minister, and inaugurate an increasingly aggressive military posture in the region, was haranguing a large crowd against accepting reparations. Begin assailed Germans as murderous Nazis, excoriating his fellow Israelis for their willingness to make deals with the nation that a few years earlier had exterminated millions of Jews. He then invoked some familiar lines from the Bible. Ta-Nehisi Coates reconstructs the scene outside the Knesset in 1952, where the parliament was debating whether to negotiate an agreement, when Begin invoked familiar lines from the Bible:

> Begin then led the crowd in an oath to never forget the victims of the Shoah, lest "my right hand lose its cunning" and "my tongue cleave to the roof of my mouth." He took the crowd through the streets toward the Knesset. From the rooftops, police repelled the crowd with tear gas and smoke bombs. But the wind shifted, and the gas blew back toward the Knesset, billowing through windows shattered by rocks. In the chaos, Begin and Prime Minister David-Ben-Gurion exchanged insults. Two hundred civilians and 140 police officers were wounded. Nearly 400 people were arrested. Knesset business was halted.[93]

The violence and threats of terror by Israeli extremists continued, but the argument for reparations won out. Israel received 3.45 billion Deutsche Marks, worth more than $7 billion in today's dollars, which provided a major share of its merchant fleet, electrical system, and railways.[94]

Theologies of Vengeance

For their part, Christians have always struggled with the Gospel's unequivocal injunction to forgive.

Writing just after the end of World War II, as the Allies prepared to impose retribution on their vanquished foes, Reinhold Niebuhr meditated on the relation between anger, justice, vengeance, hatred, and memory. "One of the tragic aspects of human history is the fact that the vanquished have longer memories than the victors," he wrote. "The victors could profitably have longer memories and the vanquished shorter ones." He repeatedly invoked the words of Ephesians 4: "Be ye angry, and sin not: *Let not the sun go down upon your wrath*: Neither give place to the devil." And from Romans 12: "Dearly beloved, avenge not yourselves, but rather give place unto wrath: for it is written, Vengeance is mine; I will repay saith the Lord."[95]

Niebuhr's biblically grounded proscriptions have been found in need of elaboration, both inside and outside the church. British theologian Robert Beckford advocates a theology of "redemptive vengeance" for situations in which straightforward forgiving and forgetting seems an abdication of justice. Reflecting on his experience of rage as an African-Caribbean Christian in Britain, and drawing on the work of South African theologian Willa Boesak, Beckford distinguishes his strategy from both *punitive vengeance* and *corrective vengeance*. Punitive vengeance focuses on retribution and retaliation; it is expressed clearly in the final three verses of Psalm 137. Corrective vengeance uses force to correct injustice, typically seeking compensation in the form of reparations.[96]

Beckford's alternative to these forms of vengeance, which ultimately fail to bring about social transformation on the part of the oppressor, is what he calls *redemptive vengeance*. At the heart of redemptive vengeance is repentance, which Beckford defines as a return to the source of all being, God. "Repentance makes space for the transformation of the victim's circumstances," he writes; "it provides the creative space for the repentance of the victimiser. Only through the creation of a new space as a result of repentance will the cycle of revenge, bitterness and violence cease."[97]

This process of grounded repentance offers manifest benefits to the psychological health of individuals as well as communities. It opens the way to forgiveness, which pointedly does not mean dropping the call for justice in the form of reparations and other compensation. Only redemptive vengeance grounded in repentance and forgiveness can create the space for genuine social transformation, reconciliation, and that rarest human good, love.[98]

Croatian-born Miroslav Volf has probed the tensions among memory, forgiveness, and justice with exceptional passion and brilliance. Given that the imperative to remember wrongdoing, and remember it forever, has become the conventional wisdom since the horrors of the twentieth century, how should we remember? What are the potential disadvantages and limitations of memory? Are there situations where memory should be time-limited?

For Volf, memory is inherently double-edged. "Memories of wrongs," he observes, "can serve to restore health and dignity, protect, and prompt the pursuit of justice. At the same time, such memories can also lead people to abase their humanity by nursing resentments and committing misdeeds. Though today many people rightly take the medicine of remembering wrongs against turmoil of the soul and violence in society, such 'medicinal' memories often poison their patients with the very diseases they are meant to cure. Medicine and poison—memories of wrongs seem to be both."[99]

"One of the key elements of rightly remembering, in my judgment, is to honor the feeling that one had when one was violated," he told me, "but at the same time to be concerned for the truthfulness in accounting for what has happened. Because I have come to believe that every untruthful memory, when it comes to a violation, is an unjust memory."[100]

Volf readily concedes that without memory we would not be functional human beings, let alone unique individuals with consciousness and a sense of self. And memory is indispensable to achieving justice. Given all that, though, he believes that memory is to some degree a matter of choice, and that we are required to make subtle distinctions regarding the exercise of memory. "Given how central memory is to human identity," he writes, "the question cannot be whether we *should* remember our past or forget it. The interesting questions are rather: *what* should we remember? *How* should we go about remembering? Should wrongs be remembered *eternally*? My argument is not that memory is bad and amnesia good, or that forgetters have a comparative advantage over rememberers, but rather that *under certain conditions the absence of the memory of wrongs suffered is desirable*."[101]

He realizes that, at this point in history, he is arguing against the grain. To explain those conditions in which the absence of memory is ethically defensible, Volf constructs a genealogy of "defenders of forgetting" that includes both Christians (Dante, Gregory of Nyssa, Martin Luther) and non-Christians (Freud, Nietzsche). It turns out that until the epic atrocities of the twentieth century that continue to weigh on us, and the popular embrace of poets of eternal remembering like Elie Wiesel, thoughtful people of a variety of religious and nonreligious persuasions were quite accepting of the necessity to forget. For Volf, as for the Christian thinkers he draws on, the "certain conditions" that justify the forgetting of wrongs suffered require belief in the redeeming Christ who, for believers, accepts and forgives human sin and renders judgment in the fullness of time.

Writing from an unapologetically Christian perspective, Volf repeatedly emphasizes that neither forgiving nor forgetting were invented by Christianity: "Christians learned it from the Hebrew Bible—the Old Testament—where it is even better attested than in the New Testament." He continues: "In the early Jewish traditions complete forgiveness involves 'forgetting.' As to the Christian tradition, so far as I can tell, the classic writers, academic theologians, popular preachers, and lay folk all thought so too—until recently."[102]

This is the problem Ricœur engages in the sweeping, fifty-page epilogue to *Memory, History, Forgetting*, which he titles "Difficult Forgiveness." Under what conditions is forgiveness possible? What role do memory and forgetting play in forgiveness? Can forgetting ever be justified in the realm of law and politics? Or, as Ricœur asks, "Is a sensible politics possible without something like a censure of memory?" He finds a satisfactory answer elusive:

> Our uneasiness concerning the right attitude to take with regard to the uses and abuses of forgetting, mainly in the practice of institutions, is finally the symptom of a stubborn uncertainty affecting the relation between forgetting and forgiveness on the level of its deep structure. The question returns with insistence: if it is possible to speak of happy memory, does there exist something like a happy forgetting?[103]

The closest he comes to an affirmative answer is a nod to Kierkegaard's praise of forgetting as *liberation from care*, captured in Jesus' exhortation to "consider the lilies of the field and the birds of the air," which neither toil, nor spin, nor sow, nor reap.[104]

Though Volf doesn't take up Psalm 137 explicitly in his published writings, I asked him about it in his office at the Yale Center for Faith and Culture, which he founded and still directs. He leads a peripatetic life, but when I've seen him, Volf has been wearing blue jeans and a sweater. He smiles frequently and charmingly.

"I read the psalm as a kind of liturgically channeled cry for justice," he tells me. "Not an unreflective scream of pain against injustice, but rather a cry after a step back has been taken. A step-removed cry, but nonetheless with full presence, complaint about injustice." He explains, "In a sense it's an implicit prayer. A search for justice, before God, is also an implicit prayer for making sure that my own articulation of injustice that has happened *to me* is just toward the one *against whom* I press the claims of justice. I find the psalm important as an expression of what one feels, as a hope of redress, but also a purification—implicit search for purification of my own remembering and longing."[105]

Volf has little patience with theologies that enshrine a nonviolent, even nonjudgmental God. "I've always felt it's something really troublingly suburban: the idea that because we should be nonviolent, God is nonviolent. That kind of connection wasn't there for the early Anabaptists, wasn't there for the early church, wasn't there all the way until relatively recently, actually." The social peace that we mostly take for granted in nations like the United States wasn't there, either. Because we assume that public order will be maintained and justice served by police "who take care that things don't rock," citizens of most liberal democracies haven't experienced the deep insecurity that characterizes the exiles of Psalm 137—or Croatia in 1995 or Syria in 2015.

"Most of us haven't seen the kind of existential upheaval that the Psalm presupposes. Inhabiting a world of violence, so that you don't know whether the violent yesterday is going to be repeated again tomorrow, shapes the soul. Perhaps it comes close to us when a bomb goes off during the Boston Marathon? But even then you have nine thousand policemen searching for one guy! Imagine how uncertainty rocks the whole fabric of society when there are no nine thousand policemen. There are no police. There is only you and the enemy: overbearing, overpowerful." Like Judah in the shadow of Babylon. "And you'll have a theology that's not quite as sanitized as suburban theologies tend to be."

Volf remembers the psalm taking on vivid meaning for him during the mid-1990s, when the former Yugoslavia was at war, riven with forced migration, ethnic cleansing, and genocide. He tells me about a sermon from those years, "probably the most powerful sermon I've ever preached."

I ask him to describe the service.

"Sunday morning service, I don't know what year," he begins. "It was in Osijek, that's a town in North Croatia on the river Drava. Serbian forces at that time were about five kilometers to the east, and also immediately across the river to the north. The city was almost completely surrounded. I think about a third of its population then were refugees. The building in which I preached used to be a Jewish synagogue that had been sold to a Pentecostal church by a Jewish community. When it was restored, its vaulted ceiling was painted like a dark blue sky with the stars of Abraham. I knew that the church would be also maybe a third filled with refugees who belonged to the small Pentecostal church up north and had been driven out.

"What I recall is that when I read the psalm, a totally hushed silence descended upon the congregation. I've never heard a text from scripture speak so powerfully. Not simply to the people, but from the people, as if it was inscribed in their faces. In the sermon I was simply narrating the background of the psalm. They were in the Psalm: *This* (their experiences) *was that* (Psalmist's experience). People were sitting on the edges of their seats. Somebody—no God—was in God's holy word singing their pain!

"And then obviously the question: What do we do as Christians? Who ought not to be enraged and full of lust for vengeance, but yet we are. And so it's not just that somebody has articulated it here, but what do I who am supposed to love my enemies do with this, how do I tie it to Jesus' journey to the Cross? For me—as for my teacher, Moltmann—the connection was the cry of dereliction: 'My God, my God, why has thou forsaken me?' as a complaint—a despairing complaint before God, and yet, in the presence of the one to whom it was directed, also always containing at least a whiff of the hope of 'resurrection.'"

Volf refers me to a passage in his book, *Exclusion and Embrace*, where the ideas behind his sermon in Osijek ended up (or vice versa). "In the imprecatory Psalms," he writes, "torrents of rage have been allowed to flow freely, channeled only by the robust structure of a ritual prayer. Strangely enough, they may point to a way out of slavery to revenge and into the freedom of forgiveness." Christians should read Psalm 137 as a reminder that

> rage belongs before God—not in the reflectively managed and man-icured form of a confession, but as a pre-reflective outburst from the depths of the soul. This is no mere cathartic discharge of pent up aggression before the Almighty who ought to care. Much more significantly, by placing unattended rage before God we place both our unjust enemy and our own vengeful self face to face with a God who loves and does justice. Hidden in the dark chambers of our hearts and nourished by the system of darkness, hate grows and seeks to infest everything with its hellish will to exclusion. In the light of the justice and love of God, however, hate recedes and the seed is planted for the miracle of forgiveness.[106]

I ask Volf about the final verses, so often expunged from the psalm.

"Well, that goes to the stone of offense in the psalm. What I have tried to say in *Exclusion and Embrace,* but also in that sermon, was whatever judgments we make about liturgy and structure of liturgy—and I think liturgies have their own permanent and very slowly changing forms—they have also their kind of pulsating heart and can be adjusted and adopted to the particularities of the situation. And whatever we do with the presence of those last verses, in particular, in the liturgy, I think it belongs to the prayer before God: articulated in private, but articulated also in public.

"And my argument would be that's exactly where the rage belongs. If it's framed properly liturgically, that's where I would want to have it. Because I think that's the only place where the rage may be safe. It's not safe simply bottled up in my own heart. It's not safe in some public space of venting our collective feelings. I think it is safe in the space where it is placed before the one God of *both* those whose children have been dashed against the rocks *and* of those who did the dashing of those children against the rocks. I think that's where rage is most safe, if it's safe anywhere at all."

After Exile

Returning once more to the Hebrew Bible: Was any vengeance of the sort envisaged in the three final verses actually perpetrated? Were any little ones dashed against stones? For that matter, was any forgiveness granted?

We might begin by noting that, however harsh conditions of forced migration and labor may have been under Nebuchadnezzar, the Babylonians and Edomites do not stand accused of crimes like genocide or the killing of innocent children (though of course these atrocities may have occurred).

As for the end of the Babylonian empire, the Bible tells us almost nothing. Judging from the sources, it appears that Babylon was taken by the Persians with virtually no conflict. The Book of Daniel, the only biblical account to give us a putative view inside Babylonia's royal court (but actually written centuries afterward), gives a historically garbled account of what other sources tell us about the major actors and chronology. Daniel refers to Belshazzar as king, for example, when that Babylonian actually ruled as vice regent while his father Nabonidus was out of country. The book indicates that Darius took power after slaying Belshazzar when in fact Darius followed Cyrus and ruled after 522 B.C.E. Then ensues a long gap in the record, before the end of exile is recounted in the Bible.

Chronicles II ends with the very same passage with which the Book of Ezra begins:

> Now in the first year of Cyrus king of Persia, so that the word of the LORD spoken through Jeremiah might be fulfilled, the LORD stirred up the heart of Cyrus king of Persia; and he issued a proclamation throughout his kingdom, both by word of mouth and in writing to this effect:
>
> This is the word of Cyrus king of Persia: The LORD the God of heaven has given me all the kingdoms of the earth, and he himself has charged me to build him a house at Jerusalem in Judah. To every man of his people now among you I say, God be with him, and let him go up to Jerusalem in Judah, and rebuild the house of the LORD the God of Israel, the God whose city is Jerusalem. And every remaining Jew, wherever he may be living may claim aid from his neighbours in that place, silver and gold, goods and cattle, in addition to the voluntary offerings for the house of God in Jerusalem. (Ezra 1:1–4)

Nowhere is there any indication of violent retribution visited on Babylonians or Edomites. What is conveyed is the purposeful euphoria of a return from exile, an expansive sense of restorative justice enacted. Israel will take up where it left off.

Surprisingly few have commented on the fact that there is only one population that suffers retribution as a result of the Babylonian conquest and destruction of the Temple. The overthrow of Babylon by Cyrus and the Persians seems to have been remarkably bloodless.[107] The only group that materially suffered were the foreign wives of the Judean captives and their children. And they suffered at the hands of—fellow Judeans!

The Book of Ezra, which narrates the return of the exiles to Jerusalem, ends with two chapters fixated on the problem of exiles' intermarriage with foreign women and their "abominable practices." Even priests and Levites were guilty of such practices, polluting the "holy race" of Israel. Ezra sits dumfounded after rending his robe and tearing his hair and beard. He offers a prayer of self-abnegation to Yahweh, who is quoted here urging exactly the opposite of Jeremiah's advice to the exiles, to assimilate cheerfully into the people that captured them. Yahweh urges, "Therefore, do not give your daughters and marriage to their sons and do not marry your sons to their daughters, and never seek their welfare or prosperity" (8:12).

As Ezra prays, "a very great crowd of Israelites assembled round him, men, women, and children, and they all wept bitterly." A large crowd gathers around the praying prophet, and a man named Shecaniah speaks up: "We have committed an offence against our God in marrying foreign wives, daughters of the foreign population. But in spite of this, there is still hope for Israel. Now, therefore, let us pledge ourselves to our God to dismiss all these women and their brood, according to your advice, my lord, and the advice of those who go in fear of the command of our God; and let us act as the law prescribes" (10:1–3).

Ezra demands an oath of loyalty from all Israelites, and issues a proclamation: all the exiles should assemble in Jerusalem within three days or face exclusion from the community; they sit shivering in a heavy rain. Rather than resolve the issue in the downpour, the assembly decides to authorize a "formal inquiry" into intermarriage, conducted by "leading men" in all the cities, with appropriate action to follow. Chapter Ten lists by name more than a hundred offenders, including priests and Levites. The Book of Ezra ends with these words: "All these had married foreign women, and they dismissed them, together with their children."

The Hebrew Bible is quite insistent on this point. The book that follows Ezra, Nehemiah, also ends with a blast against out-marrying Judeans. "I argued with them and reviled them," the prophet reports, "I beat them and tore out their hair; and I made them swear in the name of God: 'We will not marry our daughters to their sons, or take any of their daughters in marriage for our sons or for ourselves.'" Nehemiah follows this with an intriguing historical footnote: "'Was it not for such women,' I said, 'that King Solomon of Israel sinned?'" (13:23–26).

Nothing is known of the fate of these discarded women and children. To be sure, there is precedent for this concern with preserving racial purity contained in the Mosaic law, and corroborating passages can be identified in Leviticus and Deuteronomy. Nevertheless, the irony is plain; those who bear the brunt of Judah's retaliation are neither Babylonians or Edomites, nor even Babylonian babies; they are women and children who happened to marry Judeans. In his interpretation of the episode, Rob Becking concludes that the outcast women may actually have been Judeans who were demonized and scapegoated—victims of a kind of witch-hunt within the Yahwistic community rather than members of a different ethnicity. But like virtually all scholarship about the Exile and return, this is highly speculative.[108]

Ezra's account of the postexilic restoration aligns well with Regina Schwartz's argument that the religion of Yahweh, operating within an economy of scarcity, produces exclusion and violence. "Monotheism, then," she writes, "is not simply a myth of one-ness, but a doctrine of possession, of a people by God, of a land by a people of women by men. The drive to own property issues in the deep homology between possessing a woman's body and possessing land. Both are conquerable territory, it would seem, connected not only by the familiar fertility imagery of plowing and planting but also by the property images of boundaries and borders."[109]

As property, both women and land must remain pure, kept free from pollution and defilement. That requires monogamy of women, and absolute devotion to Yahweh by all of Israel. Contact with foreigners, whether through intermarriage, diplomatic alliances, religious syncretism, or sharing of actual land, represents unacceptable corruption.[110]

"Ezra wants to erect a virtual fence or a wall around Israel, to deem everything inside holy and everything outside polluted," Schwartz writes. "The demand that those who have intermarried must put away their

FIGURE 11 "By the Rivers of Babylon" exhibition billboard, Bible Lands Museum, Israel, July 2015. Courtesy of Carol and Eric Meyers.

foreign wives is framed as his effort to purify Israel of its abomination. The images he marshals to describe this contaminated land are leaking bodies of both genders: the holy seed has intermixed with the foreigner, the land is a menstruating woman. Male or female, the body of Israel has been permeable, and now Ezra wants its borders closed."[111]

By displacing some of the population, though, the Exile has complicated the question of exactly who is foreign and who is Israelite. Which faction most truly represents Judah, the Golah or those who stayed? It is an important question, which the Book of Ezra further muddies by including a list of foreign nationals as examples of "people of the land," usually taken to refer to ordinary Judeans who avoided exile. Ezra's list includes Canaanites, Hittites, Perizzites, Jebusites, Egyptians, Amorites, and others—some of whom, according to modern scholarship, had ceased to exist at the time the events narrated in Ezra were thought to be taking place.[112]

For contemporary readers, there's no mistaking the deeply gendered language deployed in prophetic accounts of the Babylonian conquest and Exile. Relatively subtle gender overtones inflect the Hebrew of Psalm 137. The direct speech attributed to the Edomites in verse seven, "Rase it, rase it, even to the foundations thereof," according to the *Anchor Bible*, is more properly translated rendered as "Strip her, strip her." The Hebrew *'ārū*, repeated twice, shares a feminine suffix. It can be translated, "make nakedness seen," used in contexts of metaphorical nakedness, such as in a euphemism for sexual intercourse, for example. And the Hebrew word for "foundations" has a secondary meaning of buttocks.[113]

Schwartz offers another revealing etymology: "that the word for 'uncover,' *galâ*, also means 'go into exile.' No longer 'covered,' the adulteress is no longer 'owned' from one point of view, no longer 'protected' from another. Israel has become a whore in exile."[114] In short, the Hebrew connotations of Psalm 137 suggest that Jerusalem under conquest is a woman being despoiled of her clothing, even subjected to sexual humiliation. This is consistent with a number of biblical texts pertaining to the plight of Judah. As we saw in Part 1, gendered and sometimes luridly sexualized language abounds in Jeremiah, Lamentations, and Ezekiel, all books that recount the causes and conditions of conquest and exile.

Which returns us in a roundabout way to the Manhattan milieu of *Mad Men*. The undercurrent of rampant misogyny and sexual harassment may be, more than the ubiquitous cigarettes and drinking, what sets the world of that series apart from the urban professional world of our own time (not that misogyny and harassment have been eradicated, of course). As the folk musicians play "Waters of Babylon" we watch scenes out of Draper's internal flow of consciousness: Rachel at the end of a long work day, Betty Draper with their children. We see Draper's boss Roger and his mistress Joan dressing coolly, impersonally, in a Manhattan hotel room after a tryst.

The song, and scene, invite us to feel we are watching Babylon, with its wealth, power, and sexual corruption, but with the knowledge that a cultural tsunami—what we remember as the sixties—is gathering force. The characters are unaware of the coming sea change; they are understandably caught up in their own reveries, the particular time and place they inhabit. New York City as Babylon—it would not be the first time that analogy has appeared (although in F. Scott Fitzgerald's short story, "Babylon Revisited," the city is Paris).

Both the series and the psalm play on a distinction Svetlana Boym draws between *restorative* and *reflective* nostalgia. "Restorative nostalgia stresses *nostos* and attempts a transhistorical reconstruction of the lost home," she writes. "Reflective nostalgia thrives in *algia*, the longing itself, and delays the homecoming—wistfully, ironically, desperately." The former promises truth and tradition, the latter ambivalence and contradiction. We would expect a twenty-first-century television series to emphasize the latter, as it does, and Psalm 137 to emphasize restorative nostalgia; but there are elements of wistful longing there as well, even desperation, a sense that homecoming, and vengeance, may be postponed indefinitely. Ezra, clearly, is all about restorative nostalgia, as are most forms of nationalism, including Zionism. "The danger of nostalgia is that it tends to confuse the actual home and the imaginary one," Boym notes. "In extreme cases it can create a phantom homeland, for the sake of which one is ready to die or kill. Unreflected nostalgia breeds monsters."[115]

Walter Brueggemann advances a different analogy for the Babylonian conquest, comparing it to the trauma suffered by the United States as a result of the 2001 attack by Al Qaeda. "I think 587 B.C.E. pierced the ideology of chosenness in which the elite thought they were immune from historical disruption," he told me. "In the same way I believe that 9/11 pierced the ideology of U.S. exceptionalism and our privilege in the world. In both cases, the main issue is not political or economic, but the disruption of an ideology grounded in a tribal notion of God."[116]

As the destruction of Jerusalem is thought to have spurred a rethinking of Hebrew Scripture and the meaning of the history it narrates, we might consider whether *Mad Men* offers a self-reflective backward glance—from the twenty-first century to an earlier, seemingly more innocent (and yet simultaneously more decadent) era, the New Frontier of the early sixties. "At first glance, nostalgia is a longing for a place," observes Boym, "but actually it is a yearning for a different time—the time of our childhood, the slower rhythms of our dreams .... The nostalgic desires to obliterate history and turn it into private or collective mythology, to revisit time like space, refusing to surrender to the irreversibility of time that plagues the human condition."[117]

Mad Men's glance faces both directions; viewers can't miss the allusion to 9/11 in the show's opening credit sequence, with a body falling in slow motion from a skyscraper past enormous billboards depicting glamorous women: all that is solid melts in the air. In which case a popular song based on Psalm 137 would represent a notably apt choice for an important early episode.

Epilogue

MAKING HISTORY OUTPACES writing history. When I began research on this book, the United States had recently launched a war (and declared victory) against Iraq, a country built on the ruins of ancient Babylon. The U.S. military tracked down and executed the former leader, Saddam Hussein, and attempted, mostly unsuccessfully, to reconstruct the nation. The territory traversed by the Tigris and Euphrates Rivers has seen endless violence and reprisals in the years since, mainly between adherents to rival strains of Islam, Sunni and Shia. The United States has invaded, drawn down its forces, reversed that with a surge strategy, and withdrawn again. Still, its legacy of intervention, even its personnel, linger.

A terrifying new power in the region, the Islamic State, also known as ISIS, has recently gathered momentum, moving methodically south out of Syria into Iraq, following the Tigris and Euphrates Rivers toward Baghdad. The Islamic State has brought slaughter of innocents, destruction of priceless antiquities, and forced migrations, many millions in Syria alone.[1] The territory comprising ancient Babylonia is once again wracked by conquest, executions, and wholesale destruction.

Grim stories emerge from beside the rivers of Babylon. During the worst sectarian fighting a decade ago, a journalist reported, "The Tigris River became so clogged with human corpses that some Iraqis stopped eating its fish, believing their taste had changed." There was the harrowing story of Ali Hussein Kadhim, an Iraqi soldier who narrowly escaped a massacre of some 1,700 Shiite soldiers stationed at an army base established in Saddam Hussein's hometown, Tikrit. As his group was methodically executed, Kadhim felt a bullet graze his head and fell into a ditch, pretending to be dead. After dark he crawled to the bank of the Tigris, where he subsisted on plants and insects for three days before drifting downriver and mounting "a nearly three-week, underground railroad–style journey through insurgent badlands, relying on sympathetic Sunnis to deliver him to safety."[2] His story could be multiplied by many thousands, but without the happy ending.

Visiting South Africa in search of lessons in reconciliation that might help heal his own country's murderous divisions, an Iraqi official was astounded to learn that "only" 125 prisoners were executed by the apartheid government during the many years Nelson Mandela was imprisoned on Robben Island. Asked to compare the challenges faced by Iraq and South Africa, the Iraqi replied, "We would have a thousand in one day." He elaborated: "The culture of Iraqis does not go for forgiveness. We come from the desert; our culture is for revenge."[3]

Meanwhile, in the lands of Judea to the southwest, cycles of vengeance continue between Israel and its enemies, most vividly in the invasion of Gaza in the summer of 2014. A United Nations report concluded that 2,251 Palestinians were killed during the fifty-day war, including 1,462 civilians. More than 6,000 Israeli airstrikes were carried out on Gaza, where 18,000 homes were destroyed, while Palestinians fired 4,881 rockets and 1,753 mortars at Israel.[4]

Making history outpaces writing about it; history can also participate in its own erasure through actions that devour the material stuff of history. The rise of the Islamic State has cast much of the archaeological heritage of Mesopotamia into jeopardy. The cities of Nimrud and Palmyra have already suffered serious damage; the ancient cities of Hatra and Assur are also in grave danger. ISIS recently beheaded the retired chief archaeologist for Palmyra after he refused to reveal information about the city's precious artifacts.[5]

The legacy of violence, the cycle of death and retribution, seems destined to play out continually in the region over the decades to come, as competition for scarce resources, land and water, sharpen. Forced migration is accelerating drastically, with 60 million people driven from their homes worldwide by the end of 2014, half of them children, according to the United Nations. Daily, tens of thousands are forced to leave home and relocate; the UN calculated that 11.5 million were displaced within Syria alone, with some 3.9 seeking refuge outside the nation, huge numbers in Turkey and Iran.[6]

As my study comes to print, the future of the lands and peoples of ancient Babylonia and Judah are unstable and unknown. It's difficult to say what will remain of Syria, or Iraq, in ten or twenty years. It's almost as challenging to imagine what the configuration of Israel will look like: One state or two? Palestinians cleansed from the land or integrated into the nation?

In the western hemisphere, the earth is shifting under Cuba, if less traumatically. The next few years will reveal just what sort of restoration, or reconciliation, will take place between those who left Cuba for the "strange land" of the United States and those who stayed "on the land." For Cubans in both camps, will the United States turn out to be more like Babylon or will it become Persia? Hegemonic oppressor or conquering liberator? "If the free market were allowed here, there would be nothing left for the Cubans in seventy-two hours," predicted a Cuban economist. "The challenge for us is to make sure the Cuban population understands that socialism is the way to vouchsafe Cuba's national sovereignty."[7] But many are betting that market reforms will bring regime change and political liberalization.

The material stuff of history may be lost, devoured in the fury of civil war. Memory, collective and individual, will endure. Partly because memory endures, forgetting and forgiveness may be the most difficult of all to imagine. But over the course of human history, apart from the occasional fleeting moment, when has that ever not been the case? The stages of response to suffering captured by Psalm 137—collective mourning, an inward-directed oath of loyalty, the articulation of explosive rage in the form of vengeful fantasy—seem as germane in the twenty-first century as a millennia (or two) ago. The psalm itself leaves little room for forgiveness, but lays some of the groundwork for that miracle, without which reconciliation is impossible.

The psalm that immediately follows offers more hope, a turn toward subdued rage and the transcendence of God. Psalm 138 begins:

> I will praise thee, O LORD, with all my heart;
> boldly, O God, will I sing psalms to thee.
> I will bow down towards thy holy temple,
> for thy love and faithfulness I will praise thy name;
> for thou has made thy promise wide as the heavens.
> When I called to thee thou didst answer me
> And make me bold and valiant-hearted.

And ends:

> The LORD will accomplish his purpose for me.
> Thy true love, O LORD, endures for ever;
> leave not thy work unfinished. (Psalm 138:1–3, 8)

* * *

I have many people to thank for their contributions to this study: fresh leads, editorial suggestions, willing to be enthused about a long manuscript on a very short psalm. I especially want to express gratitude to those who were willing to talk with me about the role of the psalm in their creative and professional lives: Peggy Bendroth, Tony Brevett, Tim Eriksen, Judy Hauff, Marjan Helms, Matisyahu, Daniel Pinker, Stephen Schwartz, Richard Slotkin, Robert Smith, Jr., John Stauffer, and Miroslav Volf.

Two intellectual collectives played an important role in incubating this project. I received early inspiration and suggestions from an eclectic group of scholars gathered by Sam Floyd of the Center for Black Music Research in Chicago: David Brackett, Yvonne Daniel, Martha Ellen Davis, Kwame Dawes, Shannon Dudley, Loren Kajikawa, Jay Rahn, Teresa Reed, and Paul Taylor. Though the edited volume on Caribbean music and religion that was the pretext for bringing us all together never came to fruition, many of the articles written for it were eventually published. Portions of *Song of Exile* are revised from "Babylon Revisited: Psalm 137 as American Protest Song," *Black Music Research Journal* 32, no. 1 (Spring 2012): 95–112; copyright 2012 by the Board of Trustees of the University of Illinois.

The other community welcomed me several years later at the most opportune time. A research fellowship at the Yale Institute of Sacred Music (ISM) provided an ideal environment in which to deepen and broaden my research while at the same time actually composing a full draft. Special thanks to the faculty and staff of the ISM, particularly director Martin Jean, Glen Segger, and Maggie Dawn. Katie Dryden artfully transcribed my interviews. Peter Hawkins and Markus Rathey generously shared with me their knowledge of the psalms in literature and music. Tom Troeger, Carolyn Sharp, and Bob Wilson provided various types of counsel and encouragement (though I in no way hold them responsible for my forays into Hebrew Bible scholarship). Thanks to Pat McCreless, Michael Denning, Ian Quinn, Judith Resnik, and Denny Curtis for their different varieties of generosity. I benefited most of all from the camaraderie of an exceptional cohort of research fellows, which that year included Robert Bates, Harald Buchinger, Melvin Butler, Kathy Foley, Andrew Irving, Deb Justice, and Ayla Lepine.

The fellowship year happened to begin fortuitously with a splendid conference at Duke University on "The Bible in the Public Square." Special thanks to conference organizers Shalom Goldman, Mark Chancey, and especially Carol and Eric Meyers, who have been consistently generous in sharing knowledge and supporting my work. An earlier version of my research appeared as a chapter in the volume that came out of that conference: "History, Memory, and Forgetting in Psalm 137," in *The Bible in the Public Square: Its Enduring Influence in American Life*, ed. Mark A. Chancey, Carol Meyers, and Eric M. Meyers, Biblical Scholarship in North America 27 (Atlanta: SBL Press, 2014), 137–57.

Closer to home, in Michigan State University's Religious Studies Department, I want to thank Arthur Versluis, Amy DeRogatis, Chris Frilingos, Bob Anderson, who helped me get started and especially Bob McKinley, who read and provided feedback on earlier versions of this work. From my other department, English, thanks to Jyotsna Singh for her encouragement, thoughtful reading, and suggestions. And John Eulenberg, who has taught me much about Judaism and music over the years. My appreciation to Dean Chris Long, who approved a course release that allowed me to finish work on this manuscript while maintaining most of my sanity. Many others have contributed psalm leads. I'm now convinced that the pool of Psalm 137 settings and allusions is virtually infinite. By the time you read this I'm sure to have stumbled across yet another reference that this book simply can't live without. Too late.

I would like to thank members of my family for their interest in this research over the years, especially Nancy Inui, who along with my mother, Virginia, listened to me "talk psalm" around the dining-room table. Caroline and Henry, you are no doubt somewhat relieved that your dad is finally closing the book on his endless psalm thing; thanks for growing into such wonderful adults. And Clare, who has been a steady loving presence throughout, with keen critical judgment and a great eye and ear, not least for resonant titles; thank you for helping me mostly keep my right hand from forgetting its cunning and my tongue from cleaving to the roof of my mouth.

Notes

PREFACE

1. David W. Stowe, *How Sweet the Sound: Music in the Spiritual Lives of Americans* (Cambridge, Mass.: Harvard University Press, 2004).

2. Paul Ricœur, *Memory, History, Forgetting*, trans. Kathleen Blamey and David Pellauer (Chicago: University of Chicago Press, 2004).

PART 1

1. *Mad Men: Season One*, created by Matthew Weiner (Santa Monica, Calif.: Lionsgate, 2008).

2. Don McLean, "Babylon," *American Pie* (Capitol Records, 1988 [1971]).

3. James L. Kugel, *In Potiphar's House: The Interpretive Life of Biblical Texts* (San Francisco: HarperSanFancisco, 1990), 173–80.

4. Susan Gillingham, "The Reception of Psalm 137 in Jewish and Christian Traditions," in *Jewish and Christian Approaches to the Psalms: Conflict and Convergence*, ed. Susan Gillingham (Oxford: Oxford University Press, 2013), 67, 68; Kugel, *In Potiphar's House*, 183.

5. Kugel, *In Potiphar's House*, 187, 193. On the iconography of Jewish musical instruments, see Benjamin Vogel, "'There on the Willows We Hung Our' . . . Violins: On Old Macewas, Synagogues and Klezmorim," *Muzykalia 7/Judaica* 2 (2009): 1–9, http://www.demusica.pl/?Pismo_Muzykalia:Muzykalia_VII%2FJudaica_2.

6. Yohanan Aharoni and Michael Avi-Yonah, *The Macmillan Bible Atlas* (New York: Macmillan, 1993), 125.

7. Rainer Albertz, "More and Less Than a Myth: Reality and Significance of Exile for the Political, Social, and Religious History of Judah," in *By the Irrigation Canals of Babylon: Approaches to the Study of the Exile*, ed. John J. Ahn and Jill Middlemas (New York: T & T Clark, 2012), 33. "The Babylonian exile still largely

remains a blank," writes Robert Wilson in the same volume, "a black hole that emits no light" (128).

8. Rainer Albertz quoted in Brad E. Kelle, "An Interdisciplinary Approach to the Exile," in *Interpreting Exile: Displacement and Deportation in Biblical and Modern Contexts*, ed. Brad E. Kelle, Frank Ritchel Ames, and Jacob L. Wright (Atlanta: Society of Biblical Literature, 2011), 5n3.

9. Albertz, "More and Less Than a Myth," 27.

10. "Thus, from a material point of view, the exiles' condition had improved," writes Shimon Bar-Efrat. "They had settled in a country richer in water and more fertile than their own; they could build houses and plant fruit trees (Jer. 29:5) and start a new life. But the material point of view is not the only one. Alongside the abundance of water was the memory of Zion, and it weighed more heavily." See Bar-Efrat, "Love of Zion: A Literary Interpretation of Psalm 137," in *Tehillah le-Moshe: Biblical and Judaic Studies in Honor of Moshe Greenberg*, ed. Mordechai Cogan, Barry L. Eichler, and Jeffrey H. Tigay (Winona Lake, Ind.: Eisenbrauns, 1997), 5.

11. Stephanie Dalley, "Occasions and Opportunities 1. To the Persian Conquest," in *The Legacy of Mesopotamia*, ed. Stephanie Dalley (New York: Oxford University Press, 1998), 29.

12. Ibid., 30.

13. Daniel L. Smith-Christopher, "Reading Exile Then: Reconsidering the Methodological Debates for Biblical Analysis in Dialogue with Sociological and Literary Analysis," in Ahn and Middlemas, *By the Irrigation Canals*, 150; Daniel L. Smith-Christopher, "Reading War and Trauma: Suggestions Toward a Social-Psychological Exegesis of Exile and War in Biblical Texts," in Kelle et al., *Interpreting Exile*, 258; David M. Carr, "Reading into the Gap: Refractions of Trauma in Israelite Prophecy," in Kelle et al., *Interpreting Exile*, 299; Hennie Viviers, "Psalm 137: Perspectives on the (Neuro-) Psychology of Loss," *Verbum et Ecclesia* 31, no. 1 (2010): 1–7; David M. Carr's ambitious study, *Holy Resilience: The Bible's Traumatic Origins* (New Haven, Conn.: Yale University Press, 2014), appeared after I had completed work on this manuscript.

14. John J. Ahn, *Exile as Forced Migrations: A Sociological, Literary, and Theological Approach on the Displacement and Resettlement of the Southern Kingdom of Judah* (Berlin: De Gruyter, 2010), 84–85, quotation from 86; see also Ahn and Middlemas, *By the Irrigation Canals*.

15. Robert R. Wilson, "Forced Migration and the Formation of the Prophetic Literature," in Ahn and Middlemas, *Irrigation Canals*; John J. Ahn, "Forced Migrations Guiding the Exile: Demarcating 597, 587, and 582 B.C.E.," in Ahn and Middlemas, *Irrigation Canals*; Kelle et al., *Interpreting Exile*; Daniel L. Smith-Christopher, *A Biblical Theology of Exile* (Minneapolis: Fortress Press, 2002). For a powerful critique of the romanticizing of exile, see Edward Said, "Reflections on Exile," in *Out There: Marginalization and Contemporary*

Cultures, ed. Russell Ferguson et al. (Cambridge, Mass.: MIT Press, 1990), 357–66.

16. Adelaida Reyes Schramm, "Music and the Refugee Experience," in *The World of Music: Music and Forced Migration*, ed. Adelaida Reyes Schramm (*Journal of the International Institute for Comparative Music Studies and Documentation 32:3*), 3–21.

17. Ahn, *Exile as Forced Migrations*, 27–28.

18. Kugel, *In Potiphar's House*, 174–80.

19. William M. Schniedewind, *How the Bible Became a Book* (Cambridge: Cambridge University Press, 2004), 156.

20. Laurie E. Pearce and Cornelia Wunsch, *Documents of Judean Exiles and West Semites in Babylonia in the Collection of David Sofer, vol. 28*, Cornell University Studies in Assyriology and Sumerology (Bethesda, Md.: CDL Press, 2014); Laurie E. Pearce, "Continuity and Normality in Sources Relating to the Judean Exile," *Hebrew Bible and Ancient Israel* 3 (2014): 163–84; Mordechai Cogan, trans. and ed., *Bound for Exile: Israelites and Judeans under Imperial Yoke: Documents from Assyria and Babylonia* (Jerusalem: Carta, 2013), 134–57. Thanks to Bob Wilson for alerting me to these findings.

21. Pearce and Wunsch, *Documents of Judean Exiles*, 3.

22. Interview with Marie (who asked not to use her full name), December 17, 2012.

23. Schniedewind, *How the Bible Became a Book*, 178–82.

24. Robert Allen Warrior, "A Native American Perspective: Canaanites, Cowboys, and Indians," in *Voices From the Margin: Interpreting the Bible in the Third World*, ed. R. S. Sugirtharajah (Maryknoll, N.Y.: Orbis, 1995), 280.

25. Daniel Smith-Christopher, "Reassessing the Historical and Sociological Impact of the Babylonian Exile (597/587–539 BCE)," in *Exile: Old Testament, Jewish, and Christian Conceptions*, ed. James M. Scott (Leiden: Brill, 1997), 33; T. M. Lemos, "The Emasculation of Exile: Hypermasculinity and Feminization in the Book of Ezekiel," in Kelle et al., *Interpreting Exile*, 377–93.

26. Lemos, "Emasculation of Exile," 391.

27. Dalley, *Legacy of Mesopotamia*, 29–30.

28. Stephen Farrell, "At War: Ezekiel's Tomb in Iraq," *New York Times*, October 20, 2010, http://www.nytimes.com/video/world/1248069187877/ezekiel-s-tomb-in-iraq.html.

29. Ibid.

30. Jill Anne Middlemas, *Troubles of Templeless Judah* (Oxford and New York: Oxford University Press), 2005; Oded Lipschitz, *The Fall and Rise of Jerusalem: Judah under Babylonian Rule* (Winona Lake, Ind.: Eisenbrauns, 2005); Hans M. Barstad, *The Myth of the Empty Land: A Study in the History and Archaeology of Judah during the "Exilic" Period* (Oslo: Scandinavia University Press, 1996).

31. Jonathan Boyarin, "Reading Exodus into History," *New Literary History* 23 (1992): 541–43; Robert Allen Warrior, "A Native American Perspective: Canaanites,

Cowboys, and Indians," in *Voices from the Margin: Interpreting the Bible in the Third World*, ed. R. S. Sugirtharajah (Maryknoll, N.Y.: Orbis, 1995), 277–85.

32. Albertz, "More and Less Than a Myth," 23–24.

33. Frank Ritchel Ames, "The Cascading Effects of Exile: From Diminished Resources to New Identities," in Kelle et al., *Interpreting Exile*, 182–84.

34. Carolyn J. Sharp, "Sites of Conflict: Textual Engagements of Dislocation and Diaspora in the Hebrew Bible," in Kelle et al., *Interpreting Exile*, 369.

35. Kugel, *In Potiphar's House*, 176–80.

36. Ibid.

37. Schniedewind, *How the Bible Became a Book*, 149.

38. Ibid., 152.

39. Elizabeth Smart, *By Grand Central Station I Sat Down and Wept* (New York: Vintage International, 1992); Joseph Leo Blotner, *Faulkner: A Biography* (Jackson: University Press of Mississippi, 2005), 399; Stephen Vincent Benét, "By the Waters of Babylon," in *Thirteen O'Clock: Stories of Several Worlds* (Salem, N.H.: Ayer, 1987), 3–20; Arthur C. Clarke, "'If I Forget Thee, Oh Earth . . . ,'" in *Expedition to Earth* (New York: Harcourt, Brace & World, 1970), 40–45.

40. Emma Lazarus, "By the Waters of Babylon: Little Poems in Prose," in *Emma Lazarus: Selections from Her Poetry and Prose*, ed. Morris U. Schappes (New York: Cooperative Book League, 1944), 43. Online: http://www.poetryfoundation.org/poem/176163#poem.

41. Emma Lazarus, "Mother of Exiles," in Daniel Marom, "Who Is the 'Mother of Exiles'? An Inquiry into Jewish Aspects of Emma Lazarus's 'The New Colossus,'" *Prooftexts* 20, no. 3 (Fall 2000): 231. Online: http://muse.jhu.edu/journals/ptx/summary/v020/20.3marom.html.

42. Robert R. Grimes, *How Shall We Sing in a Foreign Land? Music of Irish Catholic Immigrants in the Antebellum Unites States* (Notre Dame, Ind.: University of Notre Dame Press, 1998), 117.

43. Ibid., 3.

44. Thomas Day, *Why Catholics Can't Sing: The Culture of Catholicism and the Triumph of Bad Taste* (New York: Crossroad, 1991), 19.

45. Ibid., 23.

46. Grimes, *How Shall We Sing*, 184.

47. Su Yon Pak, Unzu Lee, Jung Ha Kim, and Myung Ji Cho, *Singing the Lord's Song in a New Land: Korean American Practices of Faith* (Louisville: Westminster John Knox, 2005), 3–6.

48. Bruce Cumings, *Korea's Place in the Sun: A Modern History* (New York: Norton, 2005), 176–83.

49. Pak et al., *Singing the Lord's Song*, 8.

50. Ibid., 30.

51. Ada Maria Isasi-Díaz, "'By the Rivers of Babylon': Exile as a Way of Life," in *Mujerista Theology: A Theology for the Twenty-First Century* (Maryknoll, N.Y.: Orbis, 1996), 35–36.

52. Ibid., 36–37.

53. Miguel A. De La Torre, "Constructing Our Cuban Ethnic Identity While in Babylon," in *A Dream Unfinished: Theological Reflections on America from the Margins*, ed. Eleazar S. Fernandez and Fernando F. Segovia (Maryknoll, N.Y.: Orbis), 2001), 188.

54. Ibid., 192.

55. Ibid.

56. Ibid., 199.

57. Ibid.

58. Ibid., 201.

59. Ibid., 192. For another reading of Psalm 137 in a Caribbean context (the Bahamas), see Fiona C. Black, "Read the Bible in 'Our Home and Native Land': Exploring Some Margins and Migrations in Canadian Biblical Studies (Through the Lens of Psalm 137)," in *The Future of the Biblical Past: Envisioning Biblical Studies on a Global Key*, ed. Roland Boer and Fernando F. Segovia (Atlanta: Society of Biblical Literature, 2012), 256–62.

60. Cheryl J. Sanders, *Saints in Exile: The Holiness-Pentecostal Experience in African American Religion and Culture* (New York: Oxford University Press, 1996), 143.

61. Ibid., 144.

62. Ibid., 151.

63. Sandy F. Ray, "Melodies in a Strange Land: Psalm 137," in *Journeying through a Jungle* (Nashville: Broadman Press, 1979), 57–58.

64. Joseph E. Lowery, *Singing the Lord's Song in a Strange Land* (Nashville: Abingdon Press, 2011), 70.

65. Alex Cannegieter, "From Babylon to Eternity: Appropriations of the Babylon-Motif in Christian Homiletical Constructions," in *From Babylon to Eternity: The Exile Remembered and Constructed in Text and Tradition*, ed. Bob Becking, Alex Cannegieter, Wilfred van de Pol, and Anne-Mereike Wetter (London: Equinox, 2009), 88.

66. Ibid., 86–90.

67. Don Harrán, *Salamone Rossi: Jewish Musician in Late Renaisance Mantua* (New York: Oxford University Press, 1999), 11–41; *Italy: Salomone Rossi, between Worlds*, dir. Asher Tlialim, 1995. Online: http://www.youtube.com/watch?v=ddNlAbLcLJo.

68. Gillingham, "The Reception of Psalm 137 in Jewish and Christian Traditions," 69; Harrán, *Salamone Rossi*, 201–41.

69. Martin Luther, *Three Treatises* (Philadelphia: Fortress Press, 1970), 209; Cannegieter, "From Babylon to Eternity," 91–93.

70. Henry Ainsworth, *The Booke of Psalmes: Englished both in Prose and Metre* (Amsterdam: n.p., 1612), http://eebo.chadwyck.com/search/full_rec?SOURCE=pgimages.cfg&ACTION=ByID&ID=V16069&PAGENO=165.

71. Lorraine Inserra and H. Wiley Hitchcock, *The Music of Henry Ainsworth's Psalter* (Brooklyn: Institute for Studies in American Music, 1981), 64–65.

72. Thomas Sternhold, John Hopkins, and Others, *The Whole Book of Psalms Collected into English Metre* (Oxford: Oxford University Press, 1812), http://www.cgmusic.org/workshop/oldver_frame.htm.

73. *The Bay Psalm Book: A Facsimile Reprint of the First Edition of 1640* (Chicago: University of Chicago Press, 1956).

74. Harry S. Stout, *The New England Soul: Preaching and Religious Culture in Colonial New England* (New York: Oxford University Press, 1986); David P. Barshinger, *Jonathan Edwards and the Psalms: A Redemptive-Historical Vision of Scripture* (New York: Oxford University Press, 2014), 334n107. Harry Stout confirmed in conversation that neither Mather nor Edwards preached on Psalm 137.

75. Sacvan Bercovitch, *The American Jeremiad* (Madison: University of Wisconsin Press, 1978).

76. Interview with Margaret Bendroth, November 14, 2012.

77. Dan Harper, *Yet Another Unitarian Universalist*, November 7, 2012, http://www.danielharper.org/yauu/2012/11/another-look-at-sources-of-sacred-song/.

78. Interview with Steven Schwartz, January 18, 2013.

79. Carol de Giere, *Defying Gravity: The Creative Career of Stephen Schwartz, from Godspell to Wicked* (New York: Applause Theatre and Cinema Books, 2008), 472.

80. *The Harder They Come*, dir. Perry Henzell, International Films, 1973. Criterion Collection, 2000. Cat. No. 15580.

81. Verena Reckord, "From Burru Drums to Reggae Ridims: The Evolution of Rasta Music," in *Chanting Down Babylon: The Rastafari Reader*, ed. Nathaniel Samuel Murrell, William David Spencer, and Adrian Anthony McFarlane (Philadelphia: Temple University Press, 1998), 231–65.

82. Nathaniel Samuel Murrell, "Tuning Hebrew Psalms to Reggae Rhythms: Rastas' Revolutionary Lamentations for Social Change," *Cross Currents*, http://www.crosscurrents.org/murrell.htm; Nathaniel Samuel Murrell and Burchell K. Taylor, "Rastafari's Messianic Ideology and Caribbean Theology of Liberation," in *Chanting Down Babylon: The Rastafari Reader*, ed. Murrell et al., 390–411; Nathaniel Samuel Murrell and Lewin Williams, "The Black Biblical Hermeneutics of Rastafari," in *Chanting Down Babylon: The Rastafari Reader*, ed. Murrell et al., 326–48.

83. Jean Besson, *Martha Brae's Two Histories: European Expansion and Caribbean Culture-Building in Jamaica* (Chapel Hill: University of North Carolina Press, 2002), 239–75; Reckord, "From Burru Drums to Reggae Ridims," 238, 243–44; David W. Stowe, *How Sweet the Sound: Music in the Spiritual Lives of Americans* (Cambridge, Mass: Harvard University Press, 2004), 97–105.

84. Interview with Tony Brevett, May 26, 2013.

85. "The Melodians: Community Page about Rocksteady," https://www.facebook.com/OfficialMelodians/info?tab=page_info.

86. Kenneth Bilby, email to the author, May 12, 2006.

87. "The Melodians: Community Page about Rocksteady," https://www.facebook.com/OfficialMelodians/info?tab=page_info.

88. *Shanghai Dreams*, dir. Wang Xiaoshuai. Stellar Megamedia Kingwood; Debo Films, 2005.

89. *Tulpan*, dir. Sergei Dvortsevoy. Pallas Film, ARTE, BIM Distribuzione, 2008.

90. Svetlana Boym, *The Future of Nostalgia* (New York: Basic Books, 2000l), xiv.

91. Ibid., xvii.

92. Yuval Ben-Ami, "How Shall We Sing the Lord's Song in a Strange Land," July 21, 2010, http://yuvalbenami.blogspot.com/2010/07/how-shall-we-sing-lords-song-in-strange.html.

93. Ibid.

94. "Torture at Abu Ghraib: 'The Man Behind the Hood,'" *Global Research*, April 27, 2009, http://www.globalresearch.ca/torture-at-abu-ghraib-the-man-behind-the-hood/13379.

95. Kate Zernike, "Cited as Symbol of Abu Ghraib, Man Admits He Is Not in Photo," *New York Times*, March 18, 2006, http://www.nytimes.com/2006/03/18/international/middleeast/18ghraib.html.

96. For theological reflections on this incident, see Erin Runions, "Disco-Reggae at Abu Ghraib: Music, the Bible and Torture," *Religion Dispatches*, June 22, 2009, http://religiondispatches.org/disco-reggae-at-abu-ghraib-music-the-bible-and-torture/.

PART 2

1. Matisyahu, *Youth* (Sony BMG, 2006). "Jerusalem" was written by Ivan Corraliza and Jimmy Douglass.

2. Interview with Matisyahu, November 4, 2012. For another impression of a Matisyahu show, see Hampton Stevens, "How Matisyahu's Hasidic Reggae Music Made Me Cry," *The Atlantic*, July 22, 2010, http://www.theatlantic.com/entertainment/archive/2010/07/how-matisyahus-hasidic-reggae-music-made-me-cry/60143/.

3. David Noel Freedman, "The Structure of Psalm 137," in *Near Eastern Studies in Honor of William Foxwell Albright*, ed. Hans Goedicke (Baltimore: Johns Hopkins University Press, 1971), 203. Other painstaking readings of the psalm include Harris Lenowitz, "The Mock-śimhâ of Psalm 137," in *Directions in Biblical Hebrew Poetry*, ed. Elaine R. Follis (Sheffield, U.K.: JSOT Press, 1987), 149–59; George Savran, "'How Can We Sing a Song of the Lord?' The Strategy of Lament in Psalm 137," *ZAW* 112 (2000): 43–58; William H. Bellinger Jr., "Psalm 137: Memory

and Poetry," *Horizons in Biblical Theology* 27, no. 2 (December 2005): 3–20; Christopher B. Hays, "How Shall We Sing? Psalm 137 in Historical and Canonical Context," *Horizons in Biblical Theology* 27, no. 2 (December 2005): 35–55.

4. Conversation with John Eulenberg, East Lansing, MI, 2012; on Psalm 137 and disability, including stroke, see Alex Lubet, "How Can We Sing a Song of the LORD on Alien Soil? Disability, Disaster, and the Idea of Music in Judaism," *Review of Disability Studies* 2, no. 3 (2006): 5–11.

5. Jonathan Magonet, "Psalm 37: Unlikely Liturgy or Partisan Poem? A Response to Susan Gillingham," in *Jewish and Christian Approaches to the Psalms: Conflict and Convergence*, ed. Susan Gillingham (Oxford: Oxford University Press, 2013), 84.

6. James L. Kugel, *In Potiphar's House: The Interpretive Life of Biblical Texts* (San Francisco: HarperSanFancisco, 1990), 185.

7. Augustine, *Works of Saint Augustine: A Translation for the 21st Century*, trans. Edmund Hill, ed. John E. Rotelle (Brooklyn: New City Press, 1990–2012), 227–28.

8. Christopher B. Hays, "How Shall We Sing? Psalm 137 in Historical and Canonical Context," *Horizons in Biblical Theology* 27, no. 2 (December 2005): 46–47.

9. Yosef Hayim Yerushalmi, *Zakhor: Jewish History and Jewish Memory* (Seattle: University of Washington Press, 1996), 5.

10. Gillingham, "Reception of Psalm 137," 68.

11. Ibid., 70.

12. David P. McKay and Richard Crawford, *William Billings of Boston: Eighteenth-Century Composer* (Princeton, N.J.: Princeton University Press, 1975), 64.

13. Nathaniel D. Gould, *Church Music in America, Comprising Its History and Its Peculiarities at Different Periods, with Cursory Remarks on Its Legitimate Use and Its Abuse* (Boston: A. N. Johnson, 1853), 46.

14. McKay and Crawford, *William Billings of Boston*, 155, 166.

15. Hannibal Hamlin, *Psalm Culture and Early Modern English Literature* (Cambridge: Cambridge University Press, 2004), 243, 244.

16. William Billings, *The Complete Works of William Billings: Vol. 2*, ed. Hans Nathan (Boston: American Historical Society and the Colonial Society of Massachusetts, 1977), 72–73.

17. Ralph T. Daniel, *The Anthem in New England before 1800* (Evanston, Ill.: Northwestern University Press, 1966), 69.

18. McKay and Crawford, *William Billings of Boston*, 64.

19. Billings, *Complete Works*, 136–47.

20. I had the chance to sing it with the Yale–New Haven Regular Singing group in 2013, whose convener, Professor Ian Quinn, supplied a copy in shape-note notation.

21. Samuel Williams, "A Discourse on the Love of Our Country," in *Colonies to Nation, 1763–1789: A Documentary History of the American Revolution*, ed. Jack P. Greene (New York: Norton, 1967), 377–78.

22. Ibid., 85. Perhaps surprisingly, Williams includes the king in his closing prayer, which lists the many blessings for which Americans should give thanks: "To all these mercies we may add, the life of our sovereign Lord the King has been preserved: To his family and throne, it is our duty and interest to bear a steady allegiance; and in whose royal favour and protection, we hope this country will find peace, safety and happiness, for many ages yet to come."

23. Moses Mather, "America's Appeal to the Impartial World," in *Political Sermons of the American Founding Era, 1730–1805*, ed. Ellis Sandoz (Indianapolis: Liberty Press, 1991), 481.

24. Larry Gordon and Anthony G. Barand, eds., *Northern Harmony: 4th Edition* (Plainfield, Vt.: 1998), 18–19.

25. Timothy Dwight, "Love to the Church," photocopy in author's possession.

26. David W. Stowe, *How Sweet the Sound: Music in the Spiritual Lives of Americans* (Cambridge, Mass.: Harvard University Press, 2004), 36–40.

27. Interview with John Stauffer, November 14, 2012.

28. Frederick Douglass, *The Frederick Douglass Papers. Series Three: Correspondence Vol. 1: 1842–1852*, ed. John R. McKivigan (New Haven, Conn.: Yale University Press, 2009), 73.

29. James A. Colaiaco, *Frederick Douglass and the Fourth of July* (New York: Palgrave Macmillan, 2006), 205n1.

30. Frederick Douglass, *The Frederick Douglass Papers. Series One: Speeches, Debates and Interviews. Vol. Two: 1847–54*, ed. John W. Blassingame (New Haven, Conn.: Yale University Press, 1979), 368.

31. Ibid., 368–69.

32. Douglass, *Douglass Papers. Series Three: Correspondence*, 545, 547.

33. Douglass, *Douglass Papers. Series One: Speeches, Debates and Interviews*, 368.

34. Walter Johnson, *Soul by Soul: Life Inside the Antebellum Slave Market* (Cambridge, Mass.: Harvard University Press, 1999), 68–69.

35. Harriett Beecher Stowe, *Uncle Tom's Cabin* (New York: Norton, 1994), 297.

36. Ronald Radano, *Lying Up a Nation: Race and Black Music* (Chicago: University of Chicago Press, 2003), 152–53; Eric Lott, *Love and Theft: Blackface Minstrelsy and the American Working Class* (New York: Oxford University Press, 1993), 43.

37. William L. Holladay, *The Psalms through Three Thousand Years: Prayerbook of a Cloud of Witnesses* (Minneapolis: Fortress Press, 1996), 238–39.

38. "Newport Gardner (1746–1826)," in *The Black Perspective in Music* 4, no. 2 (1976): 204.

39. Ibid., 202–7.

40. Randall K. Burkett, *Black Redemption: Churchmen Speak for the Garvey Movement* (Philadelphia: Temple University Press, 1978), 34, 77, 52.

41. Ben Glaser, "'They Require(d) of Us a Song': Psalm 137 and the New Negro Renaissance," paper delivered at the annual meeting of the American Studies Association, 2011.

42. James Weldon Johnson, *The Book of American Negro Poetry* (New York: Harcourt Brace, 1922), http://www.gutenberg.org/cache/epub/11986/pg11986.html.

43. MacKinley Helm, *Angel Mo' and Her Son, Roland Hayes* (Boston: Little Brown, 1942), 107–8.

44. Ibid., 124.

45. Sterling Brown, "Roland Hayes," *Opportunity* 30 (June 1925): 173–74.

46. Ibid.

47. John C. Tibbetts, ed., *Dvořák in America 1892–1895* (Portland, Ore.: Amadeus Press,), vi.

48. John Clapham, *Dvořák* (London: David & Charles, 1979), 197.

49. Helm, *Angel Mo'*, 106–7.

50. Tibbetts, *Dvořák in America*, 256.

51. Ibid.

52. I'm grateful to Markus Rathey for sharing his impressions of "Pri rekách babylonskych."

53. Paul Robeson, *Paul Robeson Speaks: Writings, Speeches, Interviews, 1918–1974*, ed. Philip S. Foner (London: Quartet Books, 1978), 443.

54. Ibid., 69.

55. Ibid., 392–93.

56. Ibid., 393.

57. Nick Salvatore, *Singing in a Strange Land: C. L. Franklin, the Black Church, and the Transformation of America* (New York: Little, Brown, 2005).

58. C. L. Franklin, "Without a Song," in *Give Me This Mountain: Life History and Selected Sermons*, ed. Jeff Todd Titon (Urbana: University of Illinois Press, 1989), 90.

59. Ibid.

60. Ibid., 91–92.

61. Ibid. Hayes's own accounts of the incident basically agree with Franklin's (though he doesn't mention being hoisted on any shoulders). His memoir dates the concert to 1924, before the Nazi rise to power. A *New York Times* interview implies it occurred prior to 1923: in any event, not long before Hayes received acclaim from Sterling Brown and Paul Robeson. In both accounts, Hayes stresses the importance of changing his program to begin with Schubert's "Du bist die Ruh," which apparently won over the hissing audience. Alan Rich, "'A Bouncy Seventy-Five': Roland Hayes, Despite His Age, Gives Concerts, Teaches and Reminisces," *New York Times*, June 3, 1962, 127.

62. Franklin, *Give Me This Mountain*, 92–93.

63. Ibid.

64. Interview with Robert Smith Jr., July 20, 2012.

65. George Hunter, "New Bethel Church Falls on Hard Times," *Detroit News*, December 9, 2010.

66. Ibid.

67. Robert Smith Jr., *In the Shadow of C. L. Franklin*, ed. Michael P. Williams (Joy Press, 1995), vi.

68. Jeremiah A. Wright Jr., "Faith in a Foreign Lane," in *Sermons of Joy and Strength from Jeremiah A. Wright, Jr.*, ed. Jini Kilgore Ross (Valley Forge: Judson Press, 1993), 133, 138.

69. Ibid., 138, 140.

70. David Remnick, *The Bridge: The Life and Rise of Barack Obama* (New York: Knopf, 2010), 527–28.

71. Quoted in Remnick, *The Bridge*, 525.

72. Ibid., 20.

73. Ibid., 23.

74. Yosef Hayim Yerushalmi, *Zakhor: Jewish History and Jewish Memory* (Seattle: University of Washington Press, 1996), 43.

75. Ibid., 43–44.

76. Jonathan Boyarin, "Reading Exodus into History," *New Literary History* 23, no. 3 (Summer 1992): 553n60.

77. "Newport Gardner (1746–1826)," *Black Perspective in Music* 4, no. 2 (July 1976): 204.

78. Michael Walzer, *Exodus and Revolution* (New York: Basic Books, 1984).

79. Bruce S. Feiler, *America's Prophet: Moses and the American Story* (New York: William Morrow, 2009), 296.

80. Ibid., 297–98.

81. Regina M. Schwartz, *The Curse of Cain: The Violent Legacy of Monotheism* (Chicago: University of Chicago Press, 1997), 58.

82. Robert Allen Warrior, "A Native American Perspective: Canaanites, Cowboys, and Indians," in *Voices from the Margin: Interpreting the Bible in the Third World*, ed. R. S. Sugirtharajah (Maryknoll, N.Y.: Orbis, 1995), 284–85.

83. Edward W. Said, "Michael Walzer's *Exodus and Revolution*: A Canaanite Reading," in *Blaming the Victims: Spurious Scholarship and the Palestinian Question*, ed. Edward W. Said and Christopher Hitchens (London: Verso, 2001), 166, 177.

84. Email from Marshall Linden, June 7, 2006.

85. Miguel A. De La Torre, "Constructing Our Cuban Ethnic Identity While in Babylon," in *A Dream Unfinished: Theological Reflections on America from the Margins*, ed. Eleazar S. Fernandez and Fernando F. Segovia (Maryknoll, N.Y.: Orbis, 2001), 186.

86. Anne-Mereike Wetter, "Balancing the Scales: The Construction of the Exile as Countertradition in the Bible," in Bob Becking, Alex Cannegieter, Wilfred van de Pol, and Anne-Mereike Wetter, *From Babylon to Eternity: The Exile Remembered and Constructed in Text and Tradition* (London: Equinox, 2009), 34–35.

87. John H. Yoder, "Exodus and Exile: The Two Faces of Liberation," *Cross Currents* 23, no. 1 (Fall 1973): 298.

88. Ibid., 306–7.

89. Ibid., 308.

90. Cheryl J. Sanders, *Saints in Exile: The Holiness-Pentecostal Experience in African American Religion and Culture* (New York: Oxford University Press, 1996), 143.

91. Boyarin, "Reading Exodus into History," 539, 541.

92. Ibid., 541–43.

93. Schwartz, *Curse of Cain*, 122.

94. Ari Shavit, "Lydda, 1948," *The New Yorker* (October 21, 2013), 44.

95. Paul Ricœur, *Memory, History, Forgetting*, trans. Kathleen Blamey and David Pellauer (Chicago: University of Chicago Press, 2004), 4, 15–30.

96. Ibid., 21–30.

97. Ibid., 96–102.

98. Ibid., 102–20.

99. Yerushalmi, *Zakhor*, 44–45.

100. Maurice Halwachs, *On Collective Memory*, ed. and trans. Lewis A. Coser (Chicago: University of Chicago Press, 1992); Ricoeur, *Memory*, 120–24.

101. Boym, *Future of Nostalgia*, 54–55.

102. Roger Parker, "'Va Pensiero' and the Invidious Mastery of Song," in *Leonora's Last Act: Essays in Verdian Discourse* (Princeton, N.J.: Princeton University Press, 1997), 20–41; Joseph Slater, "Byron's Hebrew Melodies," *Studies in Philology* 49, no. 1 (January 1952): 75–94. The 1815 title page announced: "Hebrew Melodies / Ancient and Modern / with appropriate Symphonies and Accompaniments / By I. Braham and I. Nathan / the Poetry written expressly for the work / By the Right Honourable / Lord Byron." The poet's first stanza, of three: "We sate down and wept by the waters / Of Babel, and thought of the day / When our foe, in the hue of his slaughters, / Made Salem's high places his prey; / And ye, oh her desolate daughters! / Were scattered all weeping away." Müller's poem, "Pause," begins: "I have hung my lute on the wall, / and wound a green ribbon around it. / I can sing no more, my heart is too full." See Philip L. Miller, ed. and trans., *The Ring of Words: An Anthology of Song Texts* (New York: Norton, 1973), 213. Thanks to Markus Rathey and Peter Hawkins for bringing the Nathan/Byron material to my attention, and to Patrick McCreless for the Schubert lead.

103. Walter Benn Michaels, *Our America: Nativism, Modernism, and Pluralism* (Durham, N.C.: Duke University Press, 1995), 128.

104. Ibid.

105. Ibid., 129.

106. Ricoeur, *Memory*, 88.

107. Ibid., 166.

108. Ibid., 278.

109. William M. Schniedewind, *How the Bible Became a Book* (Cambridge: Cambridge University Press, 2004), 19.

110. Interview with Judy Hauff, July 15, 2012.

PART 3

1. Jan T. Gross, *Neighbors: The Destruction of the Jewish Community in Jedwabne, Poland* (Princeton, N.J.: Princeton University Press, 2001), 19–20.

2. Ibid., 20. Italics added.

3. Athalya Brenner, "'On the Rivers of Babylon' (Psalm 137), or Between Victim and Perpetrator," in *Sanctified Aggression: Legacies of Biblical and Post Biblical Vocabularies of Violence*, ed. Jonneke Bekkenkamp and Yvonne Sherwood (London: T & T Clark International, 2003), 76–91.

4. Ibid., 89.

5. Ibid.

6. Personal conversation, November 2012.

7. Brenner, "'On the Rivers of Babylon' (Psalm 137)," 81, 86; William L. Holladay, *The Psalms through Three Thousand Years: Prayerbook of a Cloud of Witnesses* (Minneapolis: Fortress Press, 1996), 144.

8. Jonathan Magonet, "Psalm 37: Unlikely Liturgy or Partisan Poem? A Response to Susan Gillingham," in *Jewish and Christian Approaches to the Psalms: Conflict and Convergence*, ed. Susan Gillingham (Oxford: Oxford University Press, 2013), 87.

9. Ibid., 88.

10. Marjan Helms, *Voices of a Vanished World* (Delta Records, n.d.).

11. Interviews with Marjan Helms, August 23, 2012; August 22, 2014.

12. Norbert Troller, *Theresienstadt: Hitler's Gift to the Jews*, trans. Susan E. Cernyak-Spatz, ed. Joel Shatzky (Chapel Hill: University of North Carolina Press, 1991), 29–30.

13. David Noel Freedman, *The Nine Commandments: Uncovering a Hidden Pattern of Crime and Punishment in the Hebrew Bible* (New York: Doubleday, 2000).

14. Mitchell Dahood, *Psalms III, 100–150*, Anchor Bible 17A (Garden City, N.Y.: Doubleday, 1970), 269; C. S. Lewis, *Reflections on the Psalms* (New York: Harcourt Brace Jovanovich, 1958), 23.

15. Ellen F. Davis, *Getting Involved with God: Rediscovering the Old Testament* (Cambridge, Mass.: Cowley, 2001), 27.

16. Magonet, "Psalm 137: Unlikely Liturgy," 85.

17. Jonathan Edwards, *Original Sin (WJE Online Vol. 3)*, ed. Clyde A. Holbrook, 218, http://edwards.yale.edu/archive?path=aHRocDovL2Vkd2FyZHMueWFsZS5lZHUvY2dpLWJpbi9uZXdwaGlsby9nZXRvYmplY3QucGw/Yy4yOjQ6MS53amV; Prideaux quoted in David P. Barshinger, *Jonathan Edwards and the Psalms: A Redemptive-Historical Vision of Scripture* (New York: Oxford University Press, 2014), 324.

18. Edwards, *Original Sin*, quoted in Barshinger, *Jonathan Edwards and the Psalms*, 324.

19. Ibid., 328.

20. Davis, *Getting Involved with God*, 24.

21. Walter Brueggemann with Steve Frost, *Psalmist's Cry: Scripts for Embracing Lament* (Kansas City, Mo.: House Studio, 2010), program notes.

22. Davis, *Getting Involved with God*, 28.

23. Holladay, *The Psalms*, 311–13.

24. Augustine, *Works of Saint Augustine: A Translation for the 21st Century*, trans. Edmund Hill, ed. John E. Rotelle (Brooklyn: New City Press, 2012), 224; Susan Gillingham, "The Reception of Psalm 137 in Jewish and Christian Traditions," in *Jewish and Christian Approaches to the Psalms: Conflict and Convergence*, ed. Susan Gillingham (Oxford: Oxford University Press, 2013), 73.

25. Augustine, *Works*, 232.

26. Thanks to an anonymous reader for Oxford University Press for this point.

27. Augustine, *Works*, 240.

28. Ibid.

29. St. Benedict, *The Rule of Saint Benedict: In Latin and English With Notes*, ed. Timothy Fry (Collegeville, Minn.: Liturgical Press, 1981), 475.

30. Holladay, *The Psalms*, 372–73.

31. Ibid., 177.

32. St. Benedict, *Rule of Saint Benedict*, 163, 185. Thanks to Andrew Irving for alerting me to this reference.

33. Martin Luther, "The Babylonian Captivity of the Church," in *Three Treatises*, trans. A. T. W. Steinhäuser (Philadelphia: Fortress Press, 1970), 111.

34. Ibid., 119.

35. Ibid., 209.

36. John Calvin, *Commentary on Psalms: Volume 5*, http://www.ccel.org/ccel/calvin/calcom12.xxi.ii.html. In other words, nothing personal: God wills it.

37. Hannibal Hamlin, *Psalm Culture and Early Modern English Literature* (Cambridge: Cambridge University Press, 2004), 250, 251; Gillingham, "Reception of Psalm 137," 75n1.

38. Michael P. Kuczynski, *Prophetic Song: The Psalms as Moral Discourse in Late Medieval English* (Philadelphia: University of Pennsylvania Press, 1995), 153, 163.

39. Hamlin, *Psalm Culture*, 248–49.

40. Donald Davie, ed., *The Psalms in English* (New York: Penguin, 1996), 166–67.

41. Stephen Toulmin, *Cosmopolis: The Hidden Agenda of Modernity* (Chicago: University of Chicago Press, 1992), 54, 55–56.

42. Still, according to Toulmin, it ultimately led to a certain straitjacketing of the intellectual imagination, especially in a field like philosophy, which struggled to recreate itself in the image of science.

43. David W. Stowe, *How Sweet the Sound: Music in the Spiritual Lives of Americans* (Cambridge, Mass.: Harvard University Press, 2004), 29.

44. Davie, *Psalms in English*, 212, 211.

45. Hamlin, *Psalm Culture*, 248.

46. Quoted in Andrew Cunningham and Old Peter Grell, *The Four Horsemen of the Apocalypse: Religion, War, Famine and Death in Reformation Europe* (Cambridge: Cambridge University Press, 2000), 142.

47. Jonathan Edwards, The "Blank Bible," *WJE Online, Vol. 24*, ed. Stephen J. Stein, 537, http://edwards.yale.edu/archive?path=aHRocDovL2Vkd2FyZHMueWFsZ-

S5lZHUvY2dpLWJpbi9uZXdwaGlsby9jb250ZXhodWFsaXplLnBsP3AuMjMud2pl
by4xNzYxNDI5LjE3NjEoMzY; italics added.

48. Richard Slotkin, *Regeneration through Violence: The Mythology of the American Frontier, 1600–1860* (Middleton, Conn.: Wesleyan University Press, 1973); Richard Slotkin, *The Fatal Environment: The Myth of the Frontier in the Age of Industrialization, 1800–1890* (New York: Atheneum, 1985); Richard Slotkin, *Gunfighter Nation: The Myth of the Frontier in Twentieth-Century America* (New York: Atheneum, 1992).

49. Email from Richard Slotkin, December 12, 2012.

50. Richard Slotkin and James K. Folsom, eds., *So Dreadfull a Judgment: Puritan Responses to King Phillip's War, 1676–1677* (Middleton, Conn.: Wesleyan University Press, 1978), 3–43.

51. Ibid., 198.

52. Ibid., 302.

53. Ibid., 336–37.

54. Interview with John Stauffer, November 14, 2012.

55. Christopher B. Hays, "How Shall We Sing? Psalm 137 in Historical and Canonical Context," *Horizons in Biblical Theology* 27, no. 2 (December 2005): 46–47.

56. "War Crimes and the Gaza War," *New York Times*, June 23, 2015, A22.

57. Steve Reich, *Daniel Variations* (New York: Nonesuch, 2008).

58. Steve Reich, liner notes, *Daniel Variations*.

59. Steven Pinker, *The Better Angels of Our Nature: Why Violence Has Declined* (New York: Viking, 2011), 10.

60. Ibid., 10, 11.

61. Ibid., 11.

62. Interview with Steven Pinker, November 2, 2012.

63. Quoted in Jennifer L. Geddes, "Religious Rhetoric in Responses to Atrocity," in *The Religious in Responses to Mass Atrocity: Interdisciplinary Perspectives*, ed. Thomas Brudholm and Thomas Cushman (Cambridge: Cambridge University Press, 2009), 28.

64. George E. Berkley, *Hitler's Gift: The Story of Theresienstadt* (Boston: Branden Books, 1993), 128, 129.

65. Ibid., 267.

66. Email to author, March 24, 2015.

67. Doris L. Bergen, "Hosanna or 'Hilf, O Herr Uns': National Identity, the German Christian Movement, and the 'Dejudaization' of Sacred Music in the Third Reich," in *Music and German National Identity*, ed. Celia Applegate and Pamela Potter (Chicago: University of Chicago Press, 2002), 153.

68. Anita Lasker-Wallfisch, *Inherit the Truth: A Memoir of Survival and the Holocaust* (New York: St. Martin's Press, 2000), 76.

69. Michael H. Kater, *Different Drummers: Jazz in the Culture of Nazi Germany* (New York: Oxford University Press, 1992), 181.

70. Ibid.; Simon Wiesenthal, *The Sunflower: On the Possibilities and Limits of Forgiveness* (New York: Schocken, 1997), 12.

71. Wiesenthal, *The Sunflower*, 12.

72. Leon Szalet, *Experiment "E": A Report from an Extermination Laboratory*, trans. Catharine Bland Williams (New York: Didier, 1945), 70–71. On Kol Nidre, see Stowe, *How Sweet the Sound*, 171–95.

73. Quoted in Gillingham, "Reception of Psalm 137," 69.

74. *Hell on Earth*, dir. Vojtech Jasny, from *Broken Silence* (Universal Studios, 2004).

75. Ibid.

76. Geddes, "Religious Rhetoric in Responses to Atrocity," 23.

77. Fania Fénelon with Marcelle Routier, *Playing for Time*, trans. Judith Landry (New York: Atheneum, 1977), ix.

78. Robert Saxton, *The Wandering Jew* (NMC Recordings D170, 2011).

79. Ziva Amishai-Maisels, "Chagall's 'White Crucifixion,'" *Art Institute of Chicago Museum Studies* 17, no. 2 (1991): 138–53, 180–81; Aaron Rosen, *Imagining Jewish Art: Encounters with the Masters in Chagall, Guston, and Kitaj* (London: Legenda, 2009), 25–30.

80. Aaron Rosen, "True Lights: Seeing the Psalms through Chagall's Church Windows," in *Jewish and Christian Approaches to the Psalms: Conflict and Convergence*, ed. Susan Gillingham (Oxford: Oxford University Press, 2013), 107. Chagall quoted in Amishai-Maisels, "Chagall's 'White Crucifixion," 143.

81. Gillingham, "Reception of Psalm 137," 70.

82. Paul Ricœur, *Memory, History, Forgetting*, trans. Kathleen Blamey and David Pellauer (Chicago: University of Chicago Press, 2004), 88.

83. Ibid., 366.

84. Thomas Brudholm and Thomas Cushman, eds., *The Religious in Responses to Mass Atrocity: Interdisciplinary Perspectives* (Cambridge: Cambridge University Press, 2009), 2–4.

85. Geddes, "Religious Rhetoric in Responses to Atrocity," 21.

86. Quoted in ibid., 24–25.

87. Rudolph Otto, *The Idea of the Holy: An Inquiry into the Non-Rational Factor in the Idea of the Divine and Its Relation to the Rational*, trans. John W. Harvey (New York: Oxford University Press, 1950).

88. Geddes, "Religious Rhetoric in Responses to Atrocity," 27–32; quotation from 27.

89. Wiesenthal, *The Sunflower*, 216, 217.

90. Ibid., 171.

91. Ibid., 268, 129.

92. Thomas Brudholm, "On the Advocacy of Forgiveness after Mass Atrocities," in Thomas Brudholm and Thomas Cushman, eds., *The Religious in Responses to Mass Atrocity: Interdisciplinary Perspectives* (Cambridge: Cambridge University Press, 2009), 142.

93. Ibid.

94. Ta-Nehisi Coates, "The Case for Reparations," *The Atlantic* (June 2014), http://www.theatlantic.com/features/archive/2014/05/the-case-for-reparations/361631/.

95. Reinhold Niebuhr, *Discerning the Signs of Our Times: Sermons for Today and Tomorrow* (New York: Charles Scribner's, 1949), 23.

96. Robert Beckford, *God of the Rahtid: Redeeming Rage* (London: Darton, Longman and Todd, 2001).

97. Ibid., 60.

98. Ibid., 53–65.

99. Miroslav Volf, *End of Memory: Remembering Rightly in a Violent World* (Grand Rapids, Mich.: Eerdmans, 2006), 39.

100. Interview with Miroslav Volf, April 26, 2013.

101. Volf, *End of Memory*, 148.

102. Ibid., 134, 135.

103. Ricœur, *Memory, History, Forgetting*, 501.

104. Ibid., 505.

105. Interview with Miroslav Volf, April 26, 2013.

106. Miroslav Volf, *Exclusion and Embrace: A Theological Exploration of Identity, Otherness, and Reconciliation* (Nashville: Abingdon Press, 1996), 124.

107. Raymond Philip Dougherty, *Nabonidus and Belshazzar: A Study of the Closing Events of the Neo-Babylonian Empire* (New Haven, Conn.: Yale University Press, 1929), 166–69.

108. Bob Becking, "On the Identity of the 'Foreign' Women in Ezra 9–10," in *Exile and Restoration Revisited: Essays on the Babylonian and Persian Periods in Memory of Peter R. Ackryod*, ed. Gary N. Knoppers, Lester L. Grabbe, and Deirdre Fulton (London: T & T Clark, 2009), 43.

109. Regina M. Schwartz, *The Curse of Cain: The Violent Legacy of Monotheism* (Chicago: University of Chicago Press, 1997), 71.

110. Ibid., 64.

111. Ibid., 86.

112. Ibid., 86–87. Commenting on this account, though, David M. Carr cautions against the tendency to "critique and caricature Judaism" based on the Book of Ezra. "Standing as a tiny 'remnant' that had barely survived the exile," he asserts, "Ezra and other exile leaders felt they could not take a chance on having the next generation raised by women who were not part of the 'children of exile.'" See *Holy Resilience: The Bible's Traumatic Origins* (New Haven, Conn.: Yale University Press, 2014), 136–37.

113. Mitchell Dahood, *Psalms III, 100–150*, Anchor Bible 17A (Garden City, N.Y.: Doubleday, 1970), 273; David Noel Freedman, "The Structure of Psalm 137," in *Near Eastern Studies in Honor of William Foxwell Albright*, ed. Hans Goedicke (Baltimore: Johns Hopkins University Press, 1971), 200–201.

114. Schwartz, *Curse of Cain*, 70.

115. Svetlana Boym, *The Future of Nostalgia* (New York: Basic Books, 20001), xviii, xvi.
116. Walter Brueggemann, email to David Stowe, August 20, 2013; see also Walter Brueggemann, *The Message of the Psalms: A Theological Commentary* (Minneapolis: Fortress Press, 1984), 74–77.
117. Boym, *Future of Nostalgia*, xv.

Epilogue

1. Paul Salopek, "Fleeing Terror, Finding Refuge," *National Geographic*, March 2015, 48–71.
2. Peter Beinart, "The Surge Fallacy," *The Atlantic*, September 2015, 14; Tim Arango, "Escaping Death in Northern Iraq," *New York Times*, September 3, 2014, http://www.nytimes.com/2014/09/04/world/middleeast/surviving-isis-massacre-iraq-video.html.
3. Arango, "Escaping Death in Northern Iraq."
4. Editorial, "War Crimes and the Gaza War," *New York Times*, June 23, 2015, A22; Ben Hubbard, "Syrian Expert Who Shielded Palmyra Antiquities Meets a Grisly Death at ISIS' Hands," August 19, 2015.
5. Sarah Almukhtar, "The Islamic State's Advantage at History," *New York Times*, July 1, 2015, http://www.nytimes.com/interactive/2015/06/29/world/middleeast/isis-historic-sites-control.html; "The Crimes of Palmyra" (editorial), *New York Times*, August 25, 2015, A18, http://www.nytimes.com/2015/08/26/opinion/the-crimes-of-palmyra.html.
6. Somini Sengupta, "60 Million People Fleeing Chaotic Lands, U.N. Says," *New York Times*, June 18, 2015, A1, http://www.nytimes.com/2015/06/18/world/60-million-people-fleeing-chaotic-lands-un-says.html.
7. John Lee Anderson, "Letter from Havana: Open for Business," *The New Yorker*, July 20, 2015, 28; John Lee Anderson, "Cuba and America: The End of an Estrangement," *The New Yorker*, July 21, 2015, http://www.newyorker.com/news/daily-comment/cuba-and-america-the-end-of-an-estrangement.

Index